D1570423

WITHDRAWN

Taking Penguins

to the Movies

Taking Penguins to the Movies

Ethnic Humor
in Russia

Emil A. Draitser

Wayne State University Press
Detroit

HUMOR IN LIFE AND LETTERS SERIES

A complete listing of the books in this series can be found at the back of this volume.

General Editor

Sarah Blacher Cohen   State University of New York, Albany

Advisory Editors

Joseph Boskin   *Boston University*

Alan Dundes   *University of California, Berkeley*

William F. Fry, Jr.   *Stanford University Medical School*

Gerald Gardner   *Author and lecturer*

Jeffrey H. Goldstein   *Temple University and London University*

Don L. F. Nilsen   *Arizona State University*

June Sochen   *Northeastern Illinois University*

Copyright © 1998 by Wayne State University Press,

Detroit, Michigan 48201. All rights are reserved.

No part of this book may be reproduced without formal permission.

Manufactured in the United States of America.

02 01 00 99 98   5 4 3 2 1

Library of Congress Cataloging-in-Publication Data

Draitser, Emil, 1937–

    Taking penguins to the movies : ethnic humor in Russia / Emil A.
    Draitser.

        p.   cm. — ([Humor in life and letters])

    Includes bibliographical references and index.

    ISBN 0-8143-2327-8 (alk. paper)

    1. Russia (Federation)—Ethnic relations.   2. Russian wit and
    humor.   3. Joking—Russia (Federation)   I. Title.   II. Series.
    DK510.33.D73   1998
    305.8'00947—dc21   97-44214

A shorter version of chapter 6 originally appeared in the form of an article: "Sociological Aspects of Russian Jewish Jokes of the Exodus," in *Humor: International Humor Research Journal* 7, no. 3 (1994): 245–67.

Contents

To my father Abram and to the memory
of my mother Soybel

Preface

Although entertainment is the primary, the recognized, goal of telling jokes, the subjects they are related to are usually those that are most important to the tellers, even if they don't realize it. Humor expresses serious anxieties in lighter terms; it is this ability to alleviate frustrations that makes laughter so attractive.

At the same time, as a bit of communication, a joke dies unless the teller and the hearer share common ground. Thus it is the implicit assumptions of the culture that lie as the foundation of a joke. Analyzing and interpreting jokes makes it possible to deduce certain behavioral patterns and make explicit tacit operating knowledge of deeply held popular beliefs, the hidden underpinnings, of a culture. In his book, *The Silent Language,* anthropologist Edward Hall points out that "an understanding of a people's sense of humor is one key to the structure of that society."

Learning about Russians as people is important now as never before. Russian society is undergoing tremendous political and social changes. To deal successfully with the new Russia that is gradually emerging from the rubble of totalitarianism, we must know as much as we can about the world of the individual Russian, his or her attitudes and customs, beliefs and idiosyncrasies, and the inter- and intragroup relationships of this multinational society.

A study of Russian popular humor is not only timely, but long overdue. Though many observers of the scene have noted the Russians' penchant for jokes (which they most often call *anekdoty,* derived from the Greek *anekdota,* meaning "unpublished items"), this widespread, persistent phenomenon has long begged for exploration and interpretation.

9

My research in Russian ethnic humor has evolved from my study of Soviet underground humor. When I began my work, the Soviet Union still seemed to be going strong. Few people would have predicted its downfall. As I made ready to follow up my small collection of Soviet underground jokes, *Forbidden Laughter* (Los Angeles: Almanac, 1980), with analytical work on the subject, events in the former Soviet Union made the very notion of "Soviet" first nebulous, then totally obsolete, forcing me to shift both the focus and the scope of my study. As ethnic conflicts sprang up all over the former Soviet empire, they became the hottest political issues. Although Russian jokes about various ethnicities existed long before the fall of the Soviet Union, they became much more frequent in the late Soviet and post-Soviet periods. Ethnic humor, in fact, overshadowed political humor per se. Now free press has made old clandestine political humor obsolete. In fact, ethnic humor has become *the* major political humor in today's Russia.

Thus my original project—to study Russian political jokes—turned into a study of Russian ethnic humor. As the first extensive work on the subject, this book represents an attempt to offer to the Western reader not only a comprehensive collection of Russian ethnic humor of the second half of this century, but its content analysis and interpretation in sociopolitical and psychological terms.

While versions of some of the jokes analyzed in this work may be found in such English-language compilations as David Harris and Israel Rabinovich's *The Jokes of Oppression: Humor of Soviet Jews* and Zhanna Dolgopolova's *Russia Dies Laughing,* almost all joke entries in this book appear in English for the first time and are original translations. For my study, I consulted several Russian joke books that have appeared in recent years. Among these the most comprehensive, as far as ethnic jokelore is concerned, are O. Ivanova's *Anekdoty i tosty* (Jokes and toasts) (1994 and 1996 editions), Iosif Raskin's *Ehntsiklopediia khuliganstvuiushchego ortodoksa* (Encyclopedia of a rowdy orthodox man), Dora Shturman and Sergey Tiktin's *Sovetskii Soiuz v zerkale politicheskogo anekdota* (The Soviet Union in the mirror of a political joke), Yulius Telesin's *Tysiacha odin izbrannyi sovetskii politicheskii anekdot* (One thousand and one selected Soviet political jokes), as well as V. S. Elistratov's *Slovar' Moskovskogo argo* (Dictionary of Moscow argot). When these and other sources are not cited, the jokes discussed in this book are from my private collection, kept over three decades. Wherever possible, I have provided bibliographical data about versions of the jokes analyzed. I have also consulted the recent nine-volume publication of *Antologiia mirovogo anekdota* (Anthology of world jokes) for many Russian entries, but I have found it marred by incorrect attribution (often deliberate) of jokes to ethnicities and by the questionable authenticity of some of the entries.

As a rule, previously published Russian ethnic jokes have been presented without consideration of the concrete political and social context in which they have circulated. Publication of a joke book in the language of the culture from which the humor originated assumes the reader's close familiarity with the context in which jokes have made the rounds; publication of foreign material out of context not only deprives these jokes of much of their cultural and artistic significance, but often results in misinterpretation.

One such misinterpretation is that a number of jokes are erroneously presented as ethnic. Often the compilers make such attribution on the basis of the presence of an ethnically marked character in a joke. However, quite often in Russian jokelore an ethnic stereotype is used only for artistic purposes. Thus a number of Russian jokes involving Jews, Georgians, Ukrainians, or Chukchis are in fact not ethnic but political, in the direct sense of the word. A Jewish character could be employed to make a witty pronouncement about a political leader, a Georgian to debunk the same leader as a sexual pervert, or a Chukchi as a simpleton who, due to the effect of estrangement, provides an opportunity for deadpan humor. Sometimes a Jewish name is given to such a character just because of the joke-tellers' belief (not unknown in American culture as well) that a Jewish character makes a joke somehow funnier, no matter what it is about.

Another shortcoming of existing Russian joke books is that the collected items are usually rendered as if they are told in a vacuum. Joke-telling is a social phenomenon, first and foremost. All jokes are an expression of the spirit or mood of a group at a given time. A joke stripped of the concrete contextual circumstances in which it was recorded may be used to make different, sometimes even opposite, points. (For example, the very same Jewish joke told by a Jew in the Jewish in-group can be taken as anti-Semitic when told by a Gentile.)

Western readers may recognize some of the jokes analyzed in this book as variants of jokes that they have perceived as belonging to their own culture. This is especially possible with Russian Jewish jokes, proving that popular humor is able to cross not only spatial, but also temporal borders. Some of the Jewish jokes in Russia and America are similar because they draw on a common heritage, Eastern European Jewish folklore.

Jokes should be studied not only in their social context, but in their linguistic context as well. Many Russian jokes are tied to other forms of Russian folklore, thus striking a chord with the original listeners, who are native speakers, and so deepening the meaning. Sometimes a Russian joke is based on a proverb, with its distinct moral realized on the level of plot. In previous publications of contemporary Russian folk humor, these contextual circumstances and language ties are almost never addressed. A Western reader, unfamiliar with the deep roots of these folkloric items, is destined to see only the obvious, and to understand only the generic meaning of a joke. In fact, this stripped-to-the-bone joke is usually the only kind to cross cultural barriers.

In the rare instances when Russian ethnic humor has been analyzed, it has almost never been approached from a sociological or psychological vantage. Thus, in his *Semantic Mechanisms of Humor* (1985), Victor Raskin scrutinizes samples of Russian ethnic jokes only from the point of view of his linguistic theory of humor.

Furthermore, little has been done in Russia itself in the analysis of jokelore. With the advance of *glasnost* and *perestroika* and the lifting of official taboos on the publication of folk humor, the streets of Russian cities were soon flooded with hastily published booklets of jokes. Today, one can easily find thick and voluminous compilations of them on the Russian book market. Russian scholars, however, long isolated by Marxist ideology from Western thought, seem inadequately equipped for an in-depth analysis of this material. There is very little scholarly discussion in Russia of these joke collections. This is understandable, since many modern theories of the comic were advanced by scholars—Bergson, Freud, Koestler, and others—whose names were taboo in the Soviet Union. Only recently have there been some attempts to fill the gap. Yury Borev, Anatoly Dmitriev, and L. A. Barsky have begun to deal with the phenomenon of popular humor in their works.

The term *folklore* originally referred to the art of the "common people, especially in rural areas," as the *American Academic Encyclopedia* defines it. In the industrialized societies of the twentieth century, folkore has also involved the urban population. Because of the political conditions prevailing during most of the Soviet period, folklore (especially jokelore) circulated not only among the "common people," but among the intellectual elite as well. In fact, Soviet oral jokes became a favorite genre of Russian-speaking intelligentsia. (A Russian theorist of humor, Dr. Jury Borev, has coined a separate term for this phenomenon, called "intellectual folklore.")

I would like to warn readers who may prefer to skip the analysis and read only the jokes that, although they may find many of them enjoyable, they may run into disappointment. I have approached the selection of jokes in this book solely on the basis of their analytical interest. For that reason, readers may find that I chose not the funniest samples, but those most representative of the variants and richest in texture.

In each chapter, all jokes pertinent to the main subject are numbered. Only a handful of them remain unnumbered—either because they are very short and left in the body of the main text for a better flow of the narrative, or because they do not belong to the jokelore about the ethnicity discussed in a given chapter; they are used as an illustration of the prevailing mood within the joke teller's group in a given historical period.

I realize that there are many ways to interpret a joke. My own conclusions, although I steadfastly stand by them, could be challenged when a different approach is taken. What seems to be, nevertheless, an invariable result of any analysis of a joke is that it invokes a comic stereotype, preknowledge of which for both the teller and the hearer is a necessary condition for its success.

Although I cite a number of sociological research findings and political science assessments of the concrete historical circumstances attending the circulation of certain types of Russian ethnic jokes, this book is primarily a study of folk humor. Therefore, all references to the Russians and other ethnic groups in this work are related not to the real people, but to their image as it is portrayed or transpires in this humor. Thus, this notion of ethnic stereotype involves a comic fixed image of a group or its representative, as it is used in contemporary Russian jokelore.

Chapter 1 gives an overall assessment of the phenomenon of Russian ethnic humor and explores the sources of the repertory—the "bounded corpuses of humorous texts associated with particular social groupings" (Oring 53)—in order to establish how a separate joke fits into the whole corpus of similar folkloric material. Often a joke can be understood better when its origins are revealed and changes traced.

Chapters 2 through 4 deal with the reasons for the appearance and proliferation of the main body of contemporary Russian ethnic jokes—those about Georgians, Ukrainians, and Chukchis. (Some issues related to another large group of Russian ethnic jokes, those about the Jews, are discussed as they pertain to other material.)

Chapter 5 addresses other forms of Russian ethnic humor, such as nicknames, proverbs, and sayings. As an example of the phenomenon of "protest" humor, chapter 6 examines humor not of the Russian majority, but of a minority, as exemplified by the best-known non-Russian ethnic humor, that of the Russian Jewish.

This inquiry is a natural extension of my lifelong involvement with and interest in the phenomenon of laughter. From 1964 to 1974, under my pen name "Emil Abramov," I contributed satirical columns and humorous short stories to *Krokodil* (The crocodile), "The Club of Twelve Chairs" in *Literaturnaia gazeta,* and to other major Russian publications. In the United States, I have published a number of satirical sketches and humorous essays in the *Los Angeles Times,* the *San Francisco Chronicle,* and the *Los Angeles Herald Examiner,* as well as in *Studies in Contemporary Satire, Confrontation, The New Press Literary Quarterly,* and several other American periodicals, and in many Russian émigré publications.

I have always been intrigued by the question: what makes people laugh? My previous book *Techniques of Satire: The Case of Saltykov-Shchedrin*

(Berlin and New York: Mouton de Gruyter, 1994) concerns literary satire. Oral humor poses other questions, however: What makes a joke ethnic? Why target Georgians? Why Chukchis? Why an explosion of jokes about Ukrainians, portraying them as stingy, when their generosity is well known? How can a mediocre joke be received with enthusiasm? What makes an ethnic nickname funny or offensive? These and many other questions are addressed in this study. I hope they will interest scholars and students of folklore, ethnic studies, sociology, political science, cultural history, literature, sociolinguistics, and cultural anthropology. Lay readers may also find this book provokes their thinking about humor in general and ethnic humor in particular.

Acknowledgments

I am grateful for research grants by the Research Foundation of the City University of New York; since 1990 I have made four field trips to Russia, where I have had an opportunity to update my research database. The collection of a Muscovite (who chose to remain anonymous) helped me to fill the fifteen-year gap in my private collection (I emigrated to the United States in 1974), for which I am deeply thankful.

S. Frederick Starr, president of the Aspen Institute, has given my project steady encouragement, and my colleagues Professors Elizabeth Beaujour and Alex Alexander have provided continuing moral support. I also thank Norman Clarius of the Hunter College Interlibrary Loan Department. My loyal friend, Dr. Anthony Saidy, has helped me to stay abreast of press coverages of latest developments in Russia. I am grateful to Ruth Mathewson not only for her editing of the manuscript, but for many valuable suggestions. I would also like to express my appreciation for the benefit I received from the questions and encouragement of many participants in the following scholarly meetings at which parts of this book were presented in their initial form: Columbia University Seminar on Slavic History and Culture; American Association for Advanced Slavic Studies; Conference on Post-Soviet Cultural Studies at the University of Michigan; International Conference on "Ethnic Identity and Nationalism in Eastern Europe" (Forest City, Iowa); International Conferences on Humor Research in Birmingham, England and Sydney, Australia.

Special thanks go to my brother, Vladimir Draitser, who, with his inimitable sense of humor, has helped me to remember many jokes we exchanged in our youth.

CHAPTER 1

The Repertory of
Contemporary Russian Jokelore

As in other multiethnic societies, ethnic jokes have long been a part of Russian folklore. While the groups most frequently featured in Russian ethnic jokes of the early twentieth century were the Jews, Armenians, and Gypsies (Shmeleva and Shmelev 40), contemporary Russian ethnic jokelore has undergone a dramatic change. Jokes about the Jews have remained the main staple of the Russian ethnic repertory, but now one can find only a handful of jokes about Gypsies and only a few more about the Armenians.[1] Since the 1950s jokes about the Georgians, Chukchis, and Ukrainians have become prominent in Russian folk humor.

Because Russia is one of the world's most ethnically heterogeneous nations, in terms of both the number (more than one hundred) and the diversity of ethnic groups living in its territory, it is surprising that only a small number of distinct ethnic groups are featured in contemporary Russian jokelore. This does not necessarily signify a special friendliness toward other groups in comparison, for example, to the Americans, who have told malign jokes about thirty-nine different immigrant groups (Eisiminger 9). All the derogatory implications of ethnicity-related humor notwithstanding, to tell a joke about a certain nationality means to show awareness of its existence, of its distinctive character. Telling jokes about a group reveals at least a passing familiarity with its everyday life. Hence, the ultimate ethnic insult is the complete absence of a minority in the folklore of a majority. This explains why currently a tiny trickle of jokes built on very popular Russian Chukchi joke patterns but told about another minority group, the Koriaks, are being told by the Koriaks themselves.[2] The aim of these self-deprecating jokes is to put the group on the map of Russian mass consciousness, no matter what the cost, quite in accordance with the contemporary American saying: "I don't care what you say about me, as long as you spell my name right."

The stability of joke telling about a given targeted group in a given period varies. Anti-Georgian jokes began their steady circulation in the late 1950s. Series of jokes about Chukchis are of later vintage—dating to the early 1970s. Although jokes about the Ukrainians have long circulated among the Russians, due to their close physical proximity and their pronounced antagonism over a long historical period, these jokes have immensely intensified in the past ten years. Other groups have appeared in Russian jokelore only sporadically. There have been only a few jokes about Uzbeks or about the ethnicities of the Baltic group, including Lithuanians, Latvians, and Estonians. A Moldavian character appeared briefly in late Soviet humor.

A proper reading of an ethnic joke requires a concrete historical background of the time of their circulation. The dynamics of ethnic joke telling in Russia clearly show that with the increased tension between Russians and certain minorities, Russian jokelore has increasingly included jokes targeted at these minorities.

At least two factors contributed to the proliferation of contemporary Russian ethnic jokes in the Soviet period, both stemming from the effects of the structure and the condition of the political system that controlled Russian life for more then seven decades. The widely proclaimed Marxist-Leninist policy of internationalism; of equality among all the nationalities, however small, residing on Soviet territory; of correcting the czarist unjust treatment of minorities and solving the "nationalities question" or "nationality problems," in the end produced rather dismal results. Soviet nationality policy designed to remove the social and economic inequalities among the ethnic groups in the USSR, to end their economic and cultural backwardness, by and large failed. At the end of the 1980s, ethnic conflicts arose throughout the country, and these conflicts still present a major concern for the stability of the region formerly called the Soviet Union.

There are several reasons for the current sharpening of interracial tensions. First of all, in trying to demonstrate the supremacy of communist ideology and make it attractive to many small nations around the world, especially to the Third World countries, and in trying to prove the equality among the nationalities and take credit for it, the Soviet regime always stressed the ethnic background of persons of high achievement—unless they belonged to groups that were unpopular with the regime; at various times the Jews, the Crimean Tartars, and the Chechens each belonged to this group. As Ralph

Clem (25) notes, Soviet society had crystallized along ethnic lines as a result of "the overwhelming centrality of power in the USSR and the legitimating of ethnicity."

As John Armstrong (70–71) shows, in practice this policy was never wholly bona fide; that is, it hardly ever meant full equality with the Russians for the various ethnic groups. Throughout the Soviet period the Russians were persistently promoted in the leading role of "big brother." Constant attempts were made to Russify many ethnic cultures; this became a major social priority for Soviet leaders, starting with Stalin. The minorities may have been celebrated for their arts and crafts and their folk dancing, but they were given short shrift in decision making. As Armstrong (71) concludes, "Russians were the dominant ethnic element, the source of the unified national culture which the [Soviet] elite believed it required."

That is why, as Daniel Bell points out (cited in Clem 26), the decline of communist ideology, beginning with the Brezhnev regime, contributed further to the salience of ethnicity. The importance of the issue of national identity included not only numerous minorities living side by side with the Russians, but the Russians themselves. As a discussion of Chukchi jokes will demonstrate, the Brezhnev period of stagnation and Gorbachev's failed attempts to mend the Soviet system produced the rise in Russian ethnic consciousness, as manifested in the phenomenon of "neo-Slavophilism." William Foltz (cited in Clem 26) categorized this phenomenon as a "mirror-image response"—that is, a defensive reaction by a group threatened with loss of relative position. Western scholarly studies have found this threat to be, by and large, nonexistent. Nevertheless, the myth of such a threat came into being due to the overall frustrating economic situation in the Soviet Union at the time. As Armstrong (69) concludes, the years of economic decline, between 1968 and 1979, were the years of "the sharpest xenophobia observed in the Soviet polity."

As a result, contemporary Russian ethnic jokelore is full of gibes involving those groups that, in the Russians' view, have prospered more than they have: the Jews, the Georgians, the Armenians, and the Ukrainians. The Jews and Armenians, as members of what Armstrong (20–21) calls a "mobilized Diaspora," have always "exhibited a degree of social mobilization sufficient to enable them to occupy a special functional position in a modernizing society [and], therefore, elicited Russian resentment and, frequently, discrimination against [them]."

Since the beginning of *perestroika* in 1985, the nationality question began to be discussed in the press, and ethnic conflicts all over the vast country were brought to the fore of Russian folk awareness. As a response to this development, ethnic jokes became much more prominent in Russian folklore. In the late Soviet and post-Soviet period, the Russians' ethnic jokelore has manifested anxiety about the disturbances in Uzbekistan, Nagorno-Karabakh, Abkhazia, and other regions. Public demands from the provinces for independence or autonomy have contributed to this anxiety. Ethnic slurs have been the Russians' way of reassuring themselves; portraying an ethnicity as ignorant and inept, or insignificant as a group, served as a self-therapy of sorts that helped to allay anxieties about the possibility of confrontation.

Russian ethnic jokes, like others of this kind the world over, are based on ethnic stereotypes. Although some of these stereotypes contain a grain of truth, most of them are generalizations for the sake of disparagement of the group. In most cases, the intrinsic features of the target group have little to do with the reason for verbal assaults on it. As Christopher Wilson (215–16) observes,

> jokes are manifestly inaccurate in describing racial characteristics. For example, Negroes . . . are commonly ridiculed as deviants and religious fanatics; while Jews, a religious group, are derided in terms of physical appearance and mercenary obsessions (Barron, 1950).
>
> Characteristically, themes of racial humor bypass genuine ethnic features and ascribe common features of inferiority to several minority groups. Barron found that Irish, Negroes, and Jews alike, were all derided for their assumed verbal difficulties and blunders. Similarly, as Legman (1968) has shown, American humor attributes sexual aberration to most other nationalities. Obviously, the generality of the themes of abuse negates the specificity of any particular ethnic attribution. In the rhetoric of ridicule, the specific features of Poles are that they are stupid perverts—like all other foreigners.

Victor Raskin (chapter 6) considers jokes based on language distortion, stupidity, stinginess, and cunningness universal; they are present in many ethnic jokes around the world.[3] Before addressing Russian jokes about specific groups, one should be aware that among ethnic jokes and gibes told by the Russians, some can be described as racist, and some as relatively harmless, aimed at banter rather than at the humiliation of a target group. The racist jokes increase the Russian group cohesiveness and justify its superior status and power, as jokes of a majority group directed at minorities often do. Other purposes served are approval of the group's oppressive tactics and venting of envy toward an allegedly more prosperous minority.

Most Russian ethnic humor, like ethnic humor the world over (Apte 115), is verbal and consists of jokes (the most popular form), proverbs, sayings, children's rhymes, short folk songs the Russians call *chastushki,* nicknames, and riddles, of which the most familiar type is "Armenian Radio"—sometimes called "Radio Erevan" (Kalbouss 447).

This last genre may be confusing for an outsider. These jokes have nothing to do with radio, which in Soviet times was as severely censored as any other means of mass communication. They are also not really Armenian. They appeared in the late 1950s, in the wake of the post-Stalin "Thaw," and were given this name because of a tradition of nonsensical Armenian riddles, popular among the Russians in the late 1940s and 1950s, from which they took the format of a somewhat whimsical question and an utterly unpredictable answer. Here is a sample of a genuinely Armenian humorous riddle:

(1.1) "What is it? It's green, it hangs on the wall, and it squeaks?"
"?"
"A herring."
"Why is it green?"
"It's my herring. I can paint it any color I want."
"Why does it hang on the wall?"
"It's my herring. I can hang it wherever I want."
"Why does it squeak?"
"I'm surprised at that myself."

A few of these "radio" jokes employ ethnic scripts the Russians ascribe to Armenians, such as a tendency to homosexuality and pedophilia ("Is it true that Tchaikovsky was a homosexual?" "True. But that's not the only reason we love him"). Although a number of "radio" jokes are concerned with other sexual matters as well, by and large, the Armenian card is played to provide an "outsider's" slant, often satirical, on Soviet life and politics.

The repertory of contemporary Russian ethnic humor is comprised of original material and the borrowed jokelore of a few ethnic groups.

| Borrowing Ethnic Jokelore: Telling a Joke Within a Group

It may be perplexing to learn that a number of Russian jokes about other groups were initially (and often simultaneously) told by members of the target groups. In many cases, Russian jokes about the Georgians are nothing but retellings of indigenous jokes told by Georgian city dwellers, most of whom have to sustain themselves on meager wages. They are aimed at "those (undeservedly) rich hillbillies" who have made a quick fortune through selling their garden produce. Many Russian jokes about the Jews are of Jewish origin as well. Such borrowing from the minority jokelore by a dominant group is rather widespread and takes place in many multiethnic cultures.

There is a pronounced distinction between the functioning of a joke within the group of its origin and that outside of it. A Georgian or Jewish joke told within the respective group constitutes what Wilson (217) calls "shared ridicule," that is, "a disparaging portrait of the social, religious, ethnic or occupational group to which he [the teller] and the audience belong." Such laughter is "generally directed downward in the class structure: a middle class joker laughs at the absent lower class of the minority group."[4]

This in-group joke telling has a positive quality. As Joyce Hertzler (95) shows,

> laughter within a group is a means of expressing and maintaining the group values and standards. For example, laughter directed at the parvenu, the eccentric, the cheap climber, the troublemaker, the fool, et cetera, is a means of indicating defection from the standards of the group, as well as of underscoring principles of action. It also reaffirms for the laughers the support of the standards, and this aids in maintaining the ascendancy of the group for its members vis-à-vis other groups. Similarly, the laughter emanating from the group members is a method of attacking all insincere or seemingly harmful individual or factional claims, pretensions, and novelties within the group.

This "clearinghouse" quality of indigenous humor is often overlooked by outsiders. Sigmund Freud (1905) and Theodor Reik (1962) write of Jews telling ostensibly anti-Semitic jokes, R. Middleton and J. Moland (1959) of Negroes and anti-Negro jokes, and A. M. O'Donnell (1972; cited in Wilson 218) of self-derisive Irish jokes; many other researchers prove that members of ethnicities often make fun of their own group, using negative aspects of their stereotype (see, e.g., Josef Boskin, Lawrence LaFave, and Larry Mintz, as cited in Nilsen 219–20). This does not mean that such a phenomenon is all-inclusive or confined to minorities, however. In fact, there are plenty of Russian self-effacing jokes portraying the group as thieves, drunkards, and boors:

(1.2) An airplane is about to crash. Married couples say farewell to each other.
A husband: "Tell me, my dear, did you ever cheat on me?"
An English woman: "Yes, my dear, I did. Remember when I began to wear a pearl necklace . . . ?"
A French woman: "Yes, dear. Remember when I began to drive a new Chevrolet?"
A Russian wife: "Yes, Vassya! Remember when three shirts of yours disappeared . . ." (Barsky 158–59)

(1.3) In Africa, a cannibal captured a Russian, an Englishman, and a Frenchman. He took them to the edge of a precipice and laid down terms: he would spare the one who could pronounce a word that lasted more than five minutes.
The Englishmen shouted: "O-o-k-a-a-a-y!"

It lasted three minutes.
The Frenchman shouted: "Ma-r-r-r-r-i-i-e-e-e!"
It also lasted three minutes.
The Russian: "They're giving away vod-k-a-a-a-a!"
And the sound became: "Where? . . . Where? . . . Where? . . .
Where? . . . Where? . . ."
It kept going that way for two hours. (Anon. 322)

(1.4) How different people unacquainted with each other behave in an
unfamiliar setting.
Two Englishmen are riding in a railroad car compartment. If
nobody introduces them, they will be silent all the way from
Glasgow to London.
Two Frenchmen will begin to describe their lovers' sex appeal to
each other.
The Germans will work through the genealogical trees of their kin
till the seventeenth branch.
Our people will bark at each other without asking for names.
(Ibid.)

The fact that a member of a group tells a disparaging joke involving another member of the same group does not necessarily mean that he accepts the stereotype of the group established outside of that group.[5] Often, the opposite is true—by telling a joke about other members he wants to dissociate himself from those who, by their wrong behavior, embarrass the whole group. The following statement by Iosif Raskin (50), a Russian Jewish collector of jokes, follows this pattern: "In every nationality, there are bastards who disgrace their people. How often the Jews themselves facilitate manifestations of anti-Semitism with their behavior! Once, in my youth, I coined the expression: 'It is because of you, kikes, they don't love us, the Jews.' "

The author does not seem to realize that such a stand not only doesn't prevent racism, but, in fact, justifies it. Not unique in the Russian Jewish milieu, such an attitude, by default, approves the racist tendency to judge the whole group in terms of the (mis)behavior of a few; it calls for the impossible task of making every single member of the in-group faultless for the sake of protecting the whole group from accusations of wrongdoing.[6] In this respect, it is appropriate to recall a point made by a Russian Jewish journalist and writer, Vladimir Zhabotinsky (120, 123), back in 1911, at the time of the heightening of racial tensions between Christians and Jews, stirred by the infamous Beilis affair:[7]

We ourselves accustomed our neighbors to the thought that for any Jew who stole they might drag the whole ancient people to account, people who introduced and lived under the law in those times when our neighbors hadn't yet come up with a bast shoe. . . . We have nothing to apologize for. We are people like all peoples; we have no claims on being better. As one of the first conditions of equality, we demand the recognition of our right to have our own bastards, exactly as other peoples have them.

Russian Jewish folklore pinpoints that it is futile to attempt to pacify racists by redirecting their anger to scapegoats in a subset group. As a line of a Russian fable-cum-proverb goes: "For the strong, the weak are always guilty" *(u sil'nogo vsegda nesil'nyi vinovat):*

(1.5) A pogrom in Kishinev is in progress. They grab an old Jew right out of his warm bed.
"You, kike's mug! We'll take your guts out right now!"
"Why?"
"You still ask why?! Isn't it you who crucified our Christ?"
"I swear it's not us! It's the Odessa Jews!" (I. Raskin 50)

Even when self-defeating ethnic jokes are told by a member of a minority in the presence of members of the majority, they should not be taken at face value. They may have another function: to use self-criticism as a defensive ploy, as a way to soften the blow, to "divert hostility to amusement" (Wilson 221). Also, such ethnic jokes may seem self-degrading only because some values judged negative by an out-group are, in fact, seen as positive within the in-group (Oring 130).[8]

Retelling a Borrowed In-Group Joke

When an outsider retells an ethnic in-group joke in the company of other outsiders, contextual circumstances may sharply change the perception of its meaning. The effect of this borrowing can be rather dramatic. The very fact of an outsider's borrowed joke poking fun at a shortcoming of a subset of a given in-group, whatever the intentions, is not as innocent as it may seem. The (re)teller gives the joke's text a larger context. By default, it is then assumed that a small subset of a given in-group is a replica of the whole in-group, denying, in fact, that any subdivision of the in-group even exists. Furthermore, admitting the indigenous source of a borrowed ethnic joke gives the (re)teller, even if he or she does not realize it, an additional persuasive power: "I'm not the one who is saying this. They themselves tell this about their own."

Thus, by implication, regardless of its content and specific target, the joke's message becomes one of negative stereotyping: "Once a Jew, always a Jew," or "Once a Georgian, always a Georgian." That is, all members of a given group are one and the same. Therefore, when a member of a Russian out-group repeats an in-group Jewish or Georgian joke within his own group, it is no longer "shared ridicule," as Wilson defines it. Introducing a joke to an audience of outsiders, transplanting it from its native soil, creates a shift in the vantage of the original teller and, thus, affects the initial meaning. That is why, for example, a number of Jewish jokes aimed at certain subgroup shortcomings, contained in Zhanna Dolgopolova's (62–71) collection, are listed as anti-Semitic.

Hence, a Gentile retelling a Jewish joke in the company of other Gentiles risks being regarded as an anti-Semite, for a shortcoming initially ascribed to a subset of the Jewish in-group is then perceived, by default, as a shortcoming inherent in all Jews. The text may be a verbatim repetition of a Jewish joke by a Gentile, but such a telling represents an anti-Semitic act since it generalizes a shortcoming of a subset group to include the whole group.

The same applies to members of minorities retelling Russian self-deprecating jokes in the company of their own; under such circumstances, these jokes cannot help but sound Russophobic. Such a (re)telling cannot avoid resentment among members of the target group, whose sensitivity to criticism by outsiders is expressed by Pushkin: "Of course, I despise my Fatherland from top to bottom—but I am annoyed if a foreigner shares my feeling."[9]

What evidently happens here is that the harshest critic of his own in-group, as a rule, does not condemn it in its entirety. Even the most consummate satirist in Russian literature, Saltykov-Shchedrin, who left no stone unturned in the Russia of his time, strongly felt himself Russian,[10] and undoubtedly took for granted the existence of at least a handful of people like himself, who were spared his unmerciful satire.

In borrowing from old Jewish jokelore, there is another pitfall for the (re)teller. Created under miserable social circumstances, many Jewish shtetl jokes carried a great deal of self-irony. By telling them to one another, the Jews laughed bitterly at their own destiny: excruciating poverty, destitution of the lowest sort, combined with permanent danger of violation while living as second-class citizens. In their original design the following jokes were meant to evoke no more than a knowing smile from a fellow Jew:

(1.6) "Take bread, dear guests, spread it with butter."
"Isn't that what I'm doing?"
"No, you're piling it on. And you should spread it." (Petrosian 64; in Russian, there is an additional comic effect of sound anaphora: *namazyvat'* [to spread], *nakladyvat'* [to pile on]).

(1.7) All his relatives gather around the bed of a dying old Jew. They ask him to reveal the secret of his marvelous tea. The old man keeps silent and, when his very last moment comes, he opens his

eyes and whispers: "Fellow Jews! Don't spare the tea leaves."
(For variants, see Ivanova 1996, 292; Soloviev 2:37.)

(1.8) "Abram, I saved five kopecks."
"How?"
"I ran behind a tram."
"You would save more if you ran behind a taxi." (Petrosian 64)

When a Gentile retells these jokes today, he willy-nilly changes their meaning. Cut off from the concrete historical and social circumstances of their origin, these jokes can't help but sound anti-Semitic, as manifestations of the alleged Jewish stinginess.

A joke that is borrowed verbatim can also be read in a quite different way when the group from which the joke is borrowed and the one in which it is retold reflect conflicting sets of values or have different cultural expectations. To an anti-Semite the following joke laughs at the limitations of a provincial Jew who cannot comprehend the meaning of great power. A sympathetic teller of the same joke, however, while making gentle fun of the limitations of a shtetl Jew, may think that the joke also shows that the Jew is a not a parasite, that he is used to earning his own living and no world power can make him as proud of himself as that fact:

(1.9) "If I were the Czar," a Jewish tailor says, "I'd live better than the Czar. I'd do a little sewing on the side."[11]

Sometimes the Russians borrow an indigenous joke and subject it to alteration that significantly changes its initial tone and meaning, as in the following item, listed (correctly) as anti-Semitic in Dolgopolova's (64) collection:

(1.10) A Russian, a Ukrainian, and a Jew are traveling on a train. It is a long and boring journey.
"Let's have a game of cards," says the Russian.
"But we haven't got any cards," says the Ukrainian.
"Never mind," says the Russian. "Instead of cards we'll use food. For example, a lump of lard can be the Queen of Hearts, half a liter of vodka the King of Clubs, and so on."
They begin to play.
"Queen of Hearts," declares the Ukrainian, putting a lump of lard down on the table.
"King of Clubs," says the Russian, putting out half a liter of vodka.
"Nothing is trumps," says the Jew, putting down nothing and taking up the lard and the vodka.

This is an artistically inferior rendition of the original Jewish story, in which it is the eventual profiteer who initiates the game and suggests that food be used instead of the missing cards. It is interesting as an example of borrowing from an indigenous jokelore for what it tells us about the borrower's intentions. Anyone familiar with Jewish folklore immediately recognizes the joke as an altered version of a turn-of-the century Jewish tale about a folk hero named Herschel Ostropolier. In many tales, this poor man finds a way to feed himself by outwitting his rich skinflint fellow Jews.[12] The sympathies of the teller of the original story are fully on his side.

While keeping the main plot of the tale intact, the Russian teller has altered the original text by shifting the cast of characters, now positioning them across ethnic rather than social lines. In this way the Jew of the original, a folk jester who outwits the stingy rich of his own tribe, is replaced by a generic Jew who takes advantage of naive and trusting Slavic people, a Russian and a Ukrainian.

Redirecting Borrowed Ethnic Jokes toward Another Ethnicity

Russian ethnic jokelore of the post-Soviet period makes another use of borrowed ethnic humor: one group's indigenous jokes are told about another, which emerges as a new object of Russian resentment. In comparing old Soviet jokelore with the new, post-Soviet variety, one can easily identify the new targets of Russian gibes.

Thus many contemporary anti-Ukrainian jokes are nothing but recycled well-known ethnic jokes that initially attacked other nationalities. A number of jokes alleging Ukrainian greed closely resemble anti-Semitic jokes. A classical joke about a Jewish wife who, caught with her lover, says to her flabbergasted husband: "Abram, is that you? Oy, I'm so mixed up, so mixed up nowadays! Then who is this next to me?" now has, instead of Abram, Ostap, a Ukrainian (Dubovsky 278). Likewise, jokes featuring the Ukrainians as fools are often recycled versions of Russian jokes about the Chukchis. This does not mean, however, that the original jokes have ceased to circulate. On the contrary, almost identical tales targeting different ethnic groups may circulate simultaneously. This only proves that the joke tellers are driven not by artistic striving for originality, but by an emotional need to vent their frustration on a scapegoat at hand.

| "Ethnicizing" Old Russian Nonethnic Jokes

Another source of contemporary Russian ethnic jokelore is "ethnicized" old nonethnic jokes. Usually, a generic Russian joke originally directed downward—to ridicule a group of a lower social status—is reworked into an item aimed sidewise—across the group's ethnic boundaries. Thus the following generic joke from the Russian "stupid soldier" cycle is used in contemporary Russian jokelore to disparage several minorities. The technique of conversion is quite simple; the stupid military man is identified as a member of a targeted ethnicity:

(1.11) A guard [a Ukrainian, a Chukchi, a Georgian] shouts to a soldier
approaching his post:
"Say the watchword!"
"The watchword!"
"Pass on."

"Ethnicization" is especially conspicuous when old jokes that had attacked not a given group's shortcomings, but those of the Soviet system as a whole, are turned ethnic:

(1.12) "Haim, what are you carrying in that bag?"
"Used toilet paper."
"Where are you taking it?"
"To the cleaners." (Kharkover 1:48)

Without the given name of the person addressed, this is the very same joke that circulated in the last decades of the Soviet regime (see Draitser 1980, 26). In its previous life, the joke concerned the shortage of toilet paper throughout the country. With the advent of private enterprise, however, toilet paper became available in many places. With the addition of an ethnically marked (Jewish) name, in a different social context the very same joke has now ceased to be political and has turned ethnic, its target no longer the inefficiency of the centralized Soviet economy, unable to produce even essential items, but instead an alleged intrinsic quality of the targeted group. The implication of this 1993 version of the joke is, of course, that the Jew wants to recycle toilet paper not because of a desperate need, but because of his stinginess, a vice traditionally ascribed to the Jews and, recently, to the Ukrainians as well.

Until the early 1990s, in Russian joke books published in the USSR and abroad (e.g., Dolgopolova 1982, Telesin 1986, Shturman and Tiktin 1987) one seldom encountered any entries involving a Moldavian. As soon as the Moldavian Republic laid claims to autonomy, however, the following Soviet joke reentered the Russian repertory, this time as an ethnic joke. Again, this was accomplished simply by replacing the generic "Soviet tourist" in its old version with "a Moldavian":

(1.13) A Moldavian visiting France decided to go to a whorehouse. He
looked at the price list and bought the cheapest ticket. He walked
along the corridor and read prices posted on the doors. One room
was too expensive, another one even more so. When he couldn't

find a room at the price of his ticket, he got angry and called the Madam:
"What is this? I bought a ticket. Where and how will I be served?"
The Madam looked at his ticket and said:
"For this price you're entitled to self-service only." (Kharkover 1:52)

In its original form, this joke was self-effacing—that is, it rendered all Soviet citizens, whatever their nationality, as poor relatives of prosperous Europeans, as destitute, unable even to taste what the Russians consider the "delicacies of Western life." Now virtually the same joke ridicules not the whole "unhappy brotherhood of peoples" (to slightly change the Soviet cliché), but an estranged ethnicity.

The escalation of tension between the Russians and many minorities in the late Soviet and post-Soviet period is also reflected in the markedly increased harshness of ethnic jokes. Sometimes overtly, often covertly, the new jokelore of this period includes truly hostile gibes directed at various groups. Especially noticeable in the current folk repertory is the proliferation of the "hidden curse" joke. This is the kind of humor that A. J. Chapman, J. R. Smith, and H. C. Foot (166) find "frequently used as a vehicle for ill-disguised, non-physical attacks." In such jokes, an ethnic character is made a victim of some unpleasant turn in his life. He either is badly disfigured, is stricken with a disgusting disease, dies, or is about to die under the most humiliating, denigrating, and shameful circumstances possible.

In fact, the following jokes can be seen as narrative variants of the most popular Russian curses, such as "May you get lost!" "May you croak!" or "May you burn up!" (*Chtob ty propal! Chtob ty sdokh! Chtob ty sgorel!*"). (Givi, Rabinovich, and Ostap are nicknames of a Georgian, a Jew, and a Ukrainian.):

(1.14) "Givi, you had one ear removed surgically and now your hearing is poor. What if they did the same on your other ear?"
"Then I'd see poorly."
"How come?"
"My cap would fall over my eyes." (Ivanova 1996, 117)

(1.15) A Georgian fell into an abyss. Another one shouts to him:
"Vakhtang, are you alive?"
"Alive!"
"Your head is in one piece?
"In one."
"Your hands are OK?"

"OK!"

"Then climb out!"

"Listen, Vano, I am still falling." (Ivanova 1996, 110)

(1.16) "Will you be so kind as to call Rabinovich to the telephone?"

"Which one do you want, the old one or the young one?"

"The old one."

"They're both dead." (Ivanova 1996, 222)

(1.17) "Tell me, is Rabinovich home?"

"So far, yes."

"Why 'so far?' "

"His body will be carried out in fifteen minutes." (Ivanova 1996, 227)

(1.18) Two Ukrainians are talking. One says:

"Tell me, Ostap, do your cows smoke?"

"No."

"Do your sheep smoke?"

"No."

"Then your barn's on fire."

Apparently, most satisfying for the tellers of this kind of joke are those in which one ethnic group perishes at the hands of another:

(1.19) A ship leaving for Israel takes on passengers. One hour passes, a second, a third, and the line of passengers keeps coming aboard. A man who has come to see off a passenger asks the gallant southern [judging by the accent in the original, a Transcaucasian] captain:

"Excuse me, is your space unlimited?"

"Yes. We have made holes in the hull." (Ivanova 1996, 110)

An ethnic man is also often featured as sexually deceived by his wife, the most painful event for the folk male ego. The fact that such "hurting" jokes are intentionally minority-oriented is clearly seen in the "ethnic-blind" humorous plots they utilize. There is nothing innately ethnic in the kinds of misfortune that befall the ethnic man in these jokes; such a bad turn could happen to anyone. Thus, an old joke about a soldier who, returning home after more than nine months' absence, finds his wife with a newborn baby, has reappeared several times recently featuring a Jew, or a Chukchi, or a Ukrainian as the cuckold. These "bad wish" jokes are turned ethnic with the same simple device: the hapless character gets a name that marks him as a member of a targeted ethnicity. The situation of the following joke is also not inherently ethnic:

(1.20) Abram calls his wife and says that he is at the VDC.
"What's that?" asks Sarah.
"It's the Venereal Disease Clinic."
"What's this clinic? What kind of stuff are you giving me?"
"I'm the one who's giving you something? I'm here because of what you gave me." (Repina and Rostovtsev 212)

Without the names of the unfortunate woman and her unlucky husband, the following bit of macabre humor has circulated in Russia for the last forty years, if not longer:

(1.21) Colleagues of Sarah Abramovna's husband call her at work:
"Sarah Abramovna, don't get too agitated. . . . A terrible accident! Your husband, Abram Solomonovich, got caught under a steamroller."
"Oh, my God! Where is he?"
"We brought him to your apartment."
"How could you manage that? The keys are in my purse."
"We've slipped him under the door." (Kharkover 3:41)[13]

| Original Russian Ethnic Jokes

Besides jokes borrowed from a target ethnicity and ethnicized versions of nonethnic jokes, contemporary Russian ethnic jokelore includes a small number of new jokes, many of which use old stereotypes. For example, in the following joke three anti-Semitic stereotypes are used: "the Jews will manage no matter what," "they will go any distance to help one of their own,"[14] and "they are rarely there where the living is difficult" (as one slur goes, "they always find a little warm place [teploe mestechko] for themselves"):

(1.22) After reading a "help wanted" ad, Moisha applies for the job. To get rid of him, the boss gives him an impossible assignment; he must sell a steamship full of snow in Antarctica.
Moisha comes back with a sack full of money and an order for one million cubic meters of snow.
"How did you manage that?" asks the boss.
"It's nothing. The only thing difficult for me was finding another Jew in that place." (Repina and Rostovtsev 84)

At the same time, new Russian jokes have recently been created in which old ethnic stereotypes are broken down and replaced with new ones or long forgotten ethnic stereotypes have been revived, as is the case with Russian jokes about stupid Ukrainians and cowardly Jews. Because of Israeli victories over Arabs in the Six-Day War and in consequent military campaigns, Russian jokes about the Jews of the 1970s and 1980s had ceased to draw on a traditional stereotype of the Jew who avoids rough head-on collisions with his enemies. With the growth of grass-root anti-Semitism in the early 1990s, however, anti-Semitic jokes employing that old stereotype have resurfaced in the Russian ethnic repertory:

(1.23) "Rabinovich, are they telling the truth that Abramovich slapped your face? And you didn't react to it in any way?"
"I didn't react? How do you like that! And who fell down?"
(Petrosian 63)

(1.24) "Mister Rabinovich, they say yesterday Abramovich caught you in the forest and beat you up."
"Some forest, my foot! Just a couple of trees." (ibid.)

In addition, new stereotypes have been created that contradict the previous ones. Although a stereotype is usually perceived as negative, that is not always the case. Of four stereotypical images of Russian Jews described by Felix Dreizin (3–7), two are unquestionably anti-Semitic—"The Tradesman" (*torgash*) and "The Clever One," the cold and calculating Jew. Depending on their treatment, two others—"The Rabbi" (A Wise Man) and "The Family Man"—could be either philo- or anti-Semitic. None of these four Jewish stereotypes imply ineptness or stupidity. Not that the Russians ever consciously intended to stereotype the Jews as intelligent people; the notion of Jewish intelligence is a conclusion by default: it is difficult to present someone who is successful and foolish at the same time (unless one's success is achieved with the help of magic, as is the case with Ivan the Fool in Russian fairy tales).

Recent Russian anti-Jewish jokelore has undergone a change in this respect, however. Besides borrowing old Jewish jokes about the wise men of Chelm, which served as the Jewish in-group satire on learned men who could not handle simple everyday problems, in many editions of Russian joke books published since the early 1990s, one can find a number of items in which the Jews are rendered as incompetent fools. For example:

(1.25) The head of the Supply Department tells the head of Personnel:
"Fill out the forms for firing Rabinovich. He screwed up again! Instead of toilet paper # 3, he ordered sand paper # 2."
(Dezhnov 6)

Of course, in this joke one may see an attempt to feature the Jew in his traditional role of a saboteur who tries to injure tender Russian behinds. Yet what makes the joke even more preposterous is that, while there is no longer the notorious toilet paper shortage of Soviet years, there is no "# 3 toilet paper." Only one kind of paper, rather harsh by Western standards, is available.[15]

This is not an exceptional development in Russian humor, however, or in popular humor in general. Another reversal of a group's stereotype occurred during World War II. Despite the folkloric image of the Germans as capable,[16] during the German invasion of Russia numerous anti-German cartoons and *chastushki* portrayed the enemy as stupid.

Recent jokes devalue the Jews as a group by alluding also to their alleged sexual inadequacy:

(1.26) "Rabinovich, I heard you don't like sex? Is that true?"
"True. First, I get seasick when I'm having it. Secondly, after me, someone else has to do it."

(1.27) A husband and wife come to a rabbi:
"Rabbi, a red-headed baby was born in our family. As you can see, we are both dark-haired. Why did it happen?"
"How often do you make love? Once a week?"
"No."
"Once a month?"
"No."
"Once a year?"
"Ye, maybe . . ."
"That's it! That's where your red-headed baby comes from. It's from rust."

(1.28) A newly wed woman tells her girlfriend:
"Of course, I knew that the Jews get circumcised. But not to such a degree!"

(1.29) A Russian wife asks her Jewish husband:
"Monya, why do you have such long eyelashes?"
"They say I cried a lot in my childhood."
"It would have been better if you'd pissed a lot."

Unlike some other jokes implying the asexuality of Jewish males that are borrowed from Jewish jokelore, this last joke is a ethnicized version of a genuinely Russian joke collected by researchers in remote areas of Northern Russia based on the local sexual stereotype of identifying male and female sexuality through various features of the body (Loginov 448).

An analysis of the repertory of Russian ethnic humor shows that, while many jokes may be borrowed from the target ethnicity itself, only the teller and the audience account for their meaning at a given time.

A study of the ways of enlarging the repertory helps to better understand the jokes. Thus, simply tagging a character with an ethnic name, ethnicized versions of old nonethnic jokes clearly reveal their tendentiousness toward a target minority.

Connecting jokes to other folkloric expressions—curses, proverbs, sayings—is also helpful in discovering their true meaning.

Finally, the study of this repertory shows that a stereotype used in a joke depends on the tellers' emotional need at a given historical moment. For this purpose, an age-long stereotype can be temporarily suspended or totally altered.

CHAPTER 2

"I Didn't Buy My Driver's License: My Brother Gave It to Me for My Birthday"

Russian Jokes about Georgians and Other Southerners

Until the late 1950s, a Georgian character had appeared in Russian folk humor only sporadically. There was no Georgian stereotype to speak of, with the exception of some political jokes about Stalin that used the peculiar Georgian distortion of the Russian language for comic effect. After Stalin's death in 1953, a few jokes addressed the Georgian nationalistic pride in having a Georgian as the leader of the Soviet Union. When Stalin's mummy was placed next to Lenin's in the Mausoleum, the following item made the rounds in Russia:

(2.1) Two Georgians enter the Mausoleum. They see Lenin and Stalin lying side by side. One asks the other:
"Listen, comrade! And who is this character lying next to our Stalin?"
"Why? Don't you know? That's his order of Lenin!" (I. Raskin 394)

As is known, in 1961, after Khruschev's denunciation of Stalin's crimes against humanity, his body was removed from the Mausoleum, an action not to the liking of Georgian nationalists, as a Russian joke of that time suggests:

(2.2) A Georgian enters Lenin's tomb. He asks the guards:

"Listen, comrade! What's happened to such a handsome
mustached man, his decorations all over him, who was lying over
here? Where is he? Where did you take him?"
In order not to embitter the Georgian, one of the guards begins to
explain:
"Well, you know, his relatives came over. . . . They took him
away."
"They took him away?! Can it be? And what about him?" he
points to Lenin, "Why didn't anyone take *him* away? Is he an
orphan, or what?" (I. Raskin 394)

Since they were topical, however, these jokes ceased to circulate as soon
as the novelty of the events faded. Only one Russian joke about the Georgians
became a classic, and it is included in virtually every collection of Soviet
political jokes. Ridiculing the Soviet propaganda claim of "indestructible
friendship between the peoples of the USSR" (*nerushimaia druzhba narodov
SSSR*), it addresses the age-long animosity between Georgians and Armenians:

(2.3) "What is internationalism, Georgian style?"
"That's when people of all nationalities—Georgians, Russians,
Ukrainians, Jews, Tartars, and others—all together, as friends, go
off to slaughter the Armenians." (Telesin 123; for variants, see I.
Raskin 182; Shturman and Tiktin 412)

Due to the Georgians' "high social mobilization, avoidance of disper-
sion, and intense national consciousness"—they were a "state nation," in
Armstrong's (71) taxonomy until the late 1950s—the average Russian had
little contact with them on an everyday basis. Only with the frequent and
rather conspicuous appearance of Georgians in Russian territories, when many
Russians began to come into direct contact with them, did numerous anti-
Georgian jokes begin to emerge in Russian folklore.

This change in Georgian behavior was caused by a rather insignificant
political decision made by the Soviet government. Shortly after Stalin's death,
in an attempt to enliven and beautify the gray landscapes of Russian cities,
the Soviet government lifted its taboo, in effect since the end of the New
Economic Policy (NEP) of the 1920s, against private enterprise, and permitted
individual, small-scale growing and selling of flowers on a free, unregulated
basis. The government also encouraged the growth of citrus fruit in order to
provide vitamin C to the cities, where—sometimes for as much as half the
year—the main cold-weather diet had been cabbage and potatoes.

Under these circumstances, owners of private plots of land in the Transcaucasian republics soon seized the opportunity. The streets and markets of
Russian towns began to be filled with oranges, flowers, and other southern

produce,[1] sold by rather distinctive-looking Transcaucasians, usually dark-haired men with mustaches. Although not all of them were Georgians, they were highly visible and easily identified on the streets and in the markets of Russian cities. (Later, beginning in the 1980s, Russian jokes about Georgians began to be replaced by such vague characterizations as "mustached southern-ers," "Caucasians," or "persons of Caucasian nationality.")[2] Georgians began to frequent places—Russian restaurants and resort areas—where big money was spent overnight. They began buying their way everywhere, beating the rigid and, at the same time, corrupt and inefficient Soviet system of distribution of goods and services.

This roused uneasy feelings among the Russians. Although less than 1 percent of the Georgian population was involved in such activities (Ehidelman 194), the stereotype was born of a Georgian making a quick fortune right in front of the Russians. Their resentment was voiced in the notorious travelogue "Fishing for Gudgeons in Georgia" by Victor Astafiev, a Russian nationalist writer. His Georgian, Otar,

> resembled that type everyone is fed up with; he can't be a true Georgian. He sticks out like a sore thumb, turning up in all the Russian town markets, up to Murmansk and Norilsk, scornfully robbing trusting Northerners blind when selling them rotten fruits or crumpled half-dead flowers. Greedy, illiterate, one the Russians belittle as a 'kopeck soul'; everywhere, without restraint, throwing his money about, taking it from overstuffed pockets made shiny from dirty hands. He's crazy about cars; he brings along his fat children, and in the hotels you can see his eight-year-old Gogiia squeezed into jeans, with sleepy eyes and stuffed cheeks.[3]

In his rebuttal of Astafiev's chauvinistic portrayal of Georgians, Ehidel-man, a Russian literary historian, focuses on Astafiev's idealized portrayal of the Russians as "the trusting Northerners" and on the denigrating charac-terization of Georgians, known for their generosity and hospitality, as having "kopeck souls" (quoted in Ehidelman 193). Astafiev claims that, while making huge amounts of money, the very same type of Georgian fruit seller he describes, "at home counts every penny when giving it to his wife, children, and parents" (ibid.). In his xenophobic zeal, Astafiev, known for the high quality of his earlier works, in this work falls into the sin of contradiction: greedy people do not part easily with their money. Besides, this is a gross distortion of reality. Only one who is completely unfamiliar with the Caucasian tradition of utter respect for parents (e.g., see Zhelvis 307) and devotion to the sanctuary of the family (at least when it comes to its financial support) could make such a statement. What seems to have happened here is that, in his righteous disgust with the prosperous Georgians he has encountered, Astafiev falls into the trap of ethnic self-stereotyping. By assigning to the Georgians those shortcomings of which they are by no means guilty, Astafiev transfers to them the Russians' own sins.[4]

The notion that Russians are entirely free of the vice of avarice is rebutted in their splendid literature. It is enough to mention such world-class misers as notorious "little Judas" Golovlyov from Saltykov-Shchedrin's novel *The Golovlyov Family* and pathological Pliushkin from Gogol's *Dead Souls*. In his novel *Oblomov* (chapter 9, part 1), Goncharov satirizes the thriftiness of Oblomovians, their total obsession with saving money, even if it means sparing candles in their homes and living in semidarkness. Even a rumor about a neighbor spending a lot of money on buying new shirts for himself horrifies them; they tell each other that, because of his insane actions, that man belongs in jail.[5]

Various aspects of the Georgian stereotype outlined by Astafiev may be found in Russian jokelore of the time. In the following item, to make the Georgian look even more villainous, Astafiev's "trusting Northerners" are replaced by a stock jocular character who evokes even more compassion—that of a perennially hungry and destitute student. (One example of a joke involving this character: "Where are you taking this skeleton?" "This is not a skeleton. It's my friend Vassya, a straight-A student. He's just passed his last exam.") The Georgian of the following joke not only takes advantage of a deprived student, that is, "robs [him] blind," but he gloats over his misfortune as well. The Georgian is represented as a voracious worm. The cap that the worm sports in this joke made any Russian instantly recognize who was beyond the image: at that time, Georgians often sported oversized caps that in their specific design carried a semiotic significance— because they could not be found in stores and were always made to order, they signified Georgian affluence:

(**2.4**) With his very last ruble, a student buys a dozen walnuts. He
cracks one of them. It's empty. He cracks another one—again, it's
empty. When he comes to the last one, a worm wearing a cap
crawls out and says:
"It hurts, doesn't it?" (Ivanova 1996, 98)

The private cultivation of flowers and oranges for sale was only the beginning of a flourishing "second economy," in which many people, not only Transcaucasians, took part. In addition to private owners of plots of land, moonlighters, freelance builders (whom the Russians called *shabashniki*), and underground producers of consumer goods comprised a considerable corpus of people whose incomes were many times larger than those of people who lived on only their wages.[6]

The growing new class of affluent people in the Soviet Union was "in-clined to demonstrate their opulence and well-being simply because only the satisfaction from conspicuous consumption, as well as its comfort, provided the incentives to work outside the legal work system" (Shlapentokh 224). While the Russian nouveaux riches tended to flaunt their wealth away from the eyes of their compatriots, usually in Yalta, Sochi, and other resort areas of the Crimea and Caucasus, the Transcaucasians were doing it right there where the money was made—in major Russian cities, primarily in Moscow and Leningrad. Many Russian jokes thus underscore the criminal nature of Georgian affluence, which in the Russian mind is epitomized by ownership of luxurious cars:

(2.5) A Georgian is driving a shabby subcompact "Muscovite." A new "Volga" swiftly overtakes him and stops, blocking the road. A fashionably dressed Georgian gets out and says:
"Why do you disgrace our nationality? Look at me! I'm just a year out of prison, and I'm already driving a Volga."
He slams the car door and whizzes away.
The Georgian in the Muscovite clenches his teeth and continues his journey. Sometime later a luxurious "Mercedes" overtakes him and stops, blocking the road. An even more fashionably dressed Georgian gets out and says:
"Don't you have any shame?! Why do you disgrace our nationality? Look at me! I'm only half a year out of prison, and I'm already driving a Mercedes."
He slams the door of his car and whizzes away.
The Georgian in the Muscovite utters through his clenched teeth:
"A year out of prison! Half a year out of prison! Can't you at least give me time to get home after serving my term?" (I. Raskin 161; for a variant, see Soloviev 1:45)

Thus a Georgian stereotype was born: of materialistic people—wheeler-dealers, crooks, bribe takers, and bribe givers.[7] Although many other nationalities were involved in stealing or accepting bribes for coveted foods and services (the phenomenon was rather ubiquitous and "ethnic-blind"),[8] the setting for this joke was the capital of Georgia:

(2.6) In a Tbilisi secondary school, a teacher asks her students about their fathers' professions.
"My father is a store manager," says one boy.
"My father is director of a wholesale warehouse," says another.
"My father is a director of a supermarket," says a third.
"My father is an engineer . . ."
The class explodes with laughter.
"Children," says the teacher, "it's not good to laugh at somebody else's misfortune."

The stereotypical assumption was that Georgia was where the people with money lived. Signifying this perception of Georgians as "fat cats" is the title of a sampling of jokes about them in L. A. Barsky's (190) collection: "Georgia, a Country of Millionaires." A number of gibes addressed this sore spot. What represented a material dream for the average Russian was portrayed as a mere trifle for a Georgian:

(2.7) In a church, a Georgian prays for money to buy a car. Next to him, a Russian prays for half a liter of vodka. Finally, the Georgian gets annoyed and gives the Russian ten rubles:
"Listen, get yourself a bottle and don't bother God with your trifles." (For a variant, see Ivanova 1996, 111.)

(2.8) Ivan goes on a tour of Georgia. In the course of his travels, he visits a cemetery, where the tour guide takes the group to the graves:
"Here Mister Gugashvili is buried. He was born in 1936, died in 1982. He lived eight years. And here Mr. Takhadze is buried. Born in 1920, he died in 1988. He lived thirteen years."
Ivan is perplexed:
"How come? Why eight years of life? Why thirteen?"
The guide says:
"In Georgia, a person is considered living when he has money, dacha, a car, connections. The rest doesn't count as living."
Upon returning from his trip, Ivan says to his wife:
"When I die, Marusya, engrave on my tombstone: 'Was stillborn.'" (Ivanova 1996, 114)

In the following joke, popular during *perestroika*, the Russian character gives a monthly salary figure, as is customary:

(2.9) A Georgian doctor asks a Russian doctor:
"Listen, comrade! How much does a doctor make in Russia today?"
"On average three thousand rubles."
"It's the same here. But it may differ from day to day." (Ivanova 1994, 128)

While many jokes explicitly address the disparity between the living standards of Russians and Georgians, others do it in a more subtle way. The following item turns a Russian expression about get-rich-quick people— "They rake in the shekels by the suitcase" (*den'gi chemodanami zagrebaiut*)— into a skit:

(2.10) A Georgian barges into a restaurant, takes a seat at a table, and lets fall with a thud a huge, dirty suitcase on a snow-white tablecloth. A waiter approaches him:
"Shame on you! To drop your dirty suitcase on a clean tablecloth!"
"What's with you, dear man? Where do you see a suitcase? It's my wallet." (For a variant, see Ivanova 1996, 108.)

In this joke, one notes the stark contrast between a "snow-white" Russian tablecloth, by implication representing people with "clean consciousness" (*liudi s chistoi sovest'iu*), and the dirty Georgian suitcase (read: money). One may also see in this joke an ironic twist of the Russian fairy-tale image, that of a "tablecloth" that magically covers itself with delicious food (*skatert'-samobranka*). This image of a Georgian heap of money suggests that what is possible for the Russian only in a fairy tale with the help of magic, a Georgian does in the real world with his money. The punchline of the following joke also points to the sore spot in Russian perception of Georgians—their presumed much higher standard of living:

(2.11) A telephone rings:
"Gogi, what are you doing?"
"I'm eating."
"Tell me, what are you eating?"
"It's not for a phone conversation."

In the context of Soviet life, the punchline was quite telling about current conditions. In a time of a rather scarce and bland Russian diet, the folkloric imagination ascribed an overwhelming variety and taste to the food consumed by the Georgians. By saying "It's not for a phone conversation," the Georgian in this joke seems to express the futility of even attempting to describe what he's eating. (As a refrain in Russian fairy tales goes, regarding an extraordinary beauty, "it's impossible to retell it in a fairy tale, it's impossible to describe it in writing" [*ni v skazke skazat', ni perom opisat'*]). At the same time, the punchline implies that, even if the Georgian could answer the question in detail, the mere description of his meal could prompt a police investigation of the source of his income. It was obvious at the time that no person earning regular wages could eat that well.

The growing perception of disparity in standards of living made the Georgians appear to be living not in a territory of the Soviet Union but in another, prosperous, capitalist country—implicitly in the first of the following items and explicitly in the second:

(2.12) A radio announcement at the Tbilisi rail-road station:

"From the second track, train number one leaves Tbilisi for the USSR."

(2.13) Question: "What's FRG?"
"The Federal Republic of Germany."
"Not only that. It's also the Federal Republic of Georgia."

Many jokes about the Georgians stress their corrupting power:

(2.14) Airport in Tbilisi. A ticket booth. As his turn comes up, a Georgian puts a thousand rubles in his passport, extends it to the ticket agent, and says:
"Dear man! One ticket to Moscow."
"All tickets are sold," says the agent and returns the passport.
The passenger adds another thousand rubles:
"Dear man! Give me a ticket! I'm in a big hurry!"
The agent picks up the phone: "Operator, give me the District Attorney's office."
The Georgian thinks: "Is it possible that my countryman will sell me out?"
But he hears what the ticket agent says: "Comrade Prosecutor! Your reservation is cancelled. You won't fly to Moscow." (For a variant, see I. Raskin 162.)

(2.15) A highway patrol officer stops a car. Givi is behind the wheel.
"Your driver's license," asks the officer. He examines the document for a very long time.
Taking offense about his suspiciousness, Givi says:
"You think I bought it, huh? No. My brother gave it to me for my birthday." (Barsky 191; for other variants, see Ivanova 1996, 103, 107; Petrosian 75)

(2.16) A trial in Georgia. A judge says:
"Defendant, you may say your last word to the court!"
The defendant stands and says in a low voice:
"One hundred twenty-five thousand."
"Does prosecution have any objections?"
"No."
"The case is dismissed" (*Na net i suda net*). (For a variant, see Ivanova 1996, 115.)

(2.17) In a restaurant: "Vakhtang, why don't you eat our wonderful *satsivi,* why don't you drink Mukuzani, our wonderful wine?"
"My doctor told me that my liver's in poor shape. He prohibits alcohol and spicy meals."

The next day.
"Vakhtang! What are you doing? You're drinking wine, eating *satsivi*. What about your liver? What does your doctor say?"
"Listen, I gave him one hundred rubles. He gave me his permission." (For a variant, see Ivanova 1996, 110.)

(2.18) A Georgian comes to his friend:
"*Genatsvale* (comrade)! Buy a factory from me, it's a good factory! Listen, buy the factory! It fulfills and overfulfills the state five-year plan. It has been awarded three orders of the Hero of the Socialist Labor. . . ."
"*Genatsvale*! Such a good factory! Why do you sell it?"
"I'll tell you as my friend. I want to buy the Regional Party Committee [in Russian: *obkom*]." (I. Raskin 163)

The satirical implication of the following joke is that only acts of God are not controlled by the Georgian's tremendous wealth:

(2.19) A Georgian sits in front of his TV set and watches the evening news program. The anchorman: "Beginning January 1, prices for food, cloth, hand-made carpets, cut-glass ware, cars, and hard liquor will rise significantly."
"That's OK," exclaims the Georgian. "We've been buying them before, we'll keep buying them."
The anchorman continues: "Costs for transportation and for sanatoria and resorts will also increase."
"That's OK," again exclaims the Georgian. "We've traveled to resorts, we'll keep doing it."
At the end of the program, the anchorman says: "In Georgia tomorrow strong cold winds and heavy rain are expected. In certain regions, hail is possible."
"Just look at them!" the Georgian cries out. "They do whatever they want!" (For a variant, see Ivanova 1996, 103–4.)

A subset of the series of jokes about "those filthy rich" southerners aims at Georgians lavishing money on their children, as Astafiev charged, pampering them to the point of making them look ridiculous in Russian eyes:

(2.20) A Georgian says to his son:
"Listen, Gogiia,[9] if you finish high school as an 'A' student, I'll buy you a black 'Volga.' Let everybody see how smart you are!. If you finish as a 'B' student, I'll buy you a gray 'Volga.' But if you finish as a 'C' student, I'll buy you a red one—to let everyone see what a fool you are!" (For variants, see I. Raskin 160; Ivanova 1996, 118–19.)

(2.21) Gogi comes up to his father:
"Dad, tonight's my prom night. I'm already seventeen. On this occasion, may I drink a little bit?"
"Of course, Gogi. You're already a big boy, you may drink some hard liquor."
"How much, Dad?"
His father shows three fingers—about two inches: "That much."
"Ok, Dad. And may I take some money with me?"
"Yes, Gogi. You're a big boy now, and you may take some money with you."
"How much, Dad?"
His father shows him the same three fingers: "That much . . ."
(Ivanova 1996, 102)

(2.22) A young Georgian university student writes to his mother:
"I really feel awkward. All my Russian friends come to school by bus, and I am the only one coming in his own car."
His mother answers him:
"Sonny, why should you stand out from the others? Be like everybody else. Go ahead and buy yourself a bus." (Barsky 191–92; for a variant, involving a trolley, see I. Raskin 160–61)

In several jokes, a point is made that Georgian money (not their children's abilities) buys those young people's way into the most prestigious higher-education institutions:

(2.23) A young Georgian takes entry exams to Tbilisi Conservatory. All who are on the take get their money. He passes safely all exams. Only a music exercise [*solfeggio*] is left. They tell him:
"This is very simple. We'll press a piano key, and you'll guess which one."
The young Georgian turns his back to the piano, listens to the sound of the note, and then points to one of the professors:
"You're the one who pressed it." (I. Raskin 161)

The next item makes a clear point that the aim of getting diplomas for young Georgians is not to serve society, but just to secure lucrative positions for themselves. In the Soviet Union, the position of doctor-in-chief (*glavvrach,* similar to the American "head of clinic") was assumed to be very profitable; holders of this position were often approached with bribes by both patients and subordinate doctors:

(2.25) "Well, young man," says the head of the Examination Committee to a Georgian university entrant. "So, you want to go to our medical school, to become a doctor. . . ."

"Hell no," says the young Georgian. "I don't want to be a doctor. I want to be doctor-in-chief."

It is noteworthy that, by and large, Russian jokes about the Georgians do not address the ways in which a Georgian's wealth is acquired. The premise is that to be a Georgian means being rich—period. In telling of Georgian peasants selling the fruits (often literally) of their labor in Russian marketplaces, Russian joke tellers were not concerned with the effort and risk involved in growing, storing, and transporting highly perishable goods for more than a thousand miles. Many anti-Georgian jokes express indignation and a considerable degree of envy "which [became] a leading psychological feature of Soviet life [of the time], in direct contrast to the past" (Shlapentokh 225).

Often Russian jokes addressed the irritation of the tellers with Georgians buying their way through the scarce and rigid Soviet system:

(2.26) A Georgian flies into Moscow on business for a day. In the morning, he says to his Moscow friends:
"I want to go to the Bolshoi Theater and to the Kremlin to the hall where the tsarina's diamonds are. Should be fun."
"There's no way to manage it. You can't get tickets for the Bolshoi Theater. And to see the tsarina's diamonds, there's a long waiting list."
Late the same day, the Georgian says good-bye to his friends:
"Moscow's a beautiful city! The Bolshoi Theater is good. I saw "Swan Lake" over there. . . ."
"How did you get a ticket?"
"Who needs it! I paid as much as it was necessary and they let me in and seated me in the first row. I also went to the Kremlin and I saw the diamonds. . . ."
"How come! After all, you have to get yourself on a waiting list first. . . ."
"Why bother with the waiting list? I paid as much as was necessary—and they brought the diamonds out." (Ivanova 1996, 113; for a 1970s version of this joke, involving Lenin's mummy, see Draitser 1980, 39)

A great number of Russian jokes stress Georgians' plain stupidity and utter ineptness. Here are some samples in addition to 1.11:

(2.27) "Givi, do you like tomatoes?"
"Only to eat. Otherwise—no."

(2.28) One Georgian asked his wife to put two glasses next to his bed—one empty, one with water.

"Why empty?" asked his wife.
"You're a stupid woman! Suppose I wake up in the middle of the
night. I may feel thirsty and I may feel not thirsty." (Ivanova
1996, 103)[10]

(2.29) After a water polo competition, Givi and his brother get together.
The brother says:
"Vano, why didn't you pass the ball to Gogi?"
"But I scored!"
"Yeah, but Gogi drowned." (For a variant, see Ivanova 1996,
109.)

Another means of denouncing the Georgians employed in many Russian
jokes is by stressing their strictly materialistic orientation, their slighting, even
contemptuous, attitude toward cultural values:

(2.30) On the corner of Tverskaia Street in Moscow, a mustached
southerner stands and counts a wad of money:
"Four hundred, five hundred, six hundred, seven hundred . . ."
A passerby comes up to him:
"Excuse me, would you tell me how to get to the Central
Library?"
"Hold on, dear man, hold on . . . two thousand one hundred, two
thousand two hundred, two thousand three hundred . . ."
"Excuse me, would you tell me how to get to the Central
Library?"
"Hold on, dear man . . . five thousand three hundred, five
thousand four hundred, five thousand five hundred, five thousand
six hundred . . . five thousand six hundred forty . . . that's it!
Listen, dear man, you should get yourself a real business!
Business!"

In complete disregard of the evidence that, in Soviet times, Georgian
culture reached a rather high level, and in some areas, especially cinema,
ballet, and drama, even rivaled that of the Russians, achieving well-deserved
all-Union fame, the following joke portrays the Georgian intelligentsia as
just pretending to pursue cultural interests while much more preoccupied
with its gastronomic urges. Here, in its utter disregard of reality, Russian
folk humor follows a pronouncement ascribed to Stalin, which he presumably
made during the purges of the 1930s, when infamous trials of top party leaders
and military and intellectual elite were based on fabricated evidence: "If facts
are not confirmed, it's too bad for the facts" (*esli fakty ne podtverzhdaiutsia,
tem khuzhe dlia faktov*):

(2.31) The Georgian Academic Drama Theater gives a premier performance of *Hamlet*. The cream of the Georgian intelligentsia has gathered.
The curtain goes up. The stage is completely blacked out. Then a tiny dot of light appears, which begins very slowly to grow.
There is a whisper in the hall:
"What an original take! What a wonderful director's invention!"
The dot keeps growing. Finally, in the bright light of the enlarged dot a chef in a dirty apron appears:
"The first two rows!. Shashliks are ready!" (For a variant, see I. Raskin 162.)

A few jokes portray the Georgians as hot-tempered, savage people, for whom murder is just a pastime:

(2.32) A Caucasian diary:[11]
"Monday. Its boring.
Tuesday. All day long the neighbor's boy was chasing my cockerel. He didn't catch him.
Wednesday. I slaughtered the neighbor's boy.
Thursday. The whole clan of relatives of the neighbor's youngster was chasing me. They didn't catch me.
Friday. I slaughtered the whole clan of relatives of the neighbor's youngster.
Saturday. The whole village was chasing me. They didn't catch me.
Sunday. I slaughtered the whole village.
Monday. It's boring." (Ivanova 1996, 102)

(2.33) During a math class, a teacher asks:
"What does it come to—two times two, Gogi?"
Gogi gets up. He has no answer.
From behind him, [a Russian boy] Pete whispers to him: "It's five."
Gogi repeats: "Five."
"Sit down, Gogi. You got F. And you, Pete, no prompting!"
After recess, the teacher comes into the class, looks it over, and says:
"Where's Pete?"
Nobody knows.
The teacher says: "Gogi, where's Pete?"
"I fucking slaughtered him." (Ivanova 1996, 117)

Note that the illiterate Georgian boy is juxtaposed with the presumably more knowledgeable Russian boy, Pete, the practical joker. Since, judging by the teacher's question, the action takes place in the first grade of primary school, the joke's implication is that the Georgians' savagery runs in their blood.

Portraying Georgians as uncivilized and inept imbeciles for whom culture means nothing has had a hidden psychological agenda. Such jokes imply that these people do not deserve their wealth, that no brains are needed, for they do not make their money through the competence necessary in the modern technological world. It is assumed that the Georgians are just lucky to be born in an immensely rich land where, as the Russians say, "it's enough to put a stick in the soil and it begins to bloom."

A typical device in folk humor, characterizing a person as provincial—in folk logic, stupid,—is to take him to the zoo and amaze him with an exotic species:

(2.34) A southerner hurries through the zoo. Finally, he comes to a giraffe, looks at it for a long time, and then loudly exclaims, "I still don't believe it."

(In a similar joke about the Ukrainians [3.14] the creature in question is a parrot. It seems that the farther the target group's territory is from the joke teller's, the more exotic the specimen in question is).

To the same end of denigrating the Georgians as uncultured, many jokes about them are based on language distortion, typical of many ethnic jokes told around the globe (V. Raskin 181–85). Jokes making fun of their clumsy, essentially illiterate, handling of the Russian language belong to the category in which "the butt of the jokes is a linguistic minority on the periphery whose members may have only a limited knowledge of the main language" (Davies 1990, 53). These jokes are similar to Mexican jokes about the Spanish of native speakers of Mayan, Iranian jokes about Turkish-speaking Rashtis having difficulties with Persian (Farsi), and Iraqi jokes about Kurds making weak attempts at Arabic.

The comic effect of stupidity derives from a folk association between primitive and clumsy management of language and lack of intelligence. Usually, Georgian-speakers in such gibes show their inability to recognize various grammatical forms in Russian (masculine gender vs. feminine, a noun vs. a verb, etc.). A rather skillful humorous ploy used in several jokes consists of having one Georgian teach Russian to another, with the teacher as ignorant as his pupil. Most such jokes do not fare well in translation, but the following one marginally conveys the comic idea (in Russian, the words for "a leaf" [*list*] and "a stork" [*aist*] sound close enough to make the Georgian confuse them):

(2.35) A Georgian got a job in a school, teaching Russian. He dictates in Russian:
"Autumn began. A yellow leaf flew down from a tree."
Little Vova asks:
"What's a leaf?"
The Georgian:
"I don't know. A birdie, I suppose." (Ivanova 1996, 95)

Besides ridiculing Georgian ineptness in Russian, other jokes make the point that if a Georgian doesn't master Russian, no matter how successful he may be, eventually he will perish among the Russians:

(2.36) A Georgian was swimming in the sea and suddenly began to drown. A Russian was strolling along the shore. The Georgian forgot how to call for help in Russian and began to shout the first Russian words that came to mind:
"Hey, my friend, I'm . . . taking a swim . . . for the last time! It's disappointing, yes?" (For a version involving a Chukchi, see Belianin and Butenko 100.)

Mockery of their presumed illiteracy and low cultural standards is often combined with another script of popular disparagement—the Georgians are oversexed.[12] This characterization comes in part from popular physiognomy. Some Russian men still share an ancient belief, one supported by doctors in medieval times (Bakhtin 97) and one that is alive and well today in other cultures (Simons 166), according to which the size of a man's nose signifies the size of his phallus, and therefore his reproductive ability. According to one Russian saying, "what's in a shop window is in the shop" (*chto na vitrine, to i v magazine*) (Loginov 451). According to another Russian saying, "An aquiline nose means a prick like a club" (*nos s gorbinkoi, khui dubinkoi*) (ibid.)—that is, a man with such a nose possesses great erection capability. The Russians see the Georgians as hook-nosed, and so endowed with great sexual prowess ("They asked a Georgian: 'What's your favorite bird?' 'An eagle!' 'Why?' 'Its beak is beautiful!' "):

(2.37) Two Georgians are resting under a tree:
"Listen, I can't stand it anymore! A whole week without a woman!"
"Gogi, dear man, aren't you living with your wife?"
"Why don't you mention my mother as well" (*ty by eshche mamu vspomnil*)!

(2.38) A cockerel makes love to a chicken. A Georgian comes out of his house and throws out a handful of corn. The cockerel abandons the chicken and snaps up the corn.

"Heaven forbid I should be that hungry!" says the Georgian.

(2.39) A Georgian in a doctor's office:
"Doctor, what should I do? I've begun to suffer from impotence."
"Well, what kind of sex life do you have?"
"A normal one. Every night I have my wife. Every evening I
have my mistress. During the work day, I have my secretary.
That's basically all."
"Don't you see, it's all due to your sexual overindulgence. With
such a lifestyle, impotence is bound to develop eventually."
"That's why it happens?"
"Of course."
"Thank God. And I thought it's from masturbation." (For another
version of this joke, see V. Raskin 169–70.)

Because of his uncontrollable, larger-than-life masculinity, a Georgian
gets into all sorts of embarrassing situations:

(2.40) A mustached southerner comes up to women sitting in a
gynecologist's reception room and asks who is last in line. They
look at him with interest and nod toward a seat in a far corner.
A nurse comes out from the doctor's office and asks the man:
"Citizen, who do you want to see?"
"Who, who . . . Do they install a spiral [I.U.D.] here?"
"Yes, they do."
"Well, if they install it here, it means they remove it here as well,
doesn't it?"

A number of jokes reveal Russian men's irritation with the Georgians
on sexual grounds; their money, cars, and fashionable flamboyant clothes
made the Russians feel that the Georgians were not their southern neighbors,
but living on another, futuristic, planet. Thanks to their affluence, they were
perceived as formidable competitors for the attention of Russian women:

(2.41) On a female nude beach, a flying saucer lands. Two aliens come
out in shining suits. Curious girls surround them:
"Are you extraterrestrial?"
"Yes."
"And where are you from?"
"From the Alfa Centaur."
"And does everybody there have flying saucers?"
"Yes, everybody."
"And everybody can fly to us?"
"Of course."

"And does everybody have such shining suits?"
"No, not everybody, only me and Gogi." (Ivanova 1996, 99)

Often the Georgians have been portrayed in jokes as both filthy rich and hypersexual:

(2.42) A Georgian wants to marry a girl. She sets conditions:
"I want to have our own apartment."
"If you love me, you'll have an apartment."
"I want a car."
"If you love me, you'll have a car."
"I want your penis to be 12 inches long."
"If you love me, you'll cut the extra off, and you'll have your 12 inches." (Ivanova 1994, 109)

As a way of holding the edge in sexual competitiveness, a number of Russian jokes stress the Georgians' cultural inferiority, suggesting that they are nothing but hairy, uncivilized men (gorillas) with a lot of money:

(2.43) The zoo. Near a monkey cage, a woman asks a Georgian standing nearby:
"Tell me, please, is this monkey a woman or a man?"
The man is silent. She asks again. Finally, he bursts out:
"It's a male, not a man. A man is one who has money, and this is a male!" (Kharkover 1:12)

Often both low culture and hypersexuality are combined:

(2.44) In a train compartment a German woman rides on the upper berth, and a Georgian man on the lower. The woman becomes bored. She bends down toward the Georgian and says: "*Sprechen zie Deutsch?*"
"Of course I will, my dear. Why ask?"

Here, a Georgian assumes that a German woman is not asking an innocent question in her own language, but instead, skipping all the preliminaries, is soliciting his sexual favors. In a similar joke, the setting is a Moscow bus: a French (or English) woman inadvertently stamps on a Georgian man's foot and says, "Pardon, Monsieur" (or "Excuse me, Mister"). He responds: "Of course I want it."

According to Russian jokelore, if a Georgian attends a cultural event, his actual interest is in sex. For example, at a concert by Liudmila Zykina, a famous Russian singer who happens to be full-figured, he rejoices not in her voice, but in her sexual appeal:

(2.45) At the end of a concert, the Georgians in the audience greeted
Zykina with a standing ovation and did not want her to leave the
stage.
She asked to be excused from further singing because she was
tired.
"It's OK. Don't sing. Just move around the stage, move!"

In another joke, a Georgian rushes to a ballerina, not to thank her for her
performance, but to express his righteous indignation that she is not to his
sexual taste:

(2.46) After a ballet performance, an angry Georgian hurries onstage
and asks a ballerina:
"Listen, dear, do you have boobs?"
"Of course I do," the puzzled woman answers.
"What about an ass, do you have it?"
"What do you mean? Of course, I have one."
"If so, then tell me, for God sake, why don't you wear them?"

The Georgians are sometimes depicted as chasing women just for the
sake of maintaining their reputation as philanderers:

(2.47) Sophia Loren arrived in Tbilisi. With enormous effort, the militia,
having saved her from great crowds of her fans, brought her to
her hotel and posted guards around it. When finally left alone,
the actress stepped out on the balcony, only to spot Gogiia, who
was climbing up to her from below. He had a diamond ring in his
teeth. As he ascended, the Georgian apologized for disturbing
her, introduced himself, and asked her to accept the ring as a
small token of his deep respect and appreciation of her talent.
"But this is a very expensive present! How can I reciprocate?"
"Oh! I don't need anything from you! Just one little thing. Just
before you leave, when you're boarding the plane, find me in the
crowd and say: 'Gogiia! Good-bye!' I don't need anything
more!"
The day of her departure came. The actress climbed the steps,
found the man, waved her hand and shouted:
"Gogiia! Good-bye!"
Gogiia looked sidewise at the crowd that was eyeing him with
envy and said, waving his hand:
"Aw! Listen, get going! For two weeks I've had to put up with
you!" (For variants, see Ivanova 1996, 116, I. Raskin 163.)

This image of the Georgian as a womanizer par excellence is responsible
for a newly coined verb: *prigruzinivat'sia,* "to behave like a Georgian," in

contemporary Russian slang; it connotes persistent stalking of a woman and making sexual advances toward her (Elistratov 364).[13]

As the Russians project on the Georgians (and the Jews) their own sexual taste—a preference for robust women[14]—many jokes about Georgians' sexual overindulgence carry an additional semiotic significance. In them, sexual greed and material acquisitiveness are interchangeable. In Russian folk consciousness, buying power spells sexual prowess. The Georgians' love for big women corresponds with their image as "money bags" (big money—big women, little money—skinny women):

(**2.48**) A Georgian comes to a lingerie shop. "Show me please the largest panties you have," he says to the sales clerk. "Excellent! Here is my telephone number. When someone wants to buy it, ask her to call me." (For a variant, see Petrosian 75.)

(**2.49**) On a train, a group of women have a conversation: "At home I have wonderful violets." "And I have carnations." "And I have peonies." "And I have orchids." From the upper berth, a Georgian man interjects: "By the way, about little flowers. In Tbilisi, on Rustaveli Prospect, I have a beautiful girlfriend. Her little tushi is like a table. Her name's Rose." (Ivanova 1996, 124)

Thus, tales about the Georgians' unbridled sexual exploits, their larger-than-life carnal appetites, bolster their image as "fat cats." (Incidentally, in colloquial Russian, "a cat" [*kot*] means a Don Juan; the Georgians' black mustaches reinforce this image.)

Besides disparagement of the Georgians on sexual grounds as seducers and rapists, Russian jokelore also portrays them as inclined to perversion, which includes, in the Russian folk mind, homosexuality together with pedophilia and bestiality:

(**2.50**) A mustached southerner comes to a doctor's office for a checkup. The doctor inserts a special instrument into his rectum, moves it there and asks: "Is it painful that way, comrade?" "No." "What about this way, comrade?" "Listen, doc, let's get less formal. . . ."

(**2.51**) At night, in Tbilisi, voices are heard from the courtyard:

"I love you."
"I love you too."
"What's your name?"
"Givi."
"Mine too." (Ivanova 1996, 97)[15]

(2.52) Two Georgians meet.
"Vano, they are drafting my wife into the army."
"Why? Is your wife a man?"
"What do you mean, a man! He's just a boy." (ibid. 100)

(2.53) In a remote mountain region, a commission arrived. After
attending classes and inspecting the school, the commission
went into the school yard to see how children spent time during
recess. Upon observing the scene, their hair stood on end. They
ran into the principal's office and shouted from the threshold:
"In your school yard!. A little jackass is strolling. . . . Children
approach it from behind! They do such things with it! It's
horrible!"
The principal raised his brow:
"Is the little jackass white or black?"
"White . . ."
"Then it's OK. The white one is the children's."

As noted previously, although the covert privatization of the Soviet society through wheeler-dealership, bribe taking, pilfering, and other economic
crimes was committed by many Soviet citizens, without regard to their ethnic
identity, Russian jokelore cast the Georgians as the chief perpetrators of these
acts. The Georgians, thus, joined (and often overshadowed) the Jews as money
mongers. That is why a Russian joke playing on the double meaning of the
word "Volga" (as the name of the great Russian river and of a Soviet-made
automobile) exists in two identical forms; the only difference is the name of
the target nationality: it is either a Georgian or a Jew. Because in the folk
consciousness the Volga River is referred to as "the dear mother" (as, for
instance, in the popular Russian song about her), the subliminal message of
the following joke can be easily interpreted as " 'those outsiders' are buying
up 'Mother Russia' itself:"

(2.54) "Can a Georgian [a Jew] purchase [a] Volga?"
"He can. But what does he need so much water for?"

A contemporary Russian proverb even claims the commercial superiority
of a Georgian over the traditional image of a Jew as an ingenious black
marketer: "Where a Georgian passes through, two Jews are out of business"

(*Gde odin gruzin proshel, tam dvum evreiam delat' nechego;* Kozlovsky 229).[16] Thus, the Georgians as an enterprising group have joined the Jews as scapegoats for the economical difficulties of Russian life. An urban *chastushka* is a rather crude verbal attack on the Georgians' alleged bribery of salespeople, thus depriving the Russians of highly sought-after food:

(**2.55**) Ne budet miasa v magazinakh   There won't be meat in the stores
Poka ne sdokhnut vse gruziny.   Until all Georgians croak. (Kozlovsky 314)[17]

An echo of this stereotype of the Georgian as a man of means can be heard even today, now that the nickname "New Russians," connoting nouveaux riches, is widely used. As a current joke (1996) goes,

(**2.56**) A Georgian boy asks his father:
"Daddy, what nationality am I?"
"You're a Georgian"
"And you?"
"I'm also a Georgian"
"And Mom?"
"She's a Georgian as well."
"So, Uncle Otar is also a Georgian?"
"No. He's a New Russian."

Anti-Georgian jokelore first reflected gradual internal changes in the social fabric due to the appearance of a second, "shadow" economy in the early 1960s. Russian jokes about the Georgians and other Southerners covertly expressed the Russians' dissatisfaction with the economic status quo. These conditions were seen as a violation of the implicit social contract between the Russian people and the Soviet regime, according to which egalitarianism would be observed, even if it meant equality of poverty.

Anti-Georgian jokelore is also indicative of the ways in which an ethnic stereotype takes its shape and gradually evolves. The Georgians' high visibility in Russian cities and their striking appearance made them obvious targets, a way to disparage undeserved prosperous.

Besides using the traditional scripts of disparagement of an ethnicity—that of stupidity, linguistic inadequacy, and sexual abnormality—jokes about Georgians also allege their low cultural values. Such a script in folklore contains an implicit self-congratulatory element. It compliments the tellers' group, which, despite economic hardship, continues to hold such values in high esteem.

Salt Pork in Chocolate

Russian Jokes about the Ukrainians

Since Ukrainians and Russians come from a common Slavic stock, have mutu-
ally enriching cultural influences, and speak closely related languages, it seems
especially odd that, in comparison with contemporary Russian jokes told about
other ethnicities, those aimed at the Ukrainians are unusually uncharitable,
sometimes openly malicious. These jokes send a clear message—the Russians
utterly disapprove of them, finding them without a single redeeming attribute.

Indeed, Russian jokes about the Jews render them laughable on more than
one account, but at least their mental abilities are most often recognized: a
smart Jew is an essential part of the stereotype. Although a Georgian in Russian
jokelore is berated for being oversexed, he still possesses sexual prowess—an
enviable quality from the folk point of view. While both the Georgians and
the Ukrainians are ridiculed as dim-witted, the following rather crude joke
stresses the Ukrainians' inferiority to the Georgians in this respect as well:

(3.1) A Georgian goes to a brain surgeon: "Help me, my dear man. My
head aches all the time: there's my wife to worry about, my
mother-in-law, my dissertation to finish, my house to take care of,
my car . . . I can't stand it! Operate on me! Cut where and
whatever you see fit!"
"All right," says the doctor, "but my operation will affect a
significant part of your brain."
"OK, my friend. What's a brain, anyway? It just aches!"
After the operation, the Georgian opens his eyes. The
doctor asks him:
"Well, how do you feel now?"
He answers in Ukrainian: Very well ("*O tse garno*")![1]

Today's Russian jokelore treats Africans as uncivilized, but depicts them as having at least some warm human qualities: they are trusting and generous. Even the numbskull Chukchi of the immensely popular joke series has some compensating traits of character: overall, he is a benign ethnic man. In Russian jokelore involving the Ukrainians with any other group, however, the former invariably play the part of the scoundrel. In the following item, a Negro readily shares his bananas and pineapples with a Ukrainian (here denigrated as *khokhol,* after the bushy forelock on his ancestor's head), but the latter refuses to return the favor:

(3.2) A Negro and a *khokhol* are train passengers. The Negro gets out his bananas.
Khokhol: "What's that?"
Negro: "Bananas."
Khokhol: "Let me taste them."
Negro: "Go ahead, help yourself."
Some time later, the Negro gets out his pineapples.
Khokhol: "What's that?"
Negro: "Pineapples."
Khokhol: "Let me taste them."
Negro: "Go ahead."
Some time later, the *khokhol* gets out his salt pork.
Negro: "What's that?"
Khokhol: "Salt pork."
Negro: "Let me taste it."
Khokhol: "What's there to taste? Salt pork is salt pork."
(Kharkover 3:39; for a variant, see I. Raskin 427).

In a similar tale, two Negro students are hungry and watch a Ukrainian consuming delicious food. Noticing their starving looks, he expresses pity that he has nothing to offer them, since he does not have bananas. It is a denigrating jibe aimed at both ethnicities, but the main target is clearly the Ukrainians.

This mean portrayal of the Ukrainians in contemporary Russian jokelore is especially conspicuous in jokes that compare behavior of various nationalities under the same dire circumstances:

(3.3) Pictures of hell. There are no guards around the first vat of boiling tar. One man jumps out of it and runs off.
Devil: "That's a Russian. He'll make a quick run for his half a liter of vodka. He'll come back and keep suffering, no problem."
Sure enough, the man returns and splashes back into the vat.
The second vat is also unguarded.

Devil: "Its for the Ukrainians. They would be glad to escape, but there's no hope. Here is Gritsko trying to climb out, and Taras pulls him back, down into the vat. Now Taras is making an attempt, and Gritsko does not let him get away."
The third vat is also unguarded. Tops of men's heads stick out in even rows.
Devil: "That's the Germans. They are told "*Stileegestanden!*" and they will stand forever without moving.
The fourth vat is surrounded with several rows of barbed wire and guard posts with machine guns. Vicious dogs run around it. A patrol helicopter hovers over it.
Devil: "This one is for the Jews. God forbid, if one of them runs away, he'll drag them all after him." (Shturman and Tiktin 412–13)

Thus, in this joke the Russians are unable to escape from hell due to their excusable human weakness—their heavy drinking. The Germans are shown as overly obedient. The Jews are disparaged for their excessive clannishness.[2] It is the Ukrainians whose behavior as a group is the ugliest—they cannot change their destiny because they betray each other.[3]

Grossly mistreating the Ukrainians, these contemporary Russian jokes are rarely graced with any wit or humor. They often reveal so much malevolence and loathing that many of them hardly deserve to be called jokes; they are better termed invectives. This is quite consistent with my observation about the relationship between strong negative emotions expressed in a joke and the joke's artistic quality: as a rule, when spite takes over, humor fails, for humor often reconciles hostile feelings.

The excessively harsh treatment of the Ukrainians in these jokes points to complex psychological underpinnings that have little to do with the butt of the jokes, but everything to do with their tellers. The true reasons for Russian animosity toward the Ukrainians, as expressed in this jokelore, lie in the complexity and volatile nature of contemporary ethnic, social, and political relationships between the two groups. In his seminal article on the nature of ethnic humor around the world, entitled "Ethnic Jokes, Moral Values and Social Boundaries," Christie Davies (1982, 384) writes:

All ethnic groups have two sets of boundaries that are important to their members. The first are the social and geographical boundaries of the group that define who is a member and who is not. The second are the moral boundaries of the group which define what is acceptable and characteristic behavior of the members, and what is unacceptable behavior characteristic of outsiders. Ethnic jokes police these boundaries. They mock groups who are peripheral to the central or dominant group or who are seen by them as ambiguous.

What should be added to this generally useful assessment of ethnic humor is that the need to police these borders and redefine them for the joke tellers becomes especially acute when an ambiguous or volatile historical situation arises and a definition of "who is who, ethnically" becomes particularly important. Vamik Volkan (91) observes that "The individual or group adheres more stubbornly to a sense of ethnicity when stressed by political or military crisis."

Contemporary Russian jokes about the Ukrainians are most illustrative in this respect. Tensions between the two Slavic groups have existed for a long time and have been reflected in the folklores of both peoples in the form of insulting nicknames (the Ukrainian ones directed at Russians, *moskal'* and *katsap,* versus the Russian nickname for a Ukrainian, *khokhol*) and satirical proverbs,[4] a phenomenon characteristic of many neighboring groups the world over (i.e., French vs. English, German vs. Polish and French vs. German, etc.). However, current Russian jokes about the Ukrainians redefine the borders between the groups in a new and changing sociopolitical environment.

Age-old Russian folk prejudices against the Ukrainians influenced Soviet policy decisions regarding the Ukrainian Republic and the Ukrainians (Armstrong 33). Today's Russian jokes about the Ukrainians are a rather new phenomenon, however. While, during most of the Soviet period, the Ukrainians, by and large, submitted to the role of "younger brothers,"[5] in Armstrong's terminology, and "knew their place" ("Every cricket should know its own niche" [*kazhdyi sverchok znai svoi shestok*], as the Russian proverb goes), Russian jokelore, if it addressed them at all, had been rather benevolent to the Ukrainians. Numerous collections of Soviet underground jokes of the pre-Gorbachev period include few items related to them.

Thus none of the four jokes involving them (out of a total 1,001!) in Telesin's (1986) book are even a bit malevolent. Moreover, of two jokes in which the presence of the Ukrainians is rather accidental, one is sympathetic to their plight: "What's the biggest country in the world?" "Ukraine. Its borders are in the Carpathian mountains, its capital is in Moscow, its prisons are in Siberia, and its churches are in Canada" (Telesin 124). Furthermore, despite the popular prejudice against the Ukrainians that they had been avid German collaborators during World War II, another joke dated around the end of the 1950s, at a time of heightened tension between the USSR and Red China, depicts a Ukrainian saving (albeit with an ulterior motive) a Jew from Germany:

(3.4) They summoned a Ukrainian to the KGB Headquarters:
"Explain how come you get regular parcels from Israel?"
"During the war, I hid a Jew."

"And for you, a Soviet citizen, isn't it disgraceful to receive parcels from these kikes? Have you given any thought about your future?"
"Yes, I'm hiding a Chinese now." (Telesin 143)

Beginning with Gorbachev's *glasnost* policy, when Ukrainians protested Moscow's suppression of their national culture and its wholesale Russification, the relatively stable vision of Ukraine as part and parcel of the monolithic Soviet Union of the pre-*perestroika* period began to crumble, giving way to ambivalent and ambiguous feelings about the immediate future of the relationship between the two nations. Derisive Russian jokes about the Ukrainians began reflecting the growing tension between the two groups. The underlying motif of all these jokes became the Ukrainian struggle for autonomy.

Russian public statements and debates of the time showed the unmistakeable opposition of nationalistically minded Russians to parting with the Ukrainian Republic. In his famous work, *Kak nam obustroit' Rossiiu* (How Should We Manage Russia), Solzhenitsyn sees the three Slavic nations (the Byelorussians are the third) as inseparable, sharing a common fate.[6] Russian jokes of the time reflected Russian dissatisfaction with the Ukrainians' demands for more self-government and their attempts to take a stand as a full-fledged nation. With Ukraine insisting on its distinctive national identity, including the use of the Ukrainian language as a state language and reaffirmation of the distinct nature of Ukrainian culture and its historical traditions, the old derogatory nickname for the Ukrainians in the Russian vernacular, *khokhol,* cited previously, resurfaced in the 1980s in everyday conversations and jokes as a way of stressing their intransigence.

Considering the strategic and economic importance of the Ukrainian Republic to the Russians, its moves to become an independent state could only produce high concern. As is the case in many such situations, malicious jokes aimed at the Ukrainians revealed a wide range of negative feelings, from mere irritation to open animosity:

(3.5) In a stationery store, a little boy asks the saleslady,
"Do you have notebooks I can turn into kites?"
"No. They don't exist."
"And do you have glue I can paint with?"
"No!"
A customer standing behind the boy:
"Listen, little fellow, go away and don't bother the lady with your crazy ideas."
The boy leaves, and the customer says:
"Please give me a globe of Ukraine." (Genis 2:179).

(3.6) In a birch grove, a *khokhol* breaks the trees with his head. Another *khokhol* comes over:
"What's with you, Petro?"
"A *moskal* just passed by and said: 'What a purely Russian landscape.'"

It is all too obvious that the hidden target of (3.5) is the Ukrainian thrust for freedom from Russian dominance; the teller both resents it and is annoyed with it. He treats such a move as, on the one hand, a case of a petty, "childish" whim, on a par with a little boy's childish requests, and of Ukrainian megalomania on the other.

In (3.6), the Ukrainians' stubborn—from the Russian point of view, "bullheaded"—drive for autonomy is interpreted as an anti-Russian tendency. The Russophobic Ukrainian in the joke actually behaves like a mad bull—crushing birch trees with his head. Other jokes allege that the Ukrainians are bent on hurting the Russians in any way possible; if they cannot do it themselves, they dream of a proxy:

(3.7) A Ukrainian catches a little goldfish, who says in a human voice:
"Let me go. I'll fulfill three of your wishes."
"Good," says the Ukrainian.
"Tell me your first wish," says the little goldfish.
"Let the Crimean Tartars go to war with Finland."
"Granted. Give me your second wish."
"And now let them go back to the Crimea."
"That's strange. But, as you wish."
"And my third wish: let the Tartars go to Finland again."
"But wasn't that your first wish?" The little goldfish says.
"Maybe that's so," the Ukrainian smiles. "But the thought that they would go through Moscow three times makes my heart rejoice."

Other jokes hint at the self-defeating economic consequences of Ukrainian independence. Thus, one such joke cites gas shortages in Ukraine as a result of the disputes between the two states:

(3.8) A Ukrainian caught a rabbit. He brought it to his wife and asked her to grill it.
"I can't," said his wife. "There's no gas in our gas stove."
The Ukrainian threw the rabbit out. As it ran off, it shouted [in Ukrainian]:
"Long live the independent Ukraine!" (*Khai zhive vil'na Ukraina!*)

Contemporary Russian jokes about the Ukrainians reveal two interrelated emotions characteristic of any long-term close relationship between two groups at a time when one of them is seen as straying away. One emotion can be characterized as anger for endangering a relationship that has been convenient and satisfactory for the angry party. Usually such anger takes the form of parting insults with the central motif: "OK, you want to go? Good riddance! You're no good anyway." Another emotion, apprehension about possible negative ramifications of separation, is usually reticent, in order not to give the other party the satisfaction of acknowledging its importance.[7]

Thus, shortly after *glasnost* began, numerous Russian jokes appeared that stressed the marginality of the Ukrainians as a group, their strangeness and otherness. As a way of alienating the target group, the joke tellers attributed to it the negative traits that the teller's group "does not wish to recognize among its own members" (Davies 1982, 384). As is the case with New Zealanders' jokes about the Maori, or German jokes about Swabians (see Davies 1982, 384, 386), while targeting the Ukrainians, the Russian joke tellers are also "projecting traits that they wish to remain on the moral periphery of their culture onto [those] who inhabit the social or geographical periphery of their society" (Davies 1982, 386). In a number of Russian jokes, the Ukrainians are given the very same shortcomings featured in many jokes the Russians tell about themselves, such as lack of in-group solidarity, racism, aggressiveness, ethnocentrism, and xenophobia:

(**3.9**) A *khokhol* arrives in Moscow to sell his cucumbers. Some huge fellows come up to him and demand a bribe—for the right to trade at this marketplace. He says to them:
"Oh, I don't have any money. I have cucumbers, but not money."
The fellows beat him up, stick a cucumber up his ass, and throw him out of the marketplace. The *khokhol* goes away and laughs out loud. A passerby stops him:
"Why do you laugh?"
"Tomorrow my son's godfather is coming over with melons."[8]

(**3.10**) Kiev. A father and son ride on a bus. A Negro is sitting opposite them. The son shouts:
"Dad, look—a monkey!"
The Negro begins to fidget in his seat:
"Please tell your son to stop insulting me."
The father to his son:
"Pavlo, look—a talking monkey!"[9] (For a variant, see Petrosian 73.)

(3.11) Yeltsin asks the Ukrainian president, Leonid Kravchuk:
"Listen, Lyonya, what the fuck do you need this Black Sea fleet for?"
"To conduct trade with Europe."
"But it's a military fleet!"
"And what if they refuse to buy our product?"[10]

(3.12) During a session in the Supreme Soviet in Kiev, the chairman of the session asks:
"Turn on the third microphone."
A delegate comes up to the mike, saying:
"Honorable deputies! Let me say a few words about kikes."
The chairman: "No. There's no need, because it's a nationalistic question."
"Then I'll talk about *moskals*."
"And you can't talk about *moskals*. It's also a nationalistic question."
"Well, then I'll talk about ecology."
"That's OK; you can talk about that."
"Honorable deputies! What's going on in our country! All the rivers are dried up, all the forests are fallen under the axe. There's nowhere to drown a kike and hang a *moskal*."[11]

To the same effect of estrangement, Russian jokes target Ukrainian onomastic rules that allow the creation of surnames in the form of composites of colloquial expressions, as in *Nechipailo* (from Ukrainian *ne chipat'*—"don't touch"). The implication of such jokes is that the Ukrainians are not like other "normal" (read: Russian) people, but an ambiguous, socially underdeveloped group, which does not even have "normal" surnames. (Obviously, this kind of joke does not fare well in translation):

(3.13) An army evening roster call:
"Sidorov!"
"Here."
"Tibishvili"
"Here."
"Cherezzabornoguzadirishchenko
[Over-the-fence-one's-own-leg-risen-ko]!"
"Here."
"*Nu ni cherta sebe familiia* [Well, the Devil alone knows what kind of surname]!"
"Here."[12]

Another way of separating one's own group from another is to highlight that group's intellectual inferiority. As Russian newspapers reported disputes between the Russian and Ukrainian governments on the division of the Soviet fleet in the Black Sea or on the future of the Crimea, hastily published booklets were sold in Moscow subway stations that contained a number of jokes in which the old stereotype of the Ukrainians as hillbillies was recreated. As Davies (1990, 67) shows, "in economies where change and modernization, enterprise and progress are associated with the cities and industrial areas," groups that are considered primarily peasants become the butt of ethnic jokes that portray them as backward, slow-witted, unsophisticated, and stupid. Despite the existence of highly developed centers of heavy industry in Kiev, Kharkov, Zaporozhie, and Dnepropetrovsk, the coal mines of Donbass, and electrical and nuclear power stations located in Ukraine,[13] this association of Ukraine with peasantry in Russian folk consciousness comes from its image as the "granary of the Soviet Union," an image endlessly reinforced by the Soviet press.

Thus, contemporary Russian jokes about the Ukrainians are typical jests of city slickers about "country cousins." By and large, they are similar to jokes told about rednecks and country bumpkins in the United States and in many other countries, such as Japan, Singapore, and Thailand (see Davies 1990, 67). For example, in the following item a Ukrainian is portrayed as so provincial that he has never seen a parrot, a plot typical of "backwardness" jokes (see, for example, the one about a Georgian puzzled by a giraffe's appearance in [2.34]):

(3.14) A Ukrainian took his son to the zoo. He asked a zoo attendant
where they should spend their last two hours. It was too late to
go to the terrarium. It was also too late to go and see the bears.
"Then go and see the parrot," the attendant said.
The Ukrainian and his boy talked to the parrot. It didn't answer.
They shouted at it. No response. Then the father said:
"Take a stick and bang it over its cage."
The son did as advised.
The parrot suddenly screamed: "I'll tear you to pieces!"
"Don't worry, uncle," said the frightened father. "We're just
kidding. . . ." (For a variant, see Petrosian 72.)

A denigrating attitude toward a Ukrainian is also based on his alleged naiveté and stupidity:

(3.15) A Russian and a *khokhol* go on a reconnaissance mission. As they
crawl they touch a barbed wire, and the enemy's sentry shouts:
"Halt! Who's there?"
The Russian says: "Meow!" and the sentry calms down.

In a few hours, the scouts crawl back and again touch a barbed wire.

"Halt! Who's there?"

The *khokhol* responds: "It's just us cats, we're crawling back!"

In other jokes the Ukrainians are portrayed as dirty, thick skinned, and vulgar:

(3.16) A Russian asks a Ukrainian: "What, you don't have bathtubs in your hut? Where do you bathe yourself then?"

"In the river."

"What about winter?"

"What's winter in Ukraine!" (Petrosian 74)

In reference to the Chernobyl catastrophe, the following two-line *chastushka* was composed:

(3.17) We are a Ukrainian nation!

What's it to us, radiation! (I. Raskin 450)

(3.18) A young Ukrainian female (*khokhlushka*) is sitting with a [Russian] officer in a restaurant. The man orders a bottle of champagne.

"Oh, champagne!" *khokhlushka* says. "I love champagne so much. . . . Champagne! It's such a marvel!. Such an aroma. . . . Champagne has the scent of a bee. . . . And when I drink beer I fart. . . ." (I. Raskin 428)

In this joke, to make a contrast in manners more dramatic, the tellers cast not a male, but a young female, of whom more delicacy is expected, on the Ukrainian side of the encounter, and the Russians are represented by an officer, who traditionally is perceived as having an old-fashioned gallantry that, as the Russian self-image expressed in jokes testifies, a regular Russian does not possess.

While Ukrainians are known for having a tradition of subtle humor (in fact, two of Russia's greatest comic geniuses, Gogol and Zoschenko, came from Ukraine),[14] in contemporary Russian jokelore they are portrayed as crass hicks playing cruel and unseemly practical jokes on each other:

(3.19) Two *khokhols* sit in a pullman compartment, drink vodka, and converse on all kinds of philosophical topics:

"Gritsko, look at that fly on the window! What a miracle of nature! It shits on glass such a tiny dot that you won't even notice."

"What are you talking about, Petro! I'll shit on the tip of your nose so that you won't even feel it."

"I don't believe it, Gritsko!"
"I mean it."
"And I still don't believe it."
"Wanna bet?"
"Let's bet."
They bet. Petro offers his face to his friend. Gritsko takes down his pants and shits on his friend's face with all his might: "Well, excuse me. . . . So, I lost." (I. Raskin 428; for a variant, see Petrosian 73)

According to Davies (1990, 68), one of the factors contributing to the rural image is the special language culture of the group: "[O]nce the image of an ethnic group as comically stupid rustics is established it can often survive subsequent economic changes." Indeed, although Ukraine has undergone rapid industrialization and is a modern industrialized nation, it is its language that in the Russian folk view makes this group provincials.

Even though Ukrainian is a Slavic language in its own right that, together with Russian, derives from common Slavic linguistic roots, the Russian folk assumption is that there is no such thing as a full-fledged, separate Ukrainian language, that "those rubes" just handle the language of the city—that is, Russian—poorly. One of the denigrating Russian colloquial references to the Ukrainian language is, characteristically, as "a cow's language" (usually referred to by the Russians in Ukrainian: *korov'ia mova*); witticisms about the language have circulated among the Russians for a long time. Disparagement of the Ukrainian language has usually taken the form of folk parodies of iconic Russian literary texts, rendered in a substandard Ukrainian vernacular. For example:

(3.20) "Do you know how it sounds in Ukrainian: "*Padu li ia, streloi pronzennyi, il' mimo proletit ona?*" (from Pushkin's *Eugene Onegin,* chapter 6, stanza 21) ["Am I to perish, pierced with the [swift] arrow of fate's decree, or be spared?"]
Answer: "*Chi gepnus' ia, driuchkom propertyi, chi mymo proshpurliae vyn!*"

To understand the sly linguistic trick employed here, one need only translate the parodic line back into substandard Russian, keeping the same stylistic level of this Ukrainian version and then comparing the original with Pushkin's text:

"*Il' shmiaknus' ia probityi palkoi il' mimo proshmygnet ona?*" [Approximately, "Would I drop dead cut down by a blade or will it whiz by me?"]

Russians' jokes about the Ukrainian language not only stress its seeming oddity; much more irritation is expressed at the Ukrainians' resolute insistence on speaking their own language. Such behavior is interpreted as an act of defiance of the Russians, a refusal to do what they are told in a larger sense:

(3.21) "Are there any *moskals?*" one Ukrainian says to another in Ukrainian.
"There aren't any here."
"Let's talk in Russian then." (Shmeleva and Shmelev 40)

Some Russians regard the Ukrainian language not as "a slow or old-fashioned version of their own language" (Davies 1990, 61), as is the case with other languages featured in jokes told around the world, but as a willful Ukrainian attempt to present what they perceive as an artificial and crudely imitative version of Russian as another, separate, language that is totally their own.[15]

In the Soviet period, the Communist press often reinforced this folk tendency to treat the Ukrainian language as inferior. It was also assumed that the Ukrainians' insistence on their own language came out of stubborn defiance of the Russians and was a demonstration of their will to achieve independence. When talking in a mocking tone about the Ukrainians who objected to the Russification of Ukrainian culture, the propagandistic articles in *Pravda* and similar Russian-language papers would sarcastically incorporate such Ukrainian words as "separatists" (*samostiiniki*) and "people of the yellow and blue" (*zhovto-blakitniki*),[16] and would ridicule the dream of "free Ukraine" (*vil'na Ukraina*).

In the following contemporary joke, one can easily sense the Russian joke teller's displeasure about the persistent use of Ukrainian in a Russian-language environment:

(3.22) A roll call in an army detachment:
"First!" "Second!" "Third!" "Fourth!" "Fifth!" "Soxth!" [in the original Ukrainian: *shostyi*]
"Not 'soxth!' Sixth!" [in the original Russian: *shestoi*]
"First!" "Second!" "Third!" "Fourth!" "Fifth . . ." "Soxth!"
"Not 'soxth'—sixth!"
About fifteen minutes are spent this way. Finally:
"First!" "Second!" "Third!" "Fourth!" "Fifth . . ." "Sixth!"
"Soventh!" [in the original: Ukrainian *syomyi,* instead of the Russian *sed'moi*].

There is more to this joke, however, than mispronunciation. In 1991–92 the Russian press reported the attempts to build Ukrainian army units and bring under oath to the Ukrainian government the newly drafted troops in its territory, as well as the career military of Ukrainian origin. Behind the linguistic uneasiness that the Russian commander experienced there was a much more important and worrisome question: would the Ukrainians keep taking orders from the Russians?

It is hardly accidental, then, that a number of contemporary Russian jokes about the Ukrainians are set in military camps or are otherwise concerned with military matters (e.g., 3.11, 3.13, 3.15, 3.22). The setting reveals Russian anxiety about the loyalties of the Ukrainian contingent of the joint forces. The conceited and condescending character of the skepticism about Ukrainian military skills notwithstanding, Russian disquiet about Ukrainian behavior is quite strongly felt in 3.15. The joke is actually a plot realization of a contemporary Russian saying: "I wouldn't go with [him] on a reconnaissance mission" (*Ia by s nim v razvedku ne poshel*), used when expressing mistrust of someone.

In another joke, a wartime situation is combined with another revived stereotype of the Ukrainian as a greedy kulak (in Ukrainian, *kurkul'*):

(**3.23**) Two *khokhols* lie in a trench. One is wounded and moans:
"Mykola, finish me off. Shoot me! The Germans will come and they'll torture me."
"I can't. I don't even have bullets."
"I'll sell them to you." (Genis 1:106)

The term *kulak* (meaning "a fist" in Russian) became not only a nickname for peasants who used hired labor ("*batraks*") to work on their private land, but a derogatory term used in Soviet propaganda. As an epitome of exploitation and self-interested ownership, such peasants became targets of Stalin's merciless persecution during the collectivization of Soviet agriculture, when Ukraine served as the primary site.[17] For the Ukrainians, the word is a painful reminder of the injustices heaped upon them. As Armstrong (34) points out, "Ukrainians felt that this repression, carried out by Russian-speaking officials and coinciding with attacks on Ukrainian literature and a purge of Ukrainian party officials, was of a discriminatory national as well as a 'class warfare' measure."[18] Although these injustices were acknowledged after Stalin's death, many more years of forced Russification of Ukrainian culture made the Russians dread the possibility of retaliation in the form of insubordination, if not open clashes.

In contemporary Russian jokes, stereotyping the Ukrainians as "kulaks" is not blatant; rather, it is implied through portraying them as incredibly stingy and avaricious peasants. This accusation, although having no basis in reality, appears to be aimed at insulting the completely contradictory Ukrainian self-perception (cf., for example, the concept of "generous Ukraine" [*shchira Ukraina*], known to the Russians at least from the time of Gogol's *Evenings on a Farm near Dikanka*). Among many other manifestations of this Ukrainian attribute, greeting honored guests with bread and salt is an ancient Ukrainian ritual still widely practiced.

Although in his book on ethnic humor Davies does not address Russian jokes about the alleged Ukrainian stinginess, he would most likely have included them among the jokes told in many countries about "the prudent provincials," as he calls them (cf. American jokes about Iowa or Maine farmers). The Russian stereotype of the Ukrainians as rapacious proprietors can be traced back to the late 1920s and early 1930s, when Soviet propaganda took every opportunity to defame kulaks. Instances where "kulaks" hid their bread "from the toiling people of the city (*trudiashchiesia goroda*)," as the party press interpreted it, were widely publicized. Thus "kulak" both metonymically and metaphorically came to connote a covetous closefisted peasant who would not give anything away, even if keeping it meant prolonging his own misery (as in 3.23). In contemporary Russian jokelore, this spiteful individualist often acts on a premise expressed in the Russian proverb: "I'm not eating it myself but I won't give it away to anyone else" (*Sam ne gam i drugomu ne dam*), which the following joke seems to illustrate:

(3.24) They ask a Russian what he would do if they gave him an apple.
"I'd eat it."
"And two apples?"
"I would eat one apple myself and share another one with my friend."
"And a case of apples?"
"I'd sell it and buy drinks for me and my friends."
"And a carload of apples?"
"Same thing."
They asked a Jew what he would do with an apple.
"I'd sell it."
"And two?"
"I'd sell them."
"A case of them?"
"Sell."
"And a carload?"
"Same thing."
They asked a *khokhol* what he would do with an apple. He grinned:
"I'd eat it."
"And with two?"
"I'd eat them."
"And a case of them?"
"I'd eat them."

"And a carload of them?"
"I'd eat all that I could and I'd take a bite out of every one of the rest of them."

In many jokes, the alleged Ukrainian greediness is symbolized by the food that, according to the stereotype, the group treats as most coveted—salt pork (*salo*). In fact, in many Russian jokes the Ukrainians are portrayed as totally obsessed with it, putting its value above anything else:

(**3.25**) A *khokhol*'s house is on fire. He rushes there and passes boxes of salt pork to his wife.
She: "What are you doing?! Our children are in there!"
He: "If we have salt pork, we'll have more children. (Genis 2:32)

(**3.26**) From an ad in a Ukrainian newspaper:
"Will exchange a handmade carpet, two by three meters, for salt pork of the same size."

(**3.27**) "What is the best Ukrainian candy?"
"Salt pork in chocolate." (For a variant, see I. Raskin 427.)

(**3.28**) They ask a Ukrainian at the customs:
"Do you have narcotics?"
"Yes."
"Show them to us."
"Here they are!"
"But this is salt pork, not narcotics!"
"I don't know. All I know is that I'm getting high on it."
(I.Raskin 294)

(**3.29**) One *khokhol* asks another: "Listen, Petro, what would you eat if you were the president of the United States?"
"If I were the president of the United States, I would eat salt pork with salt pork" (Repina and Rostovtsev 74).

(**3.30**) A Georgian and a *khokhol* live on an uninhabited island for a whole year. The Georgian longs for women. Finally, he makes a raft and swims to another island. And—oh, joy!—it turns out that on that island, women have lived for a whole year without any men. After he enjoys himself as much as he can, the Georgian remembers his comrade. He gets on his raft and heads back to his island. From afar he shouts to the *khokhol:*
"Hey, Taras, lets go to the neighboring island. I'll show you something there! You haven't tasted such happiness for a whole year!"

Without thinking, the *khokhol* throws himself into the water and swims toward the raft with all his might and shouts triumphantly: "Salt pork! Salt pork!! Salt pork!!!" (*Salo! Salo! Salo!*)[19]

As is the case with many other food-related jokes told around the world (Davies 1990, 276–306), Russian folk humor about the alleged Ukrainian fascination with *salo,* by defining it as odd and characteristic of the Ukrainians alone, serves as a device of self-identification, of demarcation of the group's boundaries. Jokes of this kind are usually circulated to underscore a target group's otherness and strangeness.[20]

These *salo* jokes are devices of denigration as well. As in the case of Western European "sausage jokes" told about the Poles and the Germans, *salo* could also be considered "shapeless, indeterminate, and ambiguous" (Davies 1990, 306), thus ascribing similar qualities to those who partake of it, stressing their inferiority to the Russians, who consume food of more defined shape.

Salo's obvious representation of pigs, domestic animals often fed in the countryside with the leftovers of human food, makes this characterization even stronger. As in the jokes about the "sausage-Germans" (Davies 1990, 301), the grossness and coarseness of the food's shape and origin can be interpreted as the grossness and coarseness of those who eat it. Since the Ukrainians are portrayed as overeaters of this uncooked food, a part of a messy animal, the implication may be that they are themselves low and untidy. In the following item, this implication is clear:

(3.31) Two friends do not like it that a third friend, a Korean, uses dog meat as food. They take him to a hypnotist, asking that suggestion be used to convince the Korean that he is of another nationality. During the session, the hypnotist tells his patient: "You're a Korean no more. You're a *khokhol* now." After the session, the "former" Korean goes home, looks hungrily at his dog, and says: "You're not a dog anymore, you're a pig."

As a pig itself symbolizes greed and gluttony, the folk assumption is that these unattractive traits pass on to those who consume that part of the animal's body that is a direct result of its gluttony—*salo.*

However, these considerations only partly explain the pervasiveness of *salo* jokes in contemporary Russian folklore. The fact is that, although it is considered substandard by contemporary Western sensibilities and is not a part of the everyday Russian diet, salt pork is sold in Russian city markets and is valued as an appetizer and a snack (*zakuska*) that goes well with vodka. In recent history, *salo* has been treated as a meal in its own right. Due to its highly nutritious and savory qualities, it was very much in demand at a time when food was especially scarce and malnutrition of the population was rampant—during the war with the Germans in the course of World War II and in the immediate postwar period.[21]

Moreover, at least at one point in the past, *salo* was not only assumed to be intrinsically Russian, but also of world-class taste, superior to any foreign-made food—a fact that bears literary evidence. In the 1950s, in the wake of Soviet propaganda attacks on those Soviet people who admired Western goods, a satirical fable written by a conformist poet, Sergey Mikhalkov, shamed them for their "bowing before the West" (*nizkopoklonstvo pered zapadom*) and reminded them with indignation that, when it comes to the truly essential thing in life—food—they turn to what is really good—*Russian* salt pork. (The punch line of the fable: "But they eat only Russian salt pork!" (*A salo russkoe ediat!*).

Along with denigration of the group, there is another hidden psychological agenda in stereotyping the Ukrainians as *salo*-eating *kurkuls*. An acute shortage of food in Russian cities in 1990 and 1991 gave birth to speculations and predictions on the part of the Russian press and public figures about the possibility of hunger in Russian cities during the long winters. *Salo* jokes may be seen as a folk way of venting apprehension about pending acute food shortages. Considering the Russian folk image of Ukraine as a rural, food-producing nation, "the granary of the [former] Soviet Union," the highly volatile food situation in big Russian cities in the early 1990s could not help but make the Russians turn to Ukrainians. In the atmosphere of increased tension between the groups due to a number of Ukrainian moves toward autonomy, such as reported attempts to nationalize the army and replace Russian with Ukrainian as the state language, such trepidations had some basis. The caloric content of salt pork is much higher than that of usual Russian food—the semiotic meaning of it spells "abundance." By portraying the Ukrainians as gluttonous salt pork eaters, that is, people who consume many more calories than they need for survival,[22] the Russian joke tellers expressed their concern about whether those who, in their view, had more than enough food, would share it with them.

In the post-Soviet time, the image of a closefisted Ukrainian in Russian jokelore persists. Although Ukraine is economically weaker than Russia, an image of a New Ukrainian, a clone of a New Russian, has appeared in Russian jokes. In one of them (Erokaev 107–8), a New Ukrainian would rather eat two and a half kilograms of salt and be sodomized by twenty five savages than part with his money.

The insulting character of many of these jokes notwithstanding, they should not be seen as more than what they are—that is, a folkloric expression of apprehensions on the part of the Russian joke tellers about a new and constantly changing historical situation, and an unconscious attempt to deal with trepidations that this situation has produced. As an angry verbal exchange in a spousal spat does not necessarily mean a couple's complete unacceptance of each other (more often than not, it is just an attempt to reexamine and redefine the relationship), contemporary Russian jokes about the Ukrainians should also be seen as a venture in redefining the future of the relationship between two blood-related Slavic peoples. It is clear that these verbal attacks reveal not a complete and total rejection of the Ukrainians, but a basic willingness to maintain relations with them.

CHAPTER 4

Taking Penguins to the Movies

Russian Jokes about the Chukchis

Russian jokes about the Chukchi fully abide by the conditions postulated for ethnic humor: the stereotype they utilize is conventional, fictional, and mythological (V. Raskin 180). Very little of the real life of the Chukchis is reflected in jokes about them. They are known throughout the former Soviet Union for their ancient artistic carvings on walrus bones. Although the climate of the Chukotka region is severe indeed (average temperature in January ranges from 5 to -38 degrees Fahrenheit [-15 to -39 degrees Celsius], and in July only 41–50 degrees Fahrenheit [5–10 degrees Celsius]) and many amenities known to urban Russians are scarce, they are far from being just hunters and fishermen, as Russian jokelore portrays them. They breed not only deer but dairy cattle, and they grow vegetables in hothouses. The Chukchi Autonomous Region has a developed modern industry—mining of precious metals (tin, tungsten ore, gold) and coal. There is even a nuclear electrical station there (Prokhorov 2:645).

Why, then, were the Chukchi chosen as a butt of Russian ethnic humor? The answer to this question becomes apparent if one looks at the content of these jokes, which have become a staple in Russian jokelore. Over the last twenty years, Chukchi jokes have been thriving and they seem to be tickling the Russian funny bone as successfully now as they did when they first appeared in the early 1970s.

One Russian scholar, E. G. Rabinovich (100), hypothesizes that the emergence of Chukchi jokes was prompted by the publication of an English-language textbook for students of technical institutes in 1972. One of the drill exercises in the book contrasted the happy lives of Soviet Chukchis and the rather dismal fate of American Eskimos. Rabinovich suggests in his article that this heavy-handed Communist propaganda bit gave birth to the famous Chukchi joke series.

Indeed, at the first stage of their functioning, humorous tales about the Chukchi worked primarily as vehicles of folk political humor. The Chukchi was used as a mouthpiece for satirical barbs aimed at the regime's major failures, such as its inability to adequately feed and clothe its people. Ridiculing the Soviet propaganda claims that the Soviet peoples constantly express "a feeling of deep gratitude" to the Soviet regime for the great life it provides for everybody, the Russians used the comic figure of a Northern ethnic man whose image is immediately associated with harsh living conditions and permanent deprivation. As was customary for Soviet propaganda, a sharp contrast was drawn between conditions before and after the Bolshevik revolution. The following joke is in the spirit of this propaganda trick:

(4.1) A Soviet journalist interviews a Chukchi man:
"Could you tell us briefly how you lived before the October revolution?"
"Hungry and cold."
"And how do you live now?"
"Hungry, cold, and with a feeling of deep gratitude."

Of course, the stereotype of the Chukchi as deprived was not in and of itself enough to recruit him into Russian jokelore. He was brought in because he had to play the part of a fool who, as a court jester, "not only tells the truth but also sees it with the directness and insight of children, poets and the insane" (Boston 96). The Chukchi man was to play the part of Candide, a naive outsider, in order to create an effect of estrangement. The Chukchi's presumed ignorance and illiteracy made him seem unsusceptible to political indoctrination and made plausible his lack of familiarity with the pieties of the Soviet regime and its ideological sacred cows:

(4.2) A Chukchi graduates from the Institute of International Relations in Moscow and returned home. They ask him:
"Well, what did you learn in Moscow?"
"Oh, I became very smart. I know now that Marx and Engels are two different people, Ulianov and Lenin are the same person, and *Slava KPSS* [in English: "Glory to the CPSU"] is not a person at all.[1]

(4.3) A Chukchi comes to the Politburo and says:
"I want to become a Politburo member. What do I need in order to become one?"
"What are you? An idiot?"
"And is that a requirement?" (Ivanova 1994, 226)

Coming from the mouth of a Chukchi, a perfectly innocent remark is turned into an attack on the ideology:

(4.4) They sent a Chukchi to Moscow to buy sausages and told him: "Go downtown. Wherever you see a long line of people, take your place in it."
After a while the Chukchi came back without sausages and told his people:
"I went to Moscow and saw a huge line in the center of it. I spent half a day in that line. When I entered the store, I found out that the sausage was already gone and the sales clerk was in a coffin."

On the immediate level, this joke seems to be just a rather crude attack on Lenin, whose image is destroyed when he becomes a sausage seller. The joke, however, calls for a subtler reading. If Lenin can be seen as a salesman, then the only thing he is known to have sold to the Russian masses was the Communist ideology. Therefore, the Chukchi man unwittingly indicates that, contrary to the propaganda cliché that Lenin is "eternally alive," not only is he dead as a doornail, but so is his ideology, which is not even able to provide enough sausage for the population. Thus, it is not the Chukchi who is laughed at in this joke; he is only an auxiliary. The Russians laugh here at themselves, at their own preoccupation with Lenin's cult in the face of the obvious failure of his ideas. In another joke, upon entering a foreign currency "Berezka" store and being overwhelmed by the abundance of goods, the Chukchi man acts swiftly and without hesitation: he asks for political asylum.

During Konstantin Chernenko's short tenure as the head of the Soviet state, the Chukchi character was recruited by folk humor for the purpose of denigrating him. Ridiculing the propaganda claims that a Soviet man could become anyone he wished, one of the jokes implies that the incompetent and unintelligent Soviet leader was actually none other than a stupid, ignorant, and incompetent Chukchi:

(4.5) A Chukchi got his wish—to become the secretary general of the Communist Party. And he became one.[2] (Shturman and Tiktin 288)

While one group of Chukchi jokes made no use of the fact that the Chukchi man was a representative of an ethnicity, others utilized it to the fullest to debunk the regime's nationality policies. No effort was spared by the Soviet propaganda machine to create an impression of the regime's encouragement of the development of smaller nations. Through various mass media, the Chukchis, like other, mostly Asian, minorities, were often showcased by the official propaganda as a prosperous nationality that largely benefited from such Soviet policy.

To reassure the world of the triumph of these policies, the regime spared no effort to demonstrate the great advances of the numerous smaller nations living in Soviet territory. For that purpose only, the Soviet authorities often artificially promoted and publicized the presumed intellectual achievements of a half-literate member of a minority. To make the work of an ethnic poet or prose writer look professional, a Russian ghost translator, often a poet or a writer with meager chances of having a literary career of his own because of his "impure" (e.g., Jewish) origin, would completely rewrite the original text.[3]

Pricking the balloon of the official pretense that "the nationality question" was once and for all solved in the USSR, Russian Chukchi jokes mocked the fake claims about the flourishing of the education and culture of all minorities. Thus, Russian urban folklore of the early 1970s included jokes about a Chukchi as an ignorant writer or an illiterate scholar:

(4.6) A Chukchi became a member of the prestigious Writer's Union.
He was interviewed by a score of journalists.
"Tell us, please," asked one of them, "What books that you've read have made the strongest impression on you?"
The Chukchi smiled: "You are mistaken. A Chukchi's not a reader. A Chukchi's a writer."

(4.7) At an international scientific conference, they offered a Chukchi a registration form. When signing it, he put down three Xs.
"What does that mean?" they asked him.
"It's my first name, my family name, and my scholarly degree."[4]

In his book, *Arctic Mirrors: Russia and the Small Peoples of the North,* Yury Slezkine (1994, 367) writes that

> equality—to the extent that one could be non-Russian but equal in the USSR—was not forthcoming. During the stagnant 1970s, when most official values were subject to carnivalesque debunking through popular humor, the Chukchi emerged as the most popular butt of jokes that parodied Soviet claims of rapid development and spectacular cultural advances by the formerly backward. Thus, the native northerners were taken up by the folk myth makers for the same reason they had been used by the creators of socialist realism: seen as an extreme case, they provided maximum edification in the heroic genre and the most striking implausibility in the comic. The Russians expressed [their] disgust for Soviet egalitarianism by laughing at Chukchi jokes.

However, the appearance of the Chukchi in Russian jokelore was more than an artistic device of antiregime satire. Chukchi jokes had other roles to play as well. A closer look at the mood of the society when Chukchi jokes began to be especially conspicuous in the body of Russian oral folk humor may give other clues to their popularity.

It was hardly a coincidence that Chukchi jokes came to prominence in the late 1970s and early 1980s. With the dynamism and optimism of the first five-year plans of the late 1920s and the 1930s long gone, with the high hopes for improvement of life after the war not met, and with the waning of the moderate enthusiasm stirred by Khrushchev's speeches—"this generation of Soviet people will live under Communism"—a stable vision of Russian life as hopeless emerged in Russian mass consciousness.[5] By the end of Brezhnev's tenure, at the time of the regime's most pronounced stagnation, it became increasingly clear to many Russians that the great promise of the revolution that the propaganda machine still tried to keep alive was about to fail.[6] With the slowing pace of economic growth, the fundamental claim of the regime about the infallibility and superiority of its economic system over any other (i.e., capitalist) system was increasingly discredited:

A man appeared in Red Square and began to throw leaflets to the passersby. He was immediately seized by militia and taken to a precinct. Upon examination, the leaflets turned out to be blank pieces of paper. They interrogated the man:

"What does it mean? Why is there nothing on these pages?"

"Why write?" asked the man. "Isn't all clear anyway?" (In Russian: *I tak vse poniatno*).[7] (For a variant, see Shturman and Tiktin 186.)

The masses of Russians came to such conclusions about the system's major failings when they compared their lives with those of other nations. Western scholarly studies conducted some years later only confirmed what the Soviet people suspected all along: that they were hopeless losers. In the mid-1970s, per capita total consumption for the USSR was three times less than that of the United States and about half that of West Germany, France, Austria, the United Kingdom, Spain, Japan, and Italy, and their living standards were also worse than those of most of the so-called brotherhood of socialist countries (Schroeder 15, 23).

While the prosperity of such major nations as England, France, and the United States was taken for granted, especially humiliating for the Russians was the fact that even enemies recently defeated in World War II—Germany and Japan—had recuperated from the losses sustained during the war and were able to provide a much higher standard of living for their population. This fact alone made even the most uncritical Russians question the regime's excuse for the considerable lack of progress in the quality of Russian life— the grave effect of wartime destruction on the country's economy.[8] Finding a way to offset this feeling of inferiority became a psychological necessity, a subconscious agenda of the nation's psyche.

A response to this need was the rise of Russian nationalism and ethnocentrism. In the early 1980s, Vasily Rasputin, Viktor Astafiev, Vasily Belov, and other Russian writers began to talk about the Russians themselves as the deprived nationality that suffered most from the regime. It was the time of the creation of the infamous xenophobic society, "Pamiat," and the publication of Astafiev's degrading attack on Georgians.[9] Igor Shafarevich's book, *Russophobia,* can serve as the epitome of the mood of the period. In the realm of folklore, this time was marked by a sharp increase in ethnic slurs expressing a range of negative feeling—from mild resentment to overt hostility—toward Jews, Georgians, and Ukrainians.[10] By and large, these feelings have been indicative of the Russians' inferiority complex, which they have attempted to cover up or dissipate.

In the stereotypical world of Russian mass consciousness, the above-mentioned ethnic groups were assumed to be prosperous, if not on the level of Americans or Germans, at the very least faring much better in life than the Russians. The following joke from a private collection in Moscow, dated 1975, makes a point in the spirit of that time—being a Russian means being poor:

> Once upon a time an old man and his old wife lived in a mud hut near the deep blue sea. And they were Jews. One day the old man caught a goldfish and asked it to fulfill three of his wishes, one after another. As a result, he and his wife began to live in palatial quarters.
>
> But the old woman was still not satisfied. She wanted to be Russian. The old man went again to the wild blue sea and called for the goldfish to fulfill his wife's request.
>
> The goldfish agreed to please him.
>
> The old man returned to his home and saw that he was back at his old mud hut with a broken washbasin nearby. But his old wife was nowhere around. He asked his neighbors about her.
>
> They said: "She went to do the laundry for some Jews."

Stigmatizing out-groups that the Russians viewed as successful could at best help the joke tellers feel they were getting even with them. Thus, a stereotypical image that would help the Russians come to terms with their misery had to be that of an out-group that could provide them with a feeling of unquestionable supremacy. Such a feeling could be achieved only at the expense of those out-groups who, in Russian popular judgment, were *not* living better, but far worse, than the Russians. An Armenian radio joke of the time expressed this psychological imperative quite well:

> "What warms one's soul most of all?"—"An awareness that someone else is colder." (Kharkover 3:28)

Chukchi jokes fulfilled this emotional need. It is not a mere coincidence that at the period of the proliferation of Chukchi jokes, another denigrating stereotype emerged in Russian jokelore—that of black people. This phenomenon was unprecedented in Russian folk culture for the simple reason that, with the exception of a minuscule student population at the Lumumba University in Moscow, there have never been significant numbers of blacks in Russia. Citing reports in Soviet newspapers about violence against black students and tourists in Russian cities, Sergey Dovlatov (1989, 4) comes to the same conclusion regarding Russian animosity toward blacks: "A plebeian takes a stand: 'if I have a bad time, I've got to find a scapegoat.' "

Why the Chukchi?

While there have been recent tensions between the Russians and the Jews, the Russians and the Georgians, and the Russians and Ukrainians, there have been hardly any between them and the Chukchis. In fact, the Chukchis represent the only ethnic group that is prominently featured in contemporary Russian jokelore toward whom the Russians have no hostility whatsoever.

Why, then, was it the Chukchi, and not any other of the numerous minorities, who filled the humor prescription for restoring the Russians' emotional health? First of all, they belonged to that type of an out-group toward which the Russians traditionally held, if not always outright contemptuous, then invariably condescending attitudes—the Asians. For instance, the Russian word—*aziaty*—is often used as a synonym for "wild, uncivilized" (*dikie*) people.[11]

Thus, it had to be Asian people, and people of the far north, who were stereotyped as deprived: their climate is even more severe, their life is even harsher than that of the Russians. (Understandably, Southern Asian people, like Uzbeks or Turkomen, who live in a warm climate and on fertile lands that produce such delicacies as melons, grapes, peaches, and so on, that are highly sought after by the Russians, could not possibly "vie" for the "honor.") Among the reasons why the Chukchi "won" over twenty-six other ethnic groups who traditionally have been called "small peoples of the north" (Slezkine 1), such as the Nenets, Evenk, Aleut, or Nanai (to name a few), who could serve equally well as a butt of Russian superiority jokes, is the fact that the Chukchi inhabit the region farthest from major Russian industrialized centers, such as Moscow, Leningrad, or Gorky. Davies (1990, 43) notes:

Within any nation the culture of the metropolitan center or centers tends to be dominant over that of the remote periphery. Innovation, modernity, fashion begin at the center and spread outward and not the other way around; thus the people of the periphery appear slow, provincial, old-fashioned, and a fit subject of jokes about stupidity.

This is especially likely to happen if the group at the "edge" of the society has a distinctively different ethnic identity; whatever the achievements of the members of the group in their own terms, they may appear to the people at the center as failing to meet the dominant cultural standards.

Such is the case, for example, with Mexican jokes about the people of the Yucatan Peninsula, German jokes about Ostfrieslanders, and Irish jokes about the Kerry Coast inhabitants (Davies 1990, 46–49). This is also the case with the Chukchi, who occupy the most distant northeastern peninsula, geographically on the very edge of Russia. Their remoteness, plus their distinct identity and presumed traditional way of life versus that of modernity, also made the Chukchi qualify as a butt of superiority jokes, some of which are quite similar to those told about the Newfoundlanders (Newfies) in Canada, for instance (Davies 1990, 47–48).

Of course, the Chukchis are not the only people of the Chukotka Peninsula who fit the description of traits that would qualify them as a potential target of stupidity jokes. In fact, in this region the Chukchi are neither the largest nor the smallest of these groups. There are twice as many Evenks and ten times fewer Eskimos or Yukagirs than there are Chukchis (Prokhorov 2:645, 677, 705, 715)[12]. It is likely that the Chukchi were singled out as a butt of Russian jokes for linguistic reasons. In addition to geographical remoteness, the Chukchi may have "won" over other "equally qualified" ethnic groups because of their name. Not only is it most memorable, since both the peninsula and the sea of its northern shore carry their name, but, due to the unusual, hard-to-pronounce, cluster *kch* to a Russian ear, the word *chukcha* sounds funny, both "strange" and "comic."

By way of sound symbolism, then, the aural impression of the word's strangeness and comedy subconsciously extends to its bearer.[13] The word also has an element of playfulness: the sound *ch* is repeated with different vowels—*chu* and *cha*. Also, *chukcha* resembles a Russian word with negative connotations applicable to the stereotype, namely, *chuchelo* (scarecrow). In fact, an almost identical Russian dialect word, *chucha,* actually has this meaning (Vasmer 4:389).[14]

The first syllable of the word, *chuk,* has a condescending association with a child, the hero of *Chuk and Gek,* a widely known reader for elementary school children by a Soviet writer, Arkady Gaidar. Also, both syllables of the word *chukcha* resemble those of Russian words of Asian origin, such as *chuviak* (a shoe), *chuvash, parcha* (brocade), *sarancha* (locust), and so on. The Russian folk assumption is that all Chukchis live in a tent of skins called *chum,*[15] and this Russian word has an unpleasant association with the word *chuma* (plague). Moreover, the word *chukcha* can be perceived as a variant of a denigrating collective nickname for a man of any Asian ethnicity—*chuchmek* (see chapter 5, p. 114) and *churka* "blockhead" (I. Raskin 458).

Because a nationality cannot be ashamed of its own name (since it is usually a case of self-identification), the treatment of the very name *chukcha* as degrading belongs solely to the joke tellers, that is, to the Russians. In fact, the self-name of the Chukchis carries the opposite meaning; it connotes these people's innate dignity: "true people." Nevertheless, a number of Russian jokes treat the word *chukcha* as a disparaging nickname, or they play with the idea that the Chukchi want to shed it to avoid being stigmatized:

(**4.8**) An expedition is lost in a tundra during a blizzard. They begin shouting:
"Peeeo-ple! Help!"
A Chukchi crawls out from a snowdrift: "Aha, when I'm in Moscow, then I'm a 'Chukchi,' but in a blizzard, then I'm 'People' "

(**4.9**) The Chukchis began to complain that they had such an embarrassing name. The Supreme Soviet decided to grant their petition and announced that, from now on, they would be called "deer-breeding Jews."

Here, the teller uses a denigrating device of making believe that the insult is invalidated while in fact it is replaced by another insult. As if to say: "OK, you don't want to be called the Chukchis. We'll call you by the name of another despised minority."

While in jokes about the Georgians, Jews, or Ukrainians the individual names of representatives of these ethnicities appear rather frequently, this usually is not the case with Chukchi jokes: a Chukchi has no personal name. The implication is, of course, that all Chukchi look and act alike. This feature of Chukchi jokes is especially striking in the following item; even the dogs have names, but not the man who feeds them:

(**4.10**) They launched two dogs, called Belka and Strelka, into outer space with a Chukchi.
After the first orbit around the globe, they called from the earth:
"Belka!"
"Bow-wow!"
"Press the red button."
"Bow-wow! Bow-wow!"
"Strelka!"
"Bow-wow!"
"Press the white button."
"Bow-wow! Bow-wow!"

"Chukchi!"
"Bow-wow!"
"Why are you barking, motherfucker? Feed the dogs and don't touch anything."[16]

The Chukchis' association with dogs in Russian folk consciousness comes not only from the fact that they, and many other circumpolar peoples, often use dogsleds for transportation, but also because they are assumed to lead "dogs' lives."

The Chukchis' living conditions, displeasing from the Russian point of view, are not the only grounds on which they were chosen to be the butt of Russian superiority jokes:

(4.11) A Chukchi has bought himself a refrigerator. They ask him:
"What do you need the fridge for?"
"To warm myself up in the winter. It's minus 40 [both Celsius and Fahrenheit] on the street, and in the fridge only minus four [Celsius; 25 degrees Fahrenheit].

Another, perhaps more important, reason for their selection is that this ethnic stereotype, like that of Poles in American jokes (Dundes 137), could be treated as inferior in many other respects. Thus, many Chukchi jokes are racist jokes whose sole purpose is to justify their tellers' right of condescension.

Central to these jokes is the stupidity script characteristic of similar tales told around the world (V. Raskin 180); in fact, the very word *chukcha* entered contemporary Russian slang as a synonym for a fool. In 4.10, the Chukchi is not even equated with a dog; he is rendered as intellectually inferior to it. In many Chukchi jokes, the stupidity of every member of the ethnic group is taken for granted. For the sheer sake of underscoring the Chukchi's lack of mental capabilities, he is contrasted with the stereotype of the Jewish minority, which is also treated unfairly in Russian folk humor, but stereotyped as smart, in fact, too smart and too enterprising:

(4.12) "What does Rabinovich occupy himself with in exile?"
"He is occupied with scientific work: he married a Chukchi and breeds frost-proof Jews now."

The implication of this joke is that the only outstanding feature of the Chukchis is their ability to withstand deprivation.

As he appears in jokes, the Chukchi is an ideal object of exploitation. He happily accepts his hard lot and can be easily manipulated. He is like a soft toy that can be kicked around for a child's delight, the dream ethnic man one does not need to cheat. Because of his backwardness, he happily and readily cheats himself out of money:

(4.13) When a Chukchi arrives in Moscow, they tell him that taxi drivers are cheats. To his surprise, he gets an honest cab driver, who takes him to his destination and says:
"You owe me 3.25."
The Chukchi reaches for his money and begins to count twenty-five-ruble bills:
"One twenty-five bill, two twenty-five bills, three twenty-five bills."

Simpleton that he is, he doesn't feel any humiliation or exploitation by his "Big Brother," for he is too innocent even to realize that he is robbed, molested, or exploited:

(4.14) A Chukchi wearing an expensive fur coat enters an elevator. Two robbers follow him and shout:
"Take off your fur coat!"
The Chukchi spreads his hands in surprise: "What, is it summer already?"

(4.15) After serving in the army, a Chukchi comes home. His neighbors are kidding him:
"We bet you were the most stupid soldier."
"Well, no. There was one even more stupid: for two years he took me for a woman."

(4.16) A Chukchi's wife:
"Look, an iron bird flies."
The Chukchi: "It's called a plane."
His wife: "And here an iron dragonfly flies."
The Chukchi: "It's called a copter."
His wife: "Soon winter will end, spring will come. The Russians will come, they'll bring the fire water [vodka], beat you, and rape me."
The Chukchi: "It's called an ex-pe-di-tion." (For a variant, see Ivanova 1994, 227.)

The Chukchi seems numb not only to deprivation, but to insults as well. A Russian can offend him and easily get away with it because of his assumed lack of command of Russian; he does not even suspect that he is being verbally assaulted:

(4.17) A Chukchi is standing guard at a military post. Somebody passes by. The Chukchi:
"Password?"
"Fuck off!"

"What's the matter?" the Chukchi says. "Two weeks have gone by and they still haven't changed the password." (For a variant, see I. Raskin 457.)

The fact that the words the Chukchi does not comprehend are obscene ones emphasizes his linguistic ineptness in Russian, for they are highly frequent in everyday language.

While the Chukchi in jokes usually speaks in distorted language, this universal comic script (V. Raskin 181) is sometimes replaced with a script in which his complete ignorance of Russian leads him into trouble.[17] In the following joke, he is severely punished for one reason only—total ineptness in the master language, for which he alone is to blame:

(4.18) A Chukchi arrives in Moscow, but can't speak Russian. The only phrase he knows is "How do you do?". He catches a cab. The driver asks him:
"Where to?"
"How do you do?"
"Fine. So, where to?"
The Chukchi: "How do you do?"
"Fine. I'm alive, healthy, have a good wife, smart children. So, where do you want me to take you?"
"How do you do?"
The cab driver gets angry, takes the Chukchi out of the city, beats him up, and throws him out of the cab. The Chukchi walks along the highway, dirty all over, and meets a Georgian. The Chukchi: "How do you do?"
The Georgian: "Because."[18]

The ultimate dominance of a Russian over a Chukchi is symbolized by sexual conquest. While there are virtually no Russian jokes in which a Russian even attempts to sexually approach the wife of a Georgian, a Jew, or a Ukrainian, he easily gets into the bed of a Chukchi's wife.[19] Notably, he does so not because of the alleged Chukchi custom of offering their wives to guests, but because the Chukchi is too dumb to confront a Russian intruder on his sexual territory:

(4.19) Ivan used to come to a Chukchi's tent and get him accustomed to vodka. The Chukchi decides not to drink any more and warns his wife:
"As soon as Ivan comes, tell him I'm not at home. And I'll hide meanwhile."
Ivan comes with a bottle of vodka, and the Chukchi's wife tells

him that her husband isn't home. Ivan makes her drink vodka and seduces her. The Chukchi lies behind the bed-curtains and thinks: "What a predicament! I should be beating Ivan up—and I'm not home."

The sexual conquest of a Chukchi man's wife is usually most degrading. There is not even a pretense of genuine attraction toward a female Chukchi; she is stereotyped in jokes as being invariably ugly:

(4.20) While in Moscow, a Chukchi loses his wife in GUM, the big department store. He turns to the militia. The officer on duty asks him for a description of the lost woman.
"What do you mean, description? I lost my wife," the Chukchi says.
"Well, for example," says the officer, "my wife is blonde. She is tall, slim, and big-breasted. And yours?"
"No," says the Chukchi, "mine is small and stooped, and bow-legged. Well, to hell with her. Let's look for your wife."

A Chukchi woman is assumed to be next to nothing in a no-choice situation, serving the needs of sexually starved Russian men— geologists and the like:

(4.21) A Chukchi hunts for seals. He comes back to his tent. His wife is pregnant. He beats her up and demands:
"Who's the baby's father?"
She remembers who dropped by and when. In all probability, the Russian Vladimir, the geologist.
She says to her husband: "He may be the one, but we took precautions."
"How?"
"He put a pillow on my face."

Finally, the Chukchi may die as foolishly as he lives:

(4.22) "The postmortem dissection of a Chukchi man showed that he died of postmortem dissection."

| The Chukchi as a Benign Ethnic Man

While some Russian Chukchi jokes are mercilessly denigrating, others are surprisingly benign in comparison with, for instance, American jokes about Puerto Ricans, Poles, or Italians. Overall, contemporary Russian jokelore seems to treat the Chukchi people better than other minorities: they are portrayed much more benevolently than many other ethnicities, such as the greedy and gloating Ukrainians, the disgustingly wealthy Georgians, and the cunning and intellectually smug Jews. In fact, the Chukchi is an antipode to the latter, an "anti-Jew" of sorts: open, ignorant, innocent, and trustful. Money seems to be of no importance to him: while in (2.30) the Georgian carefully counts it, in (4.13), the Chukchi easily parts with it. In (4.14), he naively assumes the good intentions of others. In his simple-heartedness, since he himself is incapable of tricking anyone or hiding the truth, he cannot comprehend cheating:

(4.23) A Chukchi asks a Russian:
"Vanya, guess how many deer I have? If you guess right, I'll give you both of them." (Ivanova 1994, 204)

(4.24) A Chukchi comes up to the ticket office for the fifth time to buy a bus ticket. Finally, the cashier can't bear it any longer and says: "Why do you need so many tickets for the same bus?"
"Well, some kind of a fool is standing there, taking tickets and tearing them up." (Ivanova 1994, 216)

He doesn't understand human greed, and acts fairly, according to common sense:

(4.25) A Chukchi hires a prostitute for a night and pays her with three blue fox furs. She thinks: "Why just three—it won't be enough for a fur coat." She says to him:
"Hey, Chukchi, let's do it again."
"Let's do it."
The prostitute sees that the Chukchi puts the blue fox furs back into his suitcase.
"Why do you take them away?"
"If Chukchi wants, he pays. If you want, you pay."

At the same time, the Chukchi either sees nothing wrong with his mental capabilities ("They ask a Chukchi what nationality Lenin was. 'He was a Chukchi.' 'Why?' 'Because he was very, very smart.' "), or he humbly accepts the mental retardation ascribed to him by the Russians and doesn't seem to lose sleep over it:

(4.26) A teacher asks a Chukchi pupil which nationality is the most stupid. The Chukchi thinks for a long time and then says: "But we dance better than anybody else." (Ivanova 1994, 201)

Moreover, sometimes he finds the assumed lack of intelligence to his advantage:

(4.27) A brick falls on a Chukchi's head. He scratches the back of his head and says: "Good that I have no brains. Otherwise, I'd get a concussion. (I. Raskin 458).

In the following item, he shows that he knows his place (in this case literally) and is not too eager to take advantage of circumstances:

(**4.28**) A Chukchi gets off a train, covered with bruises. He is asked:
"Chukchi, what's happened to you?"
"Well, I was lying on the upper berth, and I kept falling off all the time."
"Why didn't you exchange places with the person who was underneath?"
"I couldn't do it. There was nobody there." (Ivanova 1994, 230)

It is easy (and profitable) to deal with Chukchis, for there is no need to treat them on an individual basis; they all look and act alike, and they know it, as the following item seems to suggest:

(**4.29**) A photographer takes pictures of many Chukchis and finds that they all come out alike. He prints all the photos from one negative and distributes them. One Chukchi wonders: "The face's mine, but the shirt's my neighbor's." (Ivanova 1994, 211)

What makes the Chukchi's image especially good-hearted is that he is a friend of nature, of animals. It is not a coincidence that in some jokes the Chukchi keeps company with those likable and endearing creatures, penguins, for he is seen almost as one of them, their human brother:

(**4.30**) A Chukchi brings a pickup truck full of penguins to a city. At a street intersection, he asks a traffic cop:
"Hey, do you know where I can take these penguins?"
"Where? What do you mean—where? Take them to the zoo."
"Good idea," says the Chukchi and whizzes away toward the zoo. After a while the traffic cop sees the Chukchi again. His pickup is still full of penguins.
"Hey," asks the cop. "What happened? Didn't you take them to the zoo?"
"I did," says the Chukchi. "And now I'm taking them to the movies."[20]

Another joke even suggests that Chuckhis and penguins are interbred:

(**4.31**) A Chukchi asks a [Russian] geologist:
"Tell me please, can a woman be totally white?"
"It happens."
"And totally black?"
"It also happens."

"And half black, half white?"
"It can't be."
A long silence.
"Ye-ee . . . Well, that was a penguin then . . ." (Ivanova
1994, 213)

If in American jokes a Pole is rendered as poor, stupid, dirty, vulgar, boorish, and tasteless (Dundes 133–35), the Chukchi man shares with him primarily the first two of these traits,[21] but even these are ultimately forgivable. He is poor because he lives at the end of the world. He does act foolishly, but most of the time not because of his innate lack of intelligence, as in American Polish jokes. In fact, the Chukchi man often exhibits common sense. His stupidity is that of a culturally backward man, ignorant of many attributes of modern civilization, a characteristic ascribed to the fact the he lives in the most remote region of the continent.

Many of the Chukchi's perplexing encounters with the world of modernity are set in Moscow, the Russian epitome of civilization, and a Moscow taxi driver is often the first Russian with whom he experiences a culture shock. In one joke, the Chukchi mistakes a car for an animal; in another, a plane for a bird:

(4.32) A Chukchi wins a "Zhiguli" car on a lottery ticket. He takes it to
the north, to his relatives. One of them looks at the headlights
and says:
"Big eyes."
Another pats the roof and says: "Such a strong skin!"
The third one looks underneath, at the exhaust pipe: "It's a male."

(4.33) They ask a Chukchi: "What is the most horrible bird?"
"A hang glider."
"Why?"
"It's big and strong. I have to shoot three times to make it release
a man from its claws."

A child of nature, he does not understand such processed food as chocolate and instant coffee (see I. Raskin 457). He cannot comprehend the working of a telephone (see Anon. 57), elevators (see Ivanova 1994, 199), condoms (209), color TV (216), electricity (227), photo processing (212), and so on. A modern apartment with all its amenities makes him feel uncomfortable and homesick for his tundra (205). Even a mirror confuses him:

(4.34) A Chukchi buys a wardrobe with a full-length mirror inside the
door. He opens the wardrobe and shouts happily to his wife:
"Wife, look, my brother has come over for a visit."

His wife runs up, looks into the mirror, and says:
"Yes, and not alone, but with his woman."

For the Chukchi, always relying on the pulling power of his dogs, a huge truck given as a present is just a warm cabin with lights:

(4.35) They give a Chukchi a huge truck. In a year they ask him:
"How do you like it?"
"It's good. It's warm in the cabin, and headlights make light in the tundra. One bad thing: dogs tire quickly. I have to change them often."

Accustomed to being carried wherever and whenever he wants by his personal dogsled, he has a hard time comprehending the idea of public transportation:

(4.36) Two Chukchis ride on a bus. One of them comes up to the driver and asks:
"Will this bus take me to the railroad station?"
"No, it won't."
The second Chukchi comes up and says:
"And what about me?"

If he allows a simple modern appliance in his life, he still has difficulty fully grasping its working principle:

(4.37) One Chukchi takes his broken alarm clock to a repair shop. The repairman, also a Chukchi, opens the clock and sees that a dead cockroach is stuck in the mechanism.
"It won't work," he says.
"Why?"
"Its mechanic has croaked."

All his backwardness notwithstanding, the Chukchi is not entirely helpless or lost. He is a survivor. While American jokes portray Poles as utterly inept in whatever they do ("Do you know why they don't give Poles a coffee break? It takes too long to retrain them." [Dundes 135]), many Russian jokes stress the fact that the Chukchi man is a good hunter. He may not be able to tell a hang glider from a bird (see 4.33), but if he shoots, he is sure not to miss. In a contemporary children's joke about a Chukchi, he is even able to perform a heroic deed of a folktale type—he catches crocodiles with his bare hands:

(4.38) A Chukchi comes to [famous pop singer] Alla Pugacheva and says to her:
"Let's get married."
"If you get me crocodile boots, we will."

The Chukchi goes to Africa. Pugacheva waits a year, and another year. By the third, she can't wait any longer and goes to Africa. She sees the Chukchi sitting on the bank of the Nile and catching a crocodile. Behind him is a big pile of crocodiles. The Chukchi puts his hand in the water and says:
"Damn, again I got one without boots." (Lurie 1989, 121)

In some jokes the Chukchi is fearless, mostly because of his unfamiliarity with modern civilization and its dangerous contraptions:

(4.39) Two Chukchis are sawing up a bomb in their vegetable garden. A third one shouts:
"What are you doing? It'll blow up any second!"
"It's OK, we have another one."

In others he simply rules out a negative outcome of an encounter with an enemy. Optimism, though offset by the implication of his ignorance of hazard, is nevertheless another appealing trait. In the following joke, he does not even doubt his victory over a numerically overwhelming enemy:

(4.40) A Chinese official comes to a Chukchi:
"We're going to fight with you. How many of you are there?"
"About five hundred. And how many of you?"
"One billion."
"Well, that's a problem. Where the hell will we be able to bury you?"

Some jokes provide clues as to the source of his courage: he embraces danger as part and parcel of a life full of peril and deprivation. In several jokes, he is portrayed as more adapted to jeopardy than a Russian. The following item is carefully set up to demonstrate the Chukchi's mental superiority even over a very smart Russian, as the folk stereotype has it—an academician, a member of the prestigious Academy of Science. Though this stereotype usually implies an aged man, to show that mental superiority, not physical fitness and skills, make the Chukchi a winner, the Russian is young and as skillful as the Chukchi:

(4.41) A young academician comes to Chukotka to hunt bears. A Chukchi, his hunting companion, asks him:
"Can you ski?"
"Top class."
"Can you shoot?"
"Top rating."
They go to look for a bear's lair.

The Chukchi tosses a stone in it, and an enraged bear crawls out
of the hole and throws himself on the hunters. The Chukchi
rushes away, the Russian rushes after him, and the bear chases
after both of them. As they run, the Russian remembers that he
has a gun on his shoulder. He stops, grabs the gun, turns around
and kills the bear with his first shot. The Chukchi comes up
and says:
"Well, a Russian is a poor hunter. Why did you kill the bear? We
should have made him run back to my house first, and then shoot
him. And now, who will drag the bear to my house?"

In another joke, he outsmarts the Russians again. He does so without resorting
to tricks: he sincerely believes that his advice is worth something in itself.
Although in this, he still shows his backwardness (what he advises is more
than obvious to the Russians), the joke demonstrates that his naive approach
to life is not always self-defeating:

(4.42) A Chukchi wanders through the tundra and spots a Russian
geological expedition. The whole group is sweating, trying to get
their truck out of the muddy pit in which it is stuck.
The Chukchi says:
"I know how to pull it out."
"How? Tell us!" the chief of the expedition shouts.
"Gimme two hundred rubles, I'll tell you," says the Chukchi.
They give him two hundred rubles. The Chukchi hides the
money deep in his pocket and says:
"To get your truck out of this pit you need a thing called
TRAC-TOR!"

His backwardness notwithstanding, some jokes portray the Chukchi as a quick
learner, in fact superior in this respect to a Russian:

(4.43) A Chukchi sits on the seashore and catches fish. Suddenly, an
American submarine surfaces.
"Hello! Did you happen to see which way the Soviet submarine
was headed?"
The Chukchi points to the left.
"Northwest!" commands the captain. "Thank you."
In half an hour, a Soviet submarine surfaces.
"Listen, comrade, did you happen to see which way the
American headed?"
"Northwest!" the Chukchi man replies.
"Hey, you, stop playing a smart aleck! Use your finger!"

In the similar setting of another joke, the Chukchi's stereotype of a stupid man is completely reversed: not only does he know a foreign language well, it is the country he lives in that is disparaged as lacking intelligence:

(4.44) A Chukchi sits on the seashore and catches fish. Suddenly, a foreign submarine surfaces, its hatch opens up, and its captain appears.
"Do you speak English?" he asks the Chukchi.
"I do," says the Chukchi, "but who the hell needs it in this idiotic country!"

| The Chukchi as a Russian

As I have shown, despite the mockery and humiliation to which the Chukchi is often subjected, many quips about him are surprisingly benign, void of the extreme harshness and spitefulness characteristic of many Russian (and not only Russian) ethnic jokes. In Chukchi jokes, one cannot help but sense a certain compassion for the simpleton. Such relatively sparing treatment of the Chukchi man can be explained by a high degree of identification of the Russian joke tellers with the butt of their jokes.

Indeed, many jokes about the Chukchi reveal a close kinship between them and the Russians. By laughing at fools' violation of the rules of society, these tales implicitly define these rules. As Boston (93) points out, "Clown, trickster, joker, buffoon, jester, fool—in various forms this strange figure, laughing or laughed at, exists both outside the norms of society and at the same time somewhere very near the center of human experience." As Sinyavsky (1981, 174) notes, Russian jokes are "most often created on the intersection or on a junction of the usual and the supernatural, the trivial and the unbelievable, the close and the remote, one's own and the strange." Davies (1990, 41) remarks that ethnic jokes about stupidity are usually told about people "whom the joke-tellers can regard not as mysterious foreigners but as a kind of inferior imitation of themselves."

If the Ukrainians, about whom the Russians also enjoy telling stupidity jokes, are close to them by blood, the Chukchis are by fate. It is apparent that, while laughing at the Chukchi's destitute way of life, with its cold climate and scarcity of food, the Russians, in fact, acknowledge their own deprivation and laugh at their own lot. As contemporary Russian jokelore attests, the Russians pride themselves on the same quality they ascribe to the Chukchis— an outstanding ability to withstand the cold—that is, hardships of life in a larger sense.[22] It is not by chance that in the following joke the Russian is the next to the last one in an international experiment to determine how long a person can survive without food; the last one is, of course, the Chukchi:

(4.45) A Russian, a Frenchman, and a Chukchi are involved in a hunger experiment. Each has a telephone in his room for emergency contact with the testers.
The Frenchman calls it quits in three days.
The Russian quits in four days.
One week passes, another one. They peek into the Chukchi's room. He is sitting by the telephone, tapping it and saying: "Telephona, telephona, Chukchi wants to eat." (Ivanova 1994, 227)

In a number of jokes, the Chukchi is a clear stand-in for the average Russian, and many of his misfortunes are real Russian misfortunes. The following joke about a Chukchi and his son in a doctor's office could be told to the same effect about a Russian boy:

(4.46) A Chukchi brought his son to a doctor:
"My son doesn't eat meat, milk, or butter."
The doctor examined the boy: "I find nothing abnormal in him. Why doesn't he eat?"
"Well, there are none of those things [in the stores]."

The Chukchi is brought into the joke solely to announce the obvious: food is scarce.

Many other jokes about the Chukchi's substandard living conditions are also told in terms of the woes of Russian life. Thus, the joke about the Chukchi standing in the line to Lenin's tomb who assumes it is for sausages (see 4.4) reflects a phenomenon of Russian life of the late 1980s: an especially acute shortage of meat products, particularly in the provinces. At that period, Moscow experienced an unusually massive influx of people from the surrounding towns and cities in search of scarce goods (*defitsit*). The joke only dramatizes the situation: the shortage is so bad that not just people from Tula, Riazan', or Iaroslavl' are pouring into the capital in search of sausage, but a Chukchi comes all the way down from the far north.

Whatever woes the Russians have had, the Chukchis in Russian jokelore have had them as well, but in a much worse form. If potatoes were the most available staple of Russian diet during long periods of cold weather for many years, the Chukchis are short of even this meager food; they cannot even spare some of it for planting:

(4.47) An interview with the chairman of an advanced *kolkhoz* in Chukotka:
"Tell us about the new method of growing potatoes that you've developed in your *kolkhoz*."

"We plant potatoes in the morning and dig them up in the
evening."
"Is it possible that they grow that fast?"
"No. We are starving to death."

It is clear that the metafunction of such jokes has little to do with the Chukchis,
but everything to do with the Russians; the sole purpose of such jokes has been
to dissipate frustration with the uncharitable circumstances of Russian life.[23]

By way of the same metaphor, Chukchi living standards compared with
those of the Russians were seen as those of the Russians themselves in comparison with the Westerners'. The huge difference between living standards in
the Chukotka region and those in Alaska, which once belonged to Russia, has
been the subject of a number of Russian Chukchi jokes, all making the same
point—the czarist government should be denounced for not selling Chukotka
as well:

(4.48) During a people's deputies meeting, a Chukchi comes up to a
microphone:
"I ask you to vote for a resolution condemning the Romanov
dynasty: Why did they sell Alaska, but not Chukotka?"

Thus, the Russian folk vision of the Chukchis' life is an exaggerated
picture of that of the Russians themselves. The Chukchi's primitive lifestyle,
as described in jokes, serves as a hyperbolic statement about the shortcomings
of Russian life of the time. It is as if by telling the Chukchi jokes, the Russians
ask each other: "Don't we, a great nation, a superpower, live like those
poor underdeveloped souls—the Chukchis?" These jokes have expressed the
ultimate despair of the Russians, who may have found a masochistic pleasure
in identifying themselves with the mythical image of what they have assumed
to be the most deprived ethnicity.

This close identification with the Chukchi is also evident in the projection
on them of the Russians' own phobias and apprehensions. This is why the
numerically overwhelming Chinese are chosen to be the Chukchi's enemy
in 4.40. Undoubtedly also as a result of strong self-identification with the
Chukchis, the Russians have endowed this stereotype with their own shortcomings, which surface in many other racist and ageist jokes unrelated to the
Chukchis:

(4.49) As the best hunter of his nomad camp, a Chukchi arrives in
Africa for a hunters' competition. They give all the participants a
route in the jungle and caution them not to shoot crocodiles or
monkeys.
After a while, the Chukchi returns and says that he killed five
"nosirs."

"What 'nosirs' are you talking about?" the judges ask.
The Chukchi:
"As I go through the jungle, a little black creature runs out in front of me. I ask it: 'Crocodile? Monkey?' It says: 'Nosir.' I shoot it. And that's happened five times. Chukchi's a good hunter!"

(4.50) A Chukchi is riding in a taxi cab in Moscow. Suddenly he sees that an old lady is rushing around in front of the car. The driver can hardly get around her. Leaving the cab, the Chukchi says to the driver:
"Well, a Russian is a poor hunter. If I hadn't opened the door in time, the old lady would have got away."

The Russians find the Chukchis' lives advantageous in certain respects. A Chukchi has nothing, but then, like the proverbial proletarian of the Communist manifesto, he has nothing to lose. He does not know fear of authorities—not because he is unaware of the possibility of political persecution under the Soviet regime, but because he really cannot be punished more then he is punished by fate. With its stern climate and remote location, far away from civilization, the Chukotka region is associated with the traditional Russian (and Soviet) places of exile and labor camps. In fact, the infamous Magadan, the epitome of Stalin's hard-labor camps, is located in Chukotka. Thus, the humor of the following joke lies precisely in the fact that it is impossible to exile the Chukchi man any farther; he is already there:

(4.51) Two Chukchis are sitting on a beach and fishing. One of them says:
"Wanna hear a political joke?"
"No. They might exile us."[24]

The Chukchi seems to be blissfully unable to fathom Soviet bureaucracy, anything that limits freedom of movement, as the notorious and dreaded Soviet passport did:

(4.52) They give a passport to a Chukchi. Next day he comes back and asks for another one.
"What do you need the other one for?"
What do you mean 'what for'? This Chukchi's a smoker."
(Ivanova 1994, 214)

The Chukchi's assumed freedom from fear of the persecution that was for many years the constant psychological preoccupation of the Russians gives his image its appeal.

This particular circumstance is only a localized case of the general quality of any folkloric (or institutionalized, as was the case with court jesters) fools who, in Ben Jonson's words, are "free from care or sorrow-taking." What sets a fool "free from sorrow" is his intrinsic quality of breaking down distinctions—"between wisdom and folly, sanity and insanity, rule and disorder" (Boston 93). What makes a reasonable man worried escapes the fool, who, by definition, does not abide by reason. Whether he is unable to reason or chooses not to make sense in a too complicated—and thus seemingly senseless—world is beside the point; for one reason or another, he always appears oblivious to the misfortunes that befall him.

The Chukchi's freedom from conventional behavior reveals in him many traits of the institutionalized figure of the fool, be it in folklore, in the mass media, on stage, or in an arena. As Boston (97) points out, "the function of the fool is to be a catalyst of laughter in society, just as the clown is on stage or screen or in the circus. Fools and clowns are disorderly, they are breakers of rules and taboos, they are agents of comic chaos." Thus, the Chukchi's presumed lack of sophistication is utilized in Soviet jokes in order to create the figure of an idiot savant who, in his naivete, cuts through the surface of things and gets to the heart of the matter. The Chukchi, like the fool in Ben Jonson's song from *Volpone,* speaks truth "free from slaughter."[25]

(4.53) A Chukchi returned home from the Communist Party Congress: "I attended the Congress. They accepted the new program. They said: 'Everything for man, everything for the benefit of man!' And this Chukchi saw this man with his own eyes. He was right there, in the Presidium."

In this respect, the Chukchi of the jokes is akin to traditional Russian folk comic figures, such as Ivan the Fool of the everyday tales and Chapaev, a real-life Civil War hero of peasant origin who became a stock figure of Soviet political propaganda in the 1930s and who has been a butt of anti-Soviet jokes since the early 1960s. Most of what Sinyavsky (1981, 175) has to say about the Chapaev of the jokes is applicable to the Chukchi of the jokes; Chapaev, he wrote in the 1970s, "remains a positive character, maybe the only stable character of contemporary Russian jokelore in this positive quality; in this combination of dullness, courage, ignorance, simple-mindedness and realistic common sense, he resembles somewhat a fairy-tale fool, though without victorious halo and exclusively in a joker's role." Like Chapaev, the Chukchi also does ostensibly foolish things, yet somehow not only survives but does not lose his joie de vivre. It is not by accident that in a recently published compilation of jokes entitled *Anekdoty o narodnykh geroiakh* (Jokes about Popular Heroes) (Smetanin and Donskaia 1994), the Chukchi is the only non-Russian among two others—Chapaev and Shtirlits, a parodic hero of the famous TV series of the early 1970s, called "Seventeen Moments of Spring" (Semnadtsat' mgnovenii vesny).[26] Like Ivan the Fool of the Russian everyday tale (*bytovaia skazka*), the Chukchi is also simpleminded and trusting. What is said about Ivan the Fool—that he "inherited primordial logic, morality, and psychological habits" (Iudin 80)—can also be said about the Chukchi. Both heroes think in external analogies. For Ivan, a table is alive: on his way home, he unloads it from his cart and expects it to trot along on its own because it has four legs. For the Chukchi man, a car's headlights are its eyes and its exhaust pipe is its phallus (see 4.32). In another joke, a trolley is just a tied-up animal:

(4.54) A Chukchi stands at a bus stop and looks at the passing city traffic. Another Chukchi comes up to him and asks:
"Well, which of these means of transport is the fastest?"
"The trolley. See how quickly it runs when it's tied up. And what if it were untied?" (Ivanova 1994, 230)

In their treatment of inanimate objects as animate, both Ivan the Fool and the Chukchi man exhibit the same trait characteristic of magical thought: they both assume the existence of a soul in all objects. By accepting words at their face value, they both reveal an archaic thinking pattern: for both, a figurative meaning of a word does not exist yet, only the literal one.

Through Russian laughter at the Chukchi's silliness, one may sense a nostalgia for those easier and happier days of childhood, a dream by those who feel burdened with the need to exert all their mental forces in order to succeed in the modern world. What seems to be revealed through this laughter is the tellers' longing for a much simpler world, a world that may lack modern amenities, but is also void of the stress and pressure that comes with a modern lifestyle. As Davies (1990, 387) points out: "Any anxieties that people have regarding their liability to failure through incompetence [in a modern workplace] are released and dissolved by laughter at the crass stupidity of ethnic outsiders."

With the collapse of the Soviet regime, the Chukchi stereotype has gradually acquired a new quality. While laughing at the Chukchi's misadventures, the Russians more often laugh not at him, but with him, empathizing with his lot. In many jokes, the Chukchi can be seen as a metaphor for Russians whose historical misfortunes during the Soviet period made the Chukchi their distorted mirror image. Chukchi jokes, more than any other Russian ethnic jokes, support Davies's notion (1990, 43) that mainstream culture views ethnic minorities as "bad imitations" of itself.[27]

Thus, the punch line of a classical Russian joke of the 1920s about a drunkard who, after getting close to a cage with a donkey, pulled the donkey's face next to his own, kissed it, and began to cry: "You poor bunny rabbit, what have the Communists done to you?" (Draitser 1980, 11) can be transferred onto the Chukchi's image. Looking at the Chukchis in the amusing mirror of folk humor, the Russians see themselves and say: "We poor Russians, what have the Communists done to us?" In this ability to reflect the sorrows of Russian life, the Chukchi has become a Russian national clown, a Petrushka of sorts, who, despite being beaten, does not lose his spirit.

CHAPTER 5

On "Chuchmeks," "Egg Yolks," and Other Strangers

Contemporary Russian Ethnic Nicknames, Proverbs, and Sayings

Nicknames contain rich data about many cultural assumptions of the group that uses them. This and other relevant folkloric material may provide an insight not only into relationships between various ethnic groups, but also into the properties of the Russian language and the artistic means employed.

Research in this ethnically colored folklore raises a number of interesting theoretical questions.

It is commonly assumed that deliberate slurs are created by the members of the *majority* for the sheer purpose of denunciation and justification of its oppressive policies or condescending attitude toward a *minority*. A. A. Roback (317), the compiler of the *Dictionary of International Slurs,* writes: "It may very well be that the low opinions were formed in justification of the bullying attitude, just as a hold-up man before robbing his victim will insult him in the vilest manner. . . . It is as if he were in the capacity of a moral agent punishing the person about to be robbed for his well-known misdeeds." Joyce Hertzler (145–46) echoes this conclusion: "The herd laughter against the victims also serves to express triumph over them. In some measure it justifies the treatment of them. In addition it is a form of draining off the common antipathy and sadistic impulses of the majority against the minority."

Another reason for the proliferation of ethnic slurs is often cited: a majority resorts to such tactics not as a way of demonstrating power, but rather as a means of relieving a feeling of inadequacy or inferiority, often unrecognized. This psychological mechanism of a group seeking blame outside of the group for its misfortunes, by means peculiar to Russians, is well described by Abram Tertz (Andrei Sinyavsky) (1976, 113) in reference to Russian anti-Semitism:

> The Russian is incapable of admitting that any evil can derive from a Russian, because deep down (like everyone else, no doubt) within his soul he is good. He cannot conceive that in the Russian state Russian people can be made unhappy through the fault of other Russians or by his own fault. A Russian is one of us, ours, [a Soviet one] (*svoi, svoiskii, sovetskii*). Nothing bad ever comes from *our* people, always from others. Russian anti-Semitism is a way of externalizing evil, a way of thrusting our own sins onto a scapegoat.

Scapegoating is not the province of the majority group exclusively: a minority may also resort to it. Scapegoating to rid oneself of the burden of guilt or shame, or any other unpleasant feeling, is a universal human trait, and few people are completely free of this vice. As individuals often find it soothing to blame others for failures, so does any group of people.

A minority often chooses a majority's discriminatory practices as justification for failures that are not necessarily the result of these practices. Such attitudes are often acknowledged and satirized by sophisticated members of the group, as in a well-known Jewish joke about a certain Rabinovich with a speech defect who blames anti-Semitism when he is turned down for a job as a radio announcer (e.g., see V. Raskin 213). As Tomas Venclova (321) observes, for non-Russian groups of the former Soviet Union, Russians frequently serve as scapegoats for all the groups' problems, whether they have anything to do with them or not.

If a majority is perceived as too formidable a power, a minority group may look for (and find) a local scapegoat, often another minority group, as in an attempt by some in the African American community to blame the Jews for their group's problems. Such is the case with many ethnic groups inside the former Soviet Union; moreover, interethnic conflicts often spill over into open hostilities, including armed conflicts, as in the case of the Armenians and the Azeris, and the Uzbeks and the Turkish Mekkhs, to name a few.

Under certain conditions a majority may find itself in the role of a minority, thus becoming the object of scapegoating. Such is currently the fate of the Russians who live in the former national republics of the Soviet Union. While in the immediate past they were a part of a privileged majority, in the now collapsed Soviet empire they have become a powerless minority, deprived of many human rights. From this standpoint, like other folkloric material belonging to the realm of popular humor, slurs of a majority directed at a minority may often be a manifestation not of power but of impotence, of anxiety created by destabilized and volatile historical circumstances,[1] or by unresolved and unclear intragroup relationships.

Many non-Russian nationalities who have long lived in the mainstream culture, the core of which was Russian language and customs, are also bitten by the bug of intolerance and hostility toward "the others," whoever they may be at a given moment. Thus, this researcher has collected several ethnic slurs about blacks, Mexicans, and Puerto Ricans used by Russian-Jewish immigrants in the United States.

| Obsolete Russian Ethnic Slurs

It goes without saying that the Russians do not have a monopoly on ethnocentrism. In his 1944 dictionary of nearly three thousand international slurs ("ethnophaulisms," as he calls them), Roback convincingly shows that hardly any nation, large or small, is free of them. In fact, although his dictionary (128–32) lists many Russian derogatory nicknames for the French, Germans, Japanese, Ukrainians, Poles, Gypsies, and Jews, the number of Russian entries is rather meager, around thirty, compared to those in English, for example— about one thousand (247).[2] Many Russian slurs also pale in comparison with English, German, or French ethnic affronts in their viciousness and ill will.

Published more than fifty years ago, Roback's dictionary is largely out- dated. Many of the Russian ethnic slurs he lists no longer circulate. It seems that tensions between the Russians and an out-group call for a disdainful nickname; once these tensions ease, the coined curse gradually goes out of circulation and out of the language itself. For example, prompted by Napoleon's invasion of Russia and prominently featured in nineteenth-century Russian literature, the anti-French slur "a little Frenchman" (*frantsuzik*) has virtually disappeared from contemporary Russian lore, and in contemporary Russian slang the words "Paris" and "Parisian" connote excellence and de- light, reflecting the age-old Russian fascination with French culture.[3]

The Russians expressed animosity toward the Germans long before Hitler's invasion of Russia in the course of World War II. The Russian name for a German means "a mute" (*nemets*) in old Russian, "one whose speech cannot be understood," (Vasmer 3:62), which makes it a generic qualifier of a foreigner and, in fact, one of the oldest obsolete Russian nicknames. A slew of either outright negative or simply unsympathetic German characters can be found in stories and novels by Gogol, Goncharov, and other nineteenth- century Russian writers. The same attitude can be seen in Russian folklore of the past, as in a proverb collected by Dal (see chapter 1, note 16).

However, anti-German slurs that were widespread in the nineteenth century, such as "a potato" (*kartoshka*) and "a sausage-glutton" (*kolbasnik*) (Roback 129) have since ceased to exist, perhaps for the simple reason that both items became Russian food staples. Some of the old anti-German slurs, such as "those damn Germans" (a rough translation of the Russian word *nemchura*) reentered the folklore during World War II, but then vanished again from the folk vocabulary. It may be surprising that, with the exception of the stereotype of a German as an obedient person, as featured in many national comparison jokes around the world, this researcher could not find many slurs directed at Germans,[4] in spite of the Russians' legitimate bitterness about German atrocities committed on Russian territory during the last war.

The only Russian ethnic nicknames listed in Roback's dictionary to survive during the half-century since its publication are concerned with Gypsies and Jews. Today old nicknames for Poles using the Polish terms *pan* and *liakh* are quite rare. Instead, a new nickname, *polak* (Shlyakhov and Adler 153), influenced by the English-American slur "Pollack," has entered contemporary Russian slang. However, Poles, an object of intense hatred in the nineteenth century, have lost their place among the scorned groups in contemporary Russian folklore.[5]

While many negative national stereotypes in Russian consciousness have disappeared, others have changed from strictly negative to ambivalent. Thus, born during the war of 1904 and listed in Roback's dictionary, the Russian slur for the Japanese—"monkeys" (*makaki*)[6]—is seldom heard today. Although a slighting attitude toward them can still be sensed in the old, but still circulating, nicknames, such as "a little Japanese" (*iaposhka*) and *samurai,* many contemporary Russian jokes respectfully portray the Japanese as a technologically advanced people. For example,

(5.1) A Japanese shows a Russian two fists and asks him:
"Which one contains my television?"
The Russian points to the right hand.
"Lucky guess," says the Japanese. "And how many sets are there?"

(5.2) Some Japanese tourists are asked what they liked most of all in Russia.
"The children," they say.
"What about the children?"
"They are wonderful. But whatever you make with your *hands* is horrible."

A Russian distorted expression, "a Japanese mother" (*iapona mat'*), is not a slur, but merely a euphemism for the Russian foul-language expression "[your] fucked mother" (*ebona mat'; the voiced "b" is substituted for the voiceless "p").

| Newly Coined Nicknames for Various Ethnic Groups

In the late Soviet and post-Soviet period, the growing tensions between Russians and many minority groups have given birth to new ethnic slurs.

Russians, by far the largest of all ethnic groups living in the former Soviet Union, also represent the dominant culture. Contemporary everyday Russian oral folklore often continues the long-standing tradition of a patronizing attitude toward many minorities whose territories were in most cases forcefully subjugated by the czars, and then kept through power and political manipulation by the Soviet regime. The chauvinism of Russian lore is strong. Echoing the world of adults, the folklore of contemporary Russian school-age children is crudely nationalistic; it regards the Russians as people superior to all foreigners. National minorities living in Russian territory are, as a rule, regarded in a derogatory way; the words "a Chinese" and "a Chukchi" are both used to mean "a stupid man"; and "a Jew" carries an invariably disparaging association (Lurie 1992, 8).

A huge influx to Moscow of refugees from the troubled Transcaucasian and Central Asian republics (known as "the Near Abroad," *blizhnee zarubezh'e*) beginning in the late 1980s, and the great number of street merchants and hustlers from the same regions, have increased both the visibility of these ethnic groups and tensions between them and the Russians. New ethnic slurs are the result of the growing Russian nationalism and ethnocentrism caused by the rise of separatism and hostility toward the Russian population in many national republics. The shortages of food and essential consumer goods, political instability, and sporadic open violence between various ethnic groups have created an atmosphere of increased intolerance and raised xenophobic feelings on both sides, as the new ethnic nicknames demonstrate. The most substantial of several similar recent publications,[7] V. S. Elistratov's (1994) *Dictionary of Moscow Argot*[8] (more than eight thousand words and three thousand idiomatic expressions based on materials from 1980–93) is full of items that are concerned with ethnicities in one way or another.

In his introduction Elistratov (8) insists on the "nonpartisan" nature of the material and claims that since "argot" (as he arbitrarily calls it) belongs to "the culture of cynics," which tends to degrade and make fun of everything and everybody, his dictionary entries are ethnic-blind; that is, they equally disparage all nationalities, including the Russians. This is not quite the case. While listing contemptuous nicknames for many ethnic groups, the volume contains only one anti-Russian slur—"a boor" (*katsap*)—which cannot be considered self-effacing since it is used by the Ukrainians. A few Russian names are employed in a slighting way, usually implying provincial stupidity and backwardness: for example, "Sasha (Masha) from the Ural Heavy Machinery Plant" (*Sasha (Masha) s Uralmasha*), "little Vanya from Presnia" (*Van'ka s Presni*), and the like.[9] However, the Russians' denigration of other national groups is much more pronounced in these dictionary entries.

| Cognitive Nicknames

Not all ethnic nicknames are necessarily slurs. Many are primarily means of identifying a person's national origin. Some are just shortened versions of a group's standard names: *latin* for a Latin American, *iug* and *iuzhok* for a Yugoslavian, *ius* (U.S.) for an American. Some foreigners are also identified through monetary denominations: a slang name for the Italians is "soldi" (*sol'di*); for the French, "francs" (*franki*); for Americans, "cents" (*tsenty*); and for the Japanese, "raccoons" (*enoty,* from *ien* "yen").[10]

Sometimes a thin line divides a benign nickname and a malign one. Occasionally, one and the same word can be both, depending on its pronunciation. A case in point is the Russian nickname "a little Kyrgyz" (*kirgizushka*). As one of my consultants, a native Kyrgyz, demonstrated, depending on which syllable is stressed, the word can convey either friendliness and even endearment (with the second "i" stressed) or disdain (with stressed "u").

Many ethnic nicknames consist of characteristic personal names, first or last, used instead of the generic name of a national group and rendered in Russian in lowercase.[11] A Georgian is designated by the indigenous given name *gogi* (domestic for Georgy), as well as by its characteristically distorted versions, *gogii, gogiia.*[12] An Armenian is called *karapet* or *khachik,* and a man from any of the southern republics of Transcaucasia and Central Asia, *mamed* (from Mukhamed; correspondingly, *Mamediia* is a nickname for the whole region). In the same way, a widespread Tartar surname, *khabibulin,* and the name of North Korea's long-term leader, *kimirsen* (Russian spelling of Kim Il Sung), are used to denote their nationalities. A Jew is identified either by a traditional Jewish first name: *abram, sarra, shmul'* (domestic of *Samuil*), *ziama* (domestic of *Zinovii*), or a Jewish last name (*rabinovich*).

A number of Jewish surnames used as nicknames are made up, that is, only sound Jewish: "iceberg" (*aizberg*), *shvonder,* "rail-road bar" (*shlagbaum*), "schnitzel" (*shnitsel'*). The first two nicknames are lowercased last names of literary origin. In Ilf and Petrov's novel *The Golden Calf* (chapter 13), upon learning that a neighbor's long absence is caused by his voyage to the Arctic in search of the lost members of an expedition among icebergs, an anti-Semitic tenant in a communal apartment rumbles suspiciously that he has endured enough of all these "Icebergs, Weissbergs, Aizenbergs, and all sorts of Rabinoviches" (*Aisbergi, Vaisbergi, Aizenbergi i vsiakie tam Rabinovichi . . .*). *Of course, the play is on the similarity between the Russian word for "iceberg" (aisberg)* and Vaisberg, a widespread Russian-Jewish surname. The second nickname, *shvonder,* is the last name of a character in Mikhail Bulgakov's novel *The Heart of a Dog*, the obnoxious member of the house committee who harasses Doctor Preobrazhensky. Although in the novel his Jewish identity is not conveyed directly, it is phonetically established by the characteristic "-er" ending of many Jewish surnames and the Yiddish-sounding phoneme *shvon,* as in "Schwanz" ("a tail," in colloquial usage "a prick").

The third nickname, *shlagbaum,* is a German word, adopted into Russian. This nickname evidently comes from Russian-Jewish jokes dealing with job discrimination and plays on the sound- similarity of the word with Jewish surnames with the same ending, such as, for example, Appelbaum:

(5.3) "Where do you work?" says one Jew to another.
"On the railroad."
"Are there many of ours working there?"
"No. Only two of us, me and Shlagbaum."

"Schnitzel" (*shnitsel'*) is just a foreign-sounding name—Jewish, to a Russian ear—for a fillet of pork or veal.

Some ethnic nicknames denote a nationality by using the language of a target group. Thus, a person of a southern nationality, usually from the Caucasus, is called "a daredevil" (*abrek,* from the Osetinian *abreg* and the Cherkessian *abrek*) or by such Georgian words as *dzhigit* ("a skillful horseman"), *katso* ("a friend"), and *ara* ("no"),[13] or an Armenian word, *serum* ("a loved one"). A Gypsy may be called by an often-used Gypsy term, *chavela.* The nickname *alorets* for an Italian is from the Italian *allora* ("now") and *iuks* for a Finn is from the Finnish *uksi* ("one").

Disdain for an ethnicity may be expressed by purely linguistic means, with the help of a variety of suffixes, most often diminutive, thus "belittling" a nationality in both literal and figurative meanings of the word, as in "a little Jew" (*evreichik;* cf., American "Jew-boy"), "a little Armenian" (*armiashka*) or "little Ashot" (*ashotik;* from an Armenian first name), and "a little Finnish man" (*finik*).[14] A "little Persian" (*persik*),[15] is an inclusive nickname for any Asian, often one of non-Turkic origin (an Afghan, an Arab, etc.). The same device is used in a nickname for Americans among some Russian immigrants in the United States—"a little American" (*amerikashka*), connoting American cultural standards presumably inferior to those held by educated Russians.

A variation of this belittling device, denigration through infantilization and zoologization, can be found in the nationalistic and xenophobic works of contemporary Russian writers. Thus, in his novel *A Sad Detective,* in referring to Jewish students in a local pedagogical institute, Victor Astafiev employs another form: "little Jewish species" (*evreichata;* cited in Ehidelman 196); the suffix *-at/-iat* is used in Russian to denote the cubs or calves of animals, as in "young hares, tigers, elephants" (*zaichata, tigriata, sloniata*).

Suffixes "*-ug/iug,*" as in Russian words for "big-time thief" or "big-time bandit" (*voriuga, bandiuga*), create offensive connotations and amplify disparagement. They are utilized in an anti-Semitic slur, *zhidiuga* (approximately, "a big-time kike," "a kike of all kikes"), and in a nickname for Westerners—*kapitalugi, kapitaliuzhniki* (similar to "capitalist pigs.") Although the official name of the Chechen region is "Chechnia," the same word in a lowercase version used as a reference to the Chechen people (instead of the grammatically correct *chechentsy*) is offensive, for the morpheme *-nia* also connotes disdain, as in *fignia* and *khernia*, both connoting "rubbish" (the same is true with *zhidovnia,* "those kikes"; Elistratov 548).

A number of ethnic nicknames in this dictionary denote a group through a variety of synecdochic techniques, usually through a feature of a group member's appearance. Such descriptive nicknames serve primarily as a means of informal ethnic cognition. They often include skin color. An Asian man is called "yellow" (*zheltyi*),[16] "citrus" (*tsitrus*), "an egg yolk" (*zheltok*), or "a colored one" (*tsvetnoi*), as in "All the colored are eager to get to Moscow" (*Vse tsvetnye khotiat v Moskvu popast'*) (Elistratov 533).

"A black one" (*chernyi*), "the black-assed" (*chernozhopyi*), and "a dirty one" (*chumazyi*) (Elistratov 555; see also Flegon 386) denote black people. These slurs have existed in Russian lore for at least four decades. Despite the absence of direct contact between them and the Russians (there was a small group at the Patrice Lumumba University Moscow), the word "Negro" acquired a disdainful connotation a few decades ago. At that time, a man who worked too hard began to be called "a Negro." Currently, an expression "a mixture of a Negro with a motorcycle" (Elistratov 277) connotes something absurd and odd. A Russian calling another Russian "comrade" may be dismissed disapprovingly with the expression "A sweaty Negro is your comrade" (Elistratov 471).

Elistratov's dictionary records a number of other folkloric items with denigrating images of blacks. Thus "an African tree" and "one who has just descended from a tree" (Elistratov 109) suggest a stupid and uncultured man. *Tumba-iumba* (Elistratov 481) is a "jokingly insulting nickname for people with a low level of culture (primarily Asian and African)."

A black person may also be given the name of something dark colored, such as "a little chocolate bar" (*shokoladka;* cf., American "chocolate drop," "hot chocolate," "sweet chocolate"—Spears 74, 208, 395), "a little coal" (*ugolek;* cf., American "charcoal"—Spears 69), "a [photo] negative" (*negativ*), "a smoked one" (*kopchenyi;* cf., American "smoke" and "smoked-Irishman"—Spears 373), and "[black] shoe polish" (*gutalin*). In contrast, the slang expression "a white man" (*belyi chelovek*) connotes "a human being," "a normal man," as in: "I'm going to America, for at least a month I'm going to live like a white man [read: like a human being]" (*Edu v Ameriku, khot' mesiats pozhivu kak belyi chelovek*). Compare this with the American expression "That's white [decent] of you."[17]

Another nickname for a black person, "a little Maxim" (*maksimka*), is a reference to the child hero of a popular film of the 1950s by the same name about a slave boy who winds up on a Russian ship and is adopted by Russian seamen. A sentimentalized attitude toward blacks was endorsed by Stalinist propaganda and emblematized by the film *Circus*. In its finale, a black baby is symbolically adopted by, as the cliché goes, "the friendly brotherhood of the people of the USSR."

Less frequently used is "a little pig-iron pot" (*chugunok*) in reference to a black child (the pot is usually black on the outside since it is often used for cooking on an open fire), as in: "My daughter wants to marry a Negro, and I [tell] her: 'If you do, bear in mind that I won't tend your little black pots' " ("*Doch' za negra khochet vyiti [zamuzh], a ia ei: esli vyidesh'—znai, chto ia ne budu tvoikh chugunkov nian'chit'"*).

In recent years, by way of folk perception of their dark hair and complexion, "the black one," "black-assed," and "the dirty one" are also used to connote people of the Transcaucasian and Central Asian republics. Accordingly, a collective word "blackness" (*chernota*) connotes the population of all southern republics and the Caucasus. For example, in Brodsky's (7) play *The Marbles* (*Mramor*), an Armenian is nicknamed "black-assed." A contemporary joke addresses this newly acquired inclusion of other ethnicities in the old slur for Negroes in Russia:

(5.4) A Negro asks a Russian to give him a light for his cigarette. The
Russian points to a Georgian and says:
"Ask that black-assed man over there."
The Negro goes over to the Georgian and says:
"Black ass, gimme a light."
The Georgian says to him:
"Listen, dear man, compared with yours, my ass is Snow White."

Other synecdochic nicknames involve the size or shape of facial features. The Jews and Caucasian people are called "big noses" (*nosany* and *nosachi*); in fact, "prominently featured" (*figurnyi*) refers to a "Jewish-Armenian" nose. A Jew is called "a big-eyed one" (*glazan*) or "pop-eyed" (*pucheglazyi*); an Asian man "a squint-eyed one" (*shchurenok*,[18] from *shchurit'sia*, "to squint"), or "cross-eyed" (*kosoglazyi*) (cf., Brodsky 10). Correspondingly, Central Asia is nicknamed "Cross-Eyeland" (*Kosoglaziia*; Elistratov 210). There is also "a narrow [8 mm] film [camera]" (*uzkoplenochnyi*), which also implies a slant-eyed person. In contemporary Russian slang, the verb "to assume an Eskimo's facial expression" (*ehskimosit'sia*) means "to squint."

A male outsider may also be identified by his hair. Here Elistratov's dictionary includes a nickname of relatively recent coinage for all Caucasian men—"mustached Southerners" (*usatye iuzhane*)—together with the age-old slur for Ukrainians, *khokhol,* a reference to the main feature of the traditional haircut of the Ukrainian Cossacks—a tuft of hair on a closely shaven head. Also rather traditional is *peis,* the nickname for a Jew (together with its diminutive and adjectival forms, *peisik* and *peisatyi*), a Russian derivative of the Yiddish-German word "pejes," for the prayer curls of Orthodox Jews (Vasmer 3:225; see also the usage of this slur in Gogol's *Taras Bulba*).

Naming a member of a group by an external feature is denigrating by implication. Addressing a person by a characteristic trait of his appearance estranges him and deprives him of individuality. While reinforcing the stereotypical image of a nationality, such nicknames imply that there is no difference between two members of the same ethnic group, as if to say "They're all the same." This is especially evident in a cross-cultural context. While the Russians call Asian people "slant-eyed" (*kosoglazye,* literally, "cross-eyed"; cf., the same American nickname—Spears 369), the Uzbeks name the Russians "white ears," the Kazakhs call them "blue eyes," and the Kyrgyzs call them "woolen heads," a reference to the Russians' much softer and finer hair in contrast to their own rather coarse hair. Thus, each group points to a feature that seems unusual and strange. At the same time, treating a subgroup synecdochically—that is, as a representative of a larger denomination—is also potentially offensive. While the Russians use the word "a Chukchi" (*chukcha*) to denote any Asian man, the Kazakhs refer to all Europeans as "Russians" (*orus*). Professor William Dirk of the University of Indiana (personal correspondence 1996) believes that a negative meaning is not intended by the Kazakh speaker. However, such a substitution of a particular name of one European group with another one that serves as a token may be insulting to, for example, a Hungarian or a Swede when he is identified by the name of a group other than his own.

Some nationalities are designated metonymically—by the name of a part of their national costume or a national dish. Thus, an Asian man is nicknamed "an [oriental] robe" (*khalat*), as in "Soon all those robes will buy out all Moscow"; Elistratov 517), "a turban" (*chalma*), or "a wide-trousered man" (*sharovarnik*). In a reference to the outsized caps (in the Russians' view) sported by many Georgians, they are sometimes called "airdromes" (*aehrodromy*).[19] The Chinese are occasionally nicknamed "eiderdowns" (*pukhoviki*) because of the Chinese-made winter jackets worn by many of them. Ethnic foods figure in the nicknames "a pasty" (*cheburek*) and "a kabob" (*shashlik*), given to any one from the Caucasus or Transcaucasian republics. There is also "dried apricot" (*uriuk*) for someone from the eastern republics of the former Soviet Union. "Rice" (*ris*) and "a rice grain" (*risinka*) refer respectively to an Asian male and female, often a Vietnamese (cf., American "rice-belly" and "riceman" for a Chinese or other Oriental person—

Spears 341–42). Correspondingly, the expression "rice students" (*risovye studenty*) means "students from Asia." All Westerners are called "hamburgers" (*gamburgery*).[20]

Although they are used primarily for interpersonal communication within the Russian group and many are not intended as slurs, almost all nicknames discussed so far are degrading by connotation. Those that use indigenous language (whether as typical names or separate words of a target group's vocabulary) invariably carry a mocking overtone. By their sheer linguistic properties, the name of a nationality in an indigenous language pronounced by a non-native speaker in the context of his own language stands out as unusual, awkward, strange, foreign. This is the nature of many slurs around the world. As was previously noted, in English, for example, such is the case with the self-names of the Russians, Poles, and Jews.

| Ethnic Invectives

While the lexical items discussed above primarily serve as a means of identification and are offensive only by way of suggestion, another group of Russian nicknames leaves no place for ambiguity: they are invariably interpreted as degrading. In these slurs a disparaging attitude is expressed through a direct negative characterization. For instance, a person from one of the Transcaucasian or Central Asian republics is referred to as "a beast" (*zver'*) and the republics themselves as "bestiary" (*zverinets*). The same people are labeled "apes" (*obez'iany*),[21] "antelopes" (*saigi*), "blockheads" (*churki*), and "bamboo" (*bambuki*); in fact, the last three nicknames are also used to denote any stupid person. To convey these peoples' exotic and allegedly cruel, uncultured, and savage nature, they are also called "khazars" (*khazary*),[22] "bandits" (*basmachi*, a reference to partisan-type military groups fighting the Soviets in the Central Asian territories in the 1920s and 1930s), "[American] Indians" (*indeitsy*),[23] and "Fridays" (*piatnitsy*), after Defoe's *Robinson Crusoe*. The same meaning is carried by such nicknames for ethnic groups in these regions as "Mamelukes" (*mamliuk, mameliuk*), an outdated name for mercenaries guarding Egyptian sultans, and "janizary" (*ianychar*), an infantry soldier in Turkish troops under sultan rule. The Russians living in Moldavia nicknamed Moldavians "peasants" (*tsarany* in Moldavian) and "mules" (*muly* in Russian).

A Westerner does not fare much better, being called by a swear word of Soviet political vocabulary—"a bourgeois" (*burzhui*, a distorted variant of *burzhua*), or "AIDS-carrier" (*SPIDonosets*) on the pattern of "mine-carrier" (*minonosets*). In contemporary Russian slang, the nickname "mustang" (*mustang*) carries two meanings—a half-wit or an American.

As for the traditional Russian arch-scapegoats, the Jews, their nicknames comprise by far the largest number. In absolute number (nearly forty variants of the key slur word, "a kike" [*zhid*] and corresponding expressions),[24] they rival only those entries that represent traditional Russian obscenities.

Elistratov's comments (135) about the key anti-Semitic slur *zhid* are rather surprising. Citing Pushkin, Gogol, Dostoevsky, and other Russian nineteenth-century writers, he claims that in their work the word, "as a rule, did not have a negative-evaluative connotation." He suggests that the contemporary (negative) semantics of the word "is connected with a tradition of dissident literature" (where the typical hero is "most often a Jew"), which "sees the word as invective." (Elistratov 645) In other words, according to this scholar, it is the Jews themselves who are guilty of treating this word as offensive.

Such a conclusion is more than doubtful. The offensiveness of the word *zhid* in the framework of the Russian culture is all too well known and dates at least from the time of the infamous Black Hundred. The word has long been perceived by both Jews and non-Jews as derogatory. Vasmer's dictionary, published in 1950–58 (Russian translation 1986, 2:53), records it as denigrating long before the appearance of the dissident literature cited by Elistratov. In fact, as Klier (1) shows, in Russia the word acquired a stable pejorative connotation by mid-nineteenth century. The derogatory meaning of the word is unmistakably clear in Elistratov's own treatment of it: he lists around two dozen derivatives of the offensive word. Thus his attempt to "whitewash" the word in its current usage is rather underhanded.

The only grain of truth that one may find in Elistratov's linguistic exercise is that the word *zhid* by itself is rather innocent; after all, it is the name of the nationality coming from the Latin word *judeus*. However, the term is not strictly linguistic, but sociolinguistic—that is, it is not the word in itself but how and in which contexts it is used that determines its emotional coloring and perceived semantics. The slighting of a nationality with a nickname rendered as its "real" name in indigenous language can be explained by the mocking effect that such rendering produces. This is the case, for example, with such terms as "Russki," "Pollack," and "Yid" in American English. The same linguistic mechanism works in usage of the word "Jude" in German. The Russian word *zhid* is of the same nature.

The fact that envy is a leading factor in the emotional need to produce anti-Semitic slurs is seen in the nickname of the Russian-made car *Zhiguli*—*zhiduli* (Elistratov 136)—which connotes a Jewish car, a car of the undeservedly rich. If anti-Asian slurs may be generally characterized as contemptuous, some anti-Semitic ones are intended to express disgust. Elistratov (437) lists "slobbery" (*sliuniavyi*) as describing a Jew, and "a crawling kike" (*zhid polzuchii;* 347), which is a travesty of a Russian expression of utter disgust and anger—"a crawling reptile" (*polzuchii gad*).

Besides all these spiteful and disdainful terms for various minorities, there are a number of "reverse slurs"—that is, the name of an ethnicity is used as derogatory. Thus, in contemporary Russian slang a stupid man may be called *mudashvili* and *pidershtein,* a symbiosis of an obscene nickname for a fool (*mudak*) or a homosexual (*pidor*) and a suffix characteristic of many Georgian (*-shvili*) and Jewish (*-shtein*) surnames. To accuse someone of greediness, a Russian may say: "Don't be a kike" (*ne zhidis'*). The verb *vytsiganit'* means to gain something in Gypsy style, that is, through cadging.

A number of names of Asian nationalities are used to characterize someone as strange, awkward, absurd, underdeveloped, stupid, incomprehensible, wild, uncultured, or simply bad. While all such epithets express antipathy toward the minorities involved, the choice of a particular group is based, by and large, on the cultural associations or phonetic qualities of the word, sometimes on both: a Nanai, a Mongol, a Korean, a Tungus (a former name for an Evenk), an Udmurt, a Turk, and a Chukchi.[25]

In Russian mass consciousness, the Nanai are associated with the widely popular humorous circus act called "The Wrestling of Nanai Boys." In this act an adult performer is dressed in a costume that makes him (or her) look like two little boys locked head-on, making believe that they are wrestling each other. There is also an expression connoting something strange and incomprehensible: "the hallucination of a drunken Nanai" (*bred p'ianogo nanaitsa;* Elistratov 51).

The choice of a Korean as a simpleton is most likely caused by the Koreans' low-status jobs and perhaps reflects an image of Northern Koreans under Kim Il Sung as obedient and industrious simpletons, human robots of sorts. A general Russian aversion to hard work, expressed in many proverbs and sayings (the best-known of them, "work isn't a wolf, it won't run away to the forest" [*rabota ne volk, v les ne ubezhit*]) finds its expression in an idiom involving a Korean name, Yong Su (Shlyakhov and Adler [87] erroneously attribute it to the Chinese): "I am slaving away like a boy Yong Su" (*ia vkalyvaiu, kak mal'chik Iun' Su*). The expression "a Korean, a Red Army soldier" (*koreets-krasnoarmeets*) is often a joking reference to any Asian man (Elistratov 207). Since there is not much contact between the Evenks and the Russians in Moscow, most likely the name "Tungus" is a reference to a line from Pushkin's famous poem "A Monument" where he speaks of the "still savage Tungus."

The choice of Udmurts, as well as Nanai and Tungus, among other Asian ethnic groups is also linguistic; their names sound funny (in both meanings of the word) due to unusual sound clusters for the Russian language. In all three words, the vowels are repeated. With its repeated sounds "*u*" and "*d/t*", together with sound symbolism of the latter as connoting something dull, the word *udmurt* resembles another folk epithet for a fool—*dunduk.*

113 |

The folk choice of a Turk (*turok*) is apparently based on the aural similarity of this word and the Russian word for a fool (*durak*). There is also an expression "[he's] a Turk, not a Cossack" (*turok ne kazak*), which connotes a coward.

Collective Denigration

As Elistratov's dictionary attests, the peoples of Central Asia are usually treated as indistinguishable from one another, as a bunch of *aziaty* "those Asians." Besides the collective nicknames already cited, the Russians have at least two other widely used ones: *natsmen* and *chuchmek* (both are surprisingly absent from Elistratov's dictionary). The first is a short form for "a national minority" (*natsional'noe men'shinstvo*), a term borrowed from the official political vocabulary of the 1920s. In contemporary Russia, it has been used to refer to a person of some nationality other than Russian, without specifying it, as in: "He's some kind of ethnic man" (*On kakoi-to natsmen*).

The other term, *chuchmek*, much more frequently used by the Russians as a disparaging nickname, designates a person of any Asian origin living in former Soviet territory. Linguistically a composite of sound clusters found in the names of three Asian nationalities, *CHUkCHa, turkMEn*, and *uzbEK* ("a Chukchi, "a Turkoman," and "an Uzbek"), the word is used to mean *any* Asian man. The deprecating implication of this nickname is clearly seen in the following *chastushka* (Telesin 121):

Khorosho, chto Iu. Gagarin	It's good that Yu. Gagarin
Ne evrei i ne tatarin,	Isn't a Jew or a Tartar,
Ne kakoi-to tam chuchmek,	And not some *chuchmek*,
A nash sovetskii chelovek.	He's ours, a Soviet man.[26]

Elistratov records another recently coined collective— a denigrating neologism that refers to all non-Russians—"foreignhood" (*inostran'*) (179), but its use is usually limited to the new notion of "the Near Abroad" (*blizhnee Zarubezh'e*), that is, the former Soviet republics. The insulting meaning of the word becomes evident from its rhyming in the following saying referring to the refugees from those regions during the unsettling time of intranational clashes: "A sea of shit from the nearest abroad" (*More srani iz blizhnei inostrani;* in the Russian the words for "shit" [*sran'*] and "foreignhood" [*inostran'*] become associated through rhyming).

Perhaps the most all-embracing Russian ethnic nickname is "a non-Russian" (*nerusskii*), used in contemporary slang for anybody who is unusual, bad, or behaves in an incomprehensible or wrong way, as in, "Why are you acting like a non-Russian today? Has your wife run away with a Georgian or what?" (Elistratov 278).

| Other Ethnicity-Related Idioms

The Russian folk attitude toward many minorities as expressed in ethnic nicknames is hardly surprising; similar attitudes are reflected in such folkloric material as proverbs, sayings, catch phrases, and the like. Some of them betray unprovoked and unmotivated derision of an ethnicity—a willingness to disparage for the sake of disparagement. While the anti-Semitic sentiment of this folk genre traditionally accuses the Jews of conspiring against the Russians—"Every Abraham has his own program" (*U kazhdogo Abrama— svoia programma*; Elistratov 17)[27]—that is, of having a secret design (or playing an entrepreneurial trick, in Elistratov's interpretation), some Russian proverbs concerned with the Georgians and Armenians are not specific and, in playful, often rhyming, terms, express general contempt: "A Georgian has a rubber [plug] up his ass" (*Gruzin—v zhope rezin*); "A little Armenian has a wooden cork up his ass" (*Armiashka—v zhope dereviahka*) (Kozlovsky 234).

A scornful attitude toward Tartars is seen in the use of their name to connote a noisy company, a horde (Elistratov 465), or to describe something absurd and incompatible with nature: "a mixture of a Tartar with a mare" (Elistratov 437).[28] A number of contemporary Russian proverbs portray Tartars as oddly patient, uninvolved, and oblivious to their own well-being, even in life or death situations. Needless to say, this image has nothing to do with reality, and, as Alexander Zholkovsky (18) suggests, is somehow conditioned by the low social status of many Tartars living in Russian territory, especially in big cities. Many of them serve as street sweepers, bathhouse workers, waiters, and such. Here are some such proverbs, all based on the theme of the Tartars' alleged "unpretentious indifference." This image may be the result of folk interpretation of the unusually (in the Russian view) noncommittal (poker-faced) expression of many Tartars in public:

Nam, tataram, vse ravno— ili nastupat' bezhat', ili otstupat' bezhat'.	It's all the same to us Tartars— whether we advance running or retreat running.
Nam, tataram, vse ravno— chto samogon, chto pulemet, lish' by s nog valilo.	It's all the same to us Tartars whether it's moonshine or a machine gun, as long as it knocks us off our feet.
Nam, tataram, vse ravno— chto malina, chto govno.	It's all the same to us Tartars, whether it's raspberry or shit.
Nam, tataram, vse ravno— chto ebat' podtaskivat', chto ebannykh ottaskivat'.	It's all the same to us Tartars— whether to drag in those to be fucked, or drag off those who are fucked.

The well-known Russian saying referring to Tartars, "An unexpected guest is worse than a Tartar" (*Nezvannyi gost' khuzhe tatarina*), is a reflection of the nightmarish national memory of the Tartar-Mongol invasion and long occupation of Russian territory during the Middle Ages. This saying has become such an integral part of everyday Russian speech that most Russians do not realize its demeaning nature. Under Gorbachev, with the renewed sensitivity toward national identity, a joke based on the use of this proverb was born:

(5.5) The Tartars complained to the Supreme Soviet that the Russians
kept embarrassing their national feelings, using the proverb: "An
unexpected guest is worse than a Tartar."
The Supreme Soviet decided that this proverb should not be
employed. It should be replaced with another one: "An
unexpected guest is *better* than a Tartar."

Since in modern times neither Tartars nor Mongols represent any real threat to the Russians (in fact, until very recently, Tartars have been fully subjugated and have formed only a small part of the vast Russian Soviet empire), the historic Russian fear of the "the yellow menace" is transferred to the Chinese. The following joke is most illuminating in terms of this fear of a rapidly growing giant nation on the immediate borders of Russia:

(5.6) Question to Armenian Radio:
"Is it possible to annihilate the Chinese people by lining them up
and killing them one by one with a machine gun?"
Answer: "Only if they would not multiply faster than you would
shoot." (Dubovsky 344)

Several decades of lingering threat of confrontation with Red China (which began back in the time of Mao Tse Tung's quest for world leadership of the Communist movement in the late 1950s) have made an imprint on the Russian perception of the Chinese as those who should not be trusted. In Elistratov's collection (196), "A Chinese man," "a Chinese spy," or "a Chinese scout" all designate a sly person.[29]

A slighting attitude toward the Chinese is revealed in the deprecating nickname "a chink" (*kitayoza*) (Elistratov 196), and in a number of Russian idioms. Referring to something puzzling and incomprehensible, a Russian may say: "This is Chinese grammar" (cf., the American expression: "It's Greek to me"). Elistratov (196, 346) also lists the adjective "Chinese" and the expression "in a Chinese way," both connoting something strange, unusual, complicated, incomprehensible, or abnormal. This perception of the Chinese is part of the general stereotype of the "impenetrable" mask of the East.

| Conclusions

Although ethnic nicknames undoubtedly reflect the Russians' low opinion of many nationalities, it would be a mistake to see this folkloric material primarily as "pure insult." In fact, very few of the slurs are used in open confrontation between the Russians and other groups. While many of these nicknames serve as only a token identification of a member of a given group, at the same time they reveal a Russian need to assert superiority. In the final analysis, such a need reflects the speakers' low opinion of themselves. As Hertzler (146) observes: "In effect, scapegoating produces satisfactions of escape, defense, and release. The scapegoat becomes the excuse for [the perpetrators'] frailties, ineptness, failure, bungling, indecency. To it they transfer their fears. Incidentally, through it they exemplify their deep-seated and annoying sense of guilt, for the scapegoat emphatically states, 'J'accuse!' "

A proper assessment of ethnic nicknames can be achieved only in the concrete social context of their circulation; they clearly belong to the sphere of sociolinguistics. One should bear in mind, for instance, that under certain circumstances, in a dyadic (close, personal, and affectionate) relationship between two individual members of different etic groups, offensive nicknames can be used with a meaning opposite to the one usually implied—as a term of endearment. When a joking (and trusting) relationship between the two is established, in using an ethnic slur the speaker sends a message: "I love you despite the fact that my group doesn't like your group."

Many Russian ethnic nicknames are little more than a by-product of lingo-centripetal tendencies characteristic of Russian folklore in general. Playing with the language is often "the name of the game" in the direct sense of the term: a member of one group avoids calling another by its given name and is bent on finding a colorful, picturesque synonym for it. As Elistratov (672) points out, these folkloric terms are highly perishable goods. Most of them are a result of improvisation and, with the exception of a handful of traditional ethnic slurs that have persisted in the Russian language over a long time, the vast majority of the new terms are hardly destined for posterity. Offensive language is a reflection of offensive attitudes. Obviously, with the changes in relationships between the Russians and other groups, many insulting words aimed at ethnicities will disappear from the Russian vocabulary, as has happened with so many of the entries in Roback's dictionary of 1944.

CHAPTER 6

"He's Abroad?
I'm the One Who's Abroad"

Contemporary Jokes Told by Russian Jews

Protest Humor

Russian folkloric denunciation of a target group is often contested. In many cases, there exists an indigenous folk response in kind to Russian humor—"protest humor," as Donald Simmons (567–70) calls a similar phenomenon. While the Russian calls a Georgian a "mustached southerner," the Georgian refers to "a Russian Vanya" (*rusuli Vanya*), which connotes a boorish simpleton. As the Russians call the Ukrainians *khokhly*, the latter have two derogatory nicknames for the Russians: *moskali*, "Moscowites," and *katsapy*, "boors." To counter *Khokhliandia*, the Russian nickname for Ukraine, the Ukrainians call Russia *Katsapshchina*. In response to Russian anti-Semitic slurs, the Russian Jews have offensive nicknames for the Russians, such as "a gentile head" (*goishe kop*), implying "a fool"; "Vanya" (*fonya*, a phonetic variant of the name); "drunkards" (*shikurim*); and "pigs" (*khazeyrim*).

Often accusations and counteraccusations are of the very same nature. If a Russian proverb says that "one Ukrainian is as sly as two Jews," a Ukrainian one claims that "a Russian is as sly as four Jews" (Roback 218), evidently considering one Jew a unit of slyness. Roback (216–18) lists other Ukrainian proverbs depicting the Russians as bad-mouthed, treacherous, and worse than the devil himself. The most striking in this respect is an international example: a cockroach in Russian vernacular is called *prusak*, "a Prussian," and in German *Russe*, "a Russian" (Roback 111).

However, in most cases there is no real exchange of hostile humor, for the sides are not on equal footing. Throughout modern history, the Russians have been "the dominant ethnic element, the source of the certified national culture which the [ruling Soviet and prerevolutionary] elite believed it required" (Armstrong 71).

Thus, a distinction should be made between two kinds of folk laughter directed at other groups: aggressive and defensive laughter. Russian folk humor, with a few exceptions, belongs to the former, described by Hertzler (45–46) as "the laughter of antipathy, antagonism and attack, the laughter directed at or against other individuals or groups, or what they stand for or do or have done, in order to control them, exclude them, reject them, humiliate them, weaken or injure them, punish them."

The folk laughter of the targeted nationalities aimed at the Russians is defensive laughter, the kind that responds to "the atmosphere of constraint, restraint, taboo; the laughter directed against the social suppressor, the oppressive authorities, the conventions, many features of social institutions, the majorities, the totalitarians, the jailers, the dominators, the 'superiors' " (Hertzler 46).

This humor plays an important role in an ethnicity's social mechanism. As Hertzler (95) observes,

> laughter within the group about some mutually satisfying situation among the members, or laughter directed against disturbing outsiders, is an important factor in enhancing the morale of the members of the in-group and in protecting it against disruptive influences from without. As between groups, when "we" laugh together, it strengthens the boundaries between us and "them" who do not know what we are laughing at, or who are not laughing with us. Furthermore, laughter at foreign groups usually helps to build the esprit de corps of the given group.

Hertzler's (146) observations about Afro-American humor are fully applicable to Russian Jewish humor; the opposition of "whites" and "blacks" is quite similar to that of "the Jews" and "the Russians." That is, Jewish humor in Russia is also "a noteworthy instance of laughter as therapeutic agent in a situation of social tension." It too "has grown out of a condition of enforced subordination and separation, which has created a background of resentment, resistance, and struggle." The Russian Jew also laughs at the contrast between his status and that of other ethnic groups, "at the contradictions in the contentions and the actions" of the oppressor, at the "impotence" of the other in coming to terms with him.

| Sociological Functions of Jewish Humor

Russian Jewish humor, as part of the whole phenomenon of East European Jewish humor, is considered by many researchers to be the source of all modern Jewish folk humor.[1] Yet it is Israeli and American Jewish humor that has interested scholars: relatively little work has been done on contemporary Russian Jewish humor. A number of collections of Russian Jewish jokes have been published in the West, of which David Harris and Israel Rabonovich's (1988) is the most representative, but a great deal remains to be done to analyze fully the wealth of this folkloric material. This situation is even more regrettable because in a country with an enormous censorship apparatus during more than seventy years of Soviet history, the oral folk humor of the Russian Jews became an invaluable source of insight into their hearts and minds. Indeed, in a country where Jewish culture was virtually annihilated on Stalin's orders (Pinkus 138–61), oral humor became the only available form of Jewish self-expression, replacing journals, books, theater, cinema, television programs, and other modern means of communication that were barred to Jews for years. Only with the beginning of *perestroika* did we see some attempts to restore Jewish cultural life. Incalculable harm had already been done.

A small but highly characteristic body of contemporary Russian Jewish jokes is concerned, explicitly and implicitly, with the mass emigration of the Jews from the USSR—the exodus that started in the early 1970s and has continued to the present with great fluctuation in its size and character. These jokes have been much more than a source of entertainment; not only have they served as an accurate gauge of the prevalent mood within the scattered Jewish community, but they have also performed several important social functions. The continuous, collective process of joke telling has always been a means of creating and reinforcing a sense of solidarity and intimacy within the Jewish group. In the absence of any formal organization aimed at representing Jewish interests, oral humor itself took on the functions normally performed by the members of a structured community.

There are two kinds of exodus jokes: those dealing with relationships within the Jewish group (intragroup jokes) and those dealing with relationships between Jews and non-Jews (intergroup jokes). My analysis of the social functions of both types of jokes uses a model suggested by William H. Martineau (114–24). According to this model, social functions of humor are analyzed in three structural settings: (1) those within a specific group; (2) those in an intergroup situation aimed at one of the two groups; and (3) those in an intergroup situation focusing on the interaction and relationship between the two groups.

In Jewish exodus jokes, two of the four major variables of social inter-action during the humorous act—that is, the actor (the agent who delivers the joke) and the audience—are taken to be Jewish or pro-Jewish, that is, they include non-Jews sympathetic to the Jewish cause. The third variable, the subject or the butt of the joke, is either the Jews themselves or an agent outside of the group who creates tension within the Jewish group (by active anti-Semitic behavior or just by demonstrating generally unsympathetic or negligent attitudes toward the Jewish in-group's interests).

The fourth variable, judgment, which is the evaluative element of the whole model, esteems or disparages a particular group. Few problems arise in finding a joke disparaging, due to its nature: it is an act of playful aggression. (Self-disparagement is highly characteristic of Jewish humor in general.) The self-esteem of this group, however, often cannot be identified. Sympathy is a better term to describe the feelings toward the Jews most often evoked in exodus jokes.

Early Jokelore on Leaving Russia

Actually, the theme of leaving the Soviet Union appeared in Russian underground humor in the late 1920s, soon after emigration from the USSR was stopped. Despite the number of Jewish protagonists in the "jumping-the-border" jokes of this period, the jokes are not concerned exclusively with the Jews; they express the wish of many people who felt trapped in the country who had more and more been stifled by Stalin's iron hand. Of the three types of jokes of the 1930s that are concerned with the Jews—Jewish jokes that deal with the specifically Jewish condition, anti-Semitic jokes, and Russian jokes in which Jewish characters are employed for artistic purposes—this last type of joke comprised the main body of the jokes about fleeing the country. In them, the Russian storyteller employs a Jewish character in order to emphasize the "no-exit" situation, as if to say that only the shrewd and ingenious folkloric Jew can find the solution to an insoluble problem. In one story, such a character goes abroad on a business trip and sends a series of postcards from the cities in the West that he visits during his trip, until he sends the last one, which comes signed not "Comrade Shapiro," but "free Shapiro." In another story, it is the Jewish character again who is destined to survive under the most perilous circumstances; he "can get out dry from the water," as the Russian saying goes:

(6.1) Rabinovich almost manages to cross the border, but at the last moment the guards spot him and rush over to him. In a desperate attempt to save his life, Rabinovich notices a pile of dog excrement, pulls down his pants, and squats over it.
"What are you doing here?" the guards shout at him.
"Don't you see, an emergency stomach problem."
The guards look at the stool and ask, "How come this turd is a dog's?"
Says the Jew: "And what kind of life is this, anyway?"

"A dog's life" is the term that the storyteller found fit to describe the life not only of a Jew but of a great many Soviet citizens in the 1930s.[2] It was only in the late 1950s and early 1960s that jokes expressing the wish to leave the country gained a genuinely Jewish coloring.

| Jewish Jokelore of Postwar Russia

This development was preceded by Stalin's growing anti-Semitism in postwar Russia. Stalin's campaigns against cosmopolitanism and Zionism in the late 1940s and early 1950s were crowned by one of the most horrifying atrocities of this century, the cold-blooded murder of Jewish poets, writers, actors, and other representatives of Jewish culture in the late 1940s, and by the infamous "doctors' case"—against "the assassins in white robes"—in the early 1950s. Jewish theater, Jewish publications, and Jewish schools virtually ceased to exist. Soon it was implied that Jews were responsible for all of the troubles of postwar Russia.

To isolate Soviet citizens from the rest of the world, the Soviet government discouraged contacts with foreigners. Soviet citizens feared writing to relatives abroad lest they be accused of giving out state secrets, a common charge in the late 1930s, still fresh in the minds of many people, both Jews and non-Jews. It was especially dangerous, however, to correspond with Jewish relatives in America and Israel. Under the pretext of the struggle with world Zionism and cosmopolitanism, Jews were forced to cut off their ties with relatives living abroad, for fear of being accused as accomplices in world Zionist intrigues. Sometimes even parents and children stopped corresponding.

In the 1960s, when the Soviet government turned to the West for subsidies, it was charged with isolating its citizens from the world. It was then that the following joke with a highly ironic punch line was created and gained instant popularity among Russian Jews:

(6.2) A Jew was summoned to KGB headquarters.
"You, Comrade Rabinovich, cause us a great deal of embarrassment. Those friends of yours in the West make ridiculous claims that we prevent you from writing to your relatives abroad. You are perfectly aware that this is a lie. When did you last write to your brother in Israel? Shame on you! No more excuses! Take this piece of paper and a pen, and write your brother right now!"
The Jew took the paper and the pen, looked uncomfortably at the KGB officer, and began to write:
"Dear brother! Finally, I've found the time and the place to write you a letter. . . ."

Jewish jokes of the late 1940s and early 1950s address the central issue of Jewish life of that period. Stalin's anti-Semitism, well documented and known to the whole world now, rekindled dormant anti-Jewish sentiments among the Russians. Having suffered tremendous losses during World War II, they needed to find a scapegoat responsible for life's continuing misery. Among drunks on city streets one could hear again the old slogan of the infamous Black Hundred, an anti-Semitic military group responsible for organizing Jewish pogroms at the beginning of the century: "Smash the Jews, and save Russia!" Jews were thought deserving of their own misery for the sheer fact of their existence, as the following joke demonstrates:

(6.3) An anti-Semite and a Jew were strolling along the street. A brick fell from a roof and hit the Jew on the head.
"Look how overpopulated we are with the damned Jews," the anti-Semite said, spitting on the ground.
"A poor brick doesn't even have a free place to fall."[3]

Shortly before his death in March of 1953, Stalin contemplated an overnight mass deportation of Jews to Siberia (Pinkus 145).[4] According to Jewish folk humor, this man, who considered himself a great internationalist and a father to all nations, claimed that the planned action was only to benefit the ancient people: the mass resettlement in areas of cold climate was supposed to produce a new breed of Jewish people in years to come—the frost-proof Jews. They would then have no fear of living anywhere on earth, the joke's Stalin explained, including the North Pole.

There is no reason to believe that Stalin wouldn't have succeeded in this plan, as in so many other of his grand undertakings. It was only his death that prevented another Holocaust, now on Russian soil. Soon after the funeral of the "father of all nations," this joke appeared:

(6.4) A little Jewish man knocked on the gates of the Kremlin:
"May I see Comrade Stalin?" he said to the guard.
"Comrade Stalin's dead. Haven't you heard?"
"Thank you," said the Jew and left, only to come back in a moment.
"I'd like to talk to Comrade Stalin," he told the guard again.
"Are you crazy?" said the guard. "Stalin's dead."
"Thank you, thank you," said the man, leaving.
But he soon returned: "Just one short word to Comrade Stalin. Please!"
"Get out of here! I'll arrest you as a stupid nuisance! I've told you ten times: Comrade Stalin's dead, dead, dead!"
"Oh, thank you so much. I just can't hear enough of it."[5]

Stalin's anti-Semitic legacy was not forgotten, however, and the Jews' troubles did not end with his death. The struggle to survive in the anti-Semitic atmosphere of postwar Russia took many forms. To escape their bitter lot, Russian Jews continued to hide their national identity, a task nearly impossible because of the carefully designed system under which no Soviet citizen could conceal his or her nationality. In all official documents—birth certificates, passports, job applications, and so on—after the first four items dealing with one's last, first, and patronymic names and date of birth, there was (and just recently [in 1997] eliminated) that "fifth item"—the question of one's nationality. It became clear to many people (not only to the Jews) that now the only function of this category was to identify Jews. This is why the punch line of the following joke, which might be incomprehensible to an outsider, left absolutely no doubt of its meaning for anyone living in postwar Russia:

(6.5) A Jew fills out one of the official applications:
"Have you been a member of any party other than the Communist Party?"
"No."
"Have you remained on any territory occupied by the enemy?"
"No."
"Have you been convicted or are you currently under investigation for any criminal activity?"
"No."
"Your nationality?"
"Yes!"

It was also clear to the listener to the following joke which nationality was implied in a parody of a newspaper ad:

(6.6) "Will exchange one nationality for two convictions. Could be long-term."

Thus, as the joke makes clear, to be a Jew in Russia then was much worse than to be a convicted criminal. Being a Jew was a kind of punishment. In fact, some jokes directly expressed this:

(6.7) They proposed a new penalty for traffic violators. For the first offense, the offender gets a hole punched in his driver's license. For the second violation, he gets another. After the third offense, the fifth item in his passport is to be changed to "a Jew." (Shturman and Tiktin 496)

There were, however, other ways to identify a Jew without looking into a passport. A person's name—first name, patronymic, and surname—also could reveal a Jew.[6] Anti-Semitism often ran so high that any last name with a European flavor was suspected of being Jewish.[7] This Russian paranoia is mocked in the following quip, undoubtedly of Jewish origin, which involves a folk hero of contemporary Russian jokelore, Vasily Ivanovich Chapaev, an unsophisticated fellow, a hero of the Civil War much celebrated by Soviet propaganda. His orderly, Pet'ka, tells him:

(6.8) "You know, Vassily Ivanovich, the Gulf Stream [in Russian one
word: *Gol'fstrim*] has frozen."
"How many times have I told you, Pet'ka, don't send those Jews
on scouts' missions. They are not cut out for it." (Telesin 491)

Anti-Discrimination Jokes

Discrimination against the Jews had an overwhelming effect on every step they took. The Jews' traditional concern for their children's education came into conflict with the practice of accepting as few Jewish students into universities as possible, no matter how brilliant the applicant might be. It was especially difficult to receive an education in the humanities, since this sphere was zealously guarded by the party in order to protect it from any ideologically unreliable elements—in practical terms, primarily Jews:

(6.9) At the entrance exam in a prestigious institute they try to
disqualify a Jewish boy. They decide to ask him a question that no
one could answer:
"Can you explain how Leo Tolstoy remembered himself from the
age of forty days?"
"So what!" the student says. "I remember myself from the time I
was seven days old."
"So, tell us what you remember."
"I remember how an old Jew with a long gray beard came to our
apartment, washed his hands, took a blade in his hand, and cut off
my chances of being admitted to your university."[8]

Especially numerous were Jewish jokes dealing with job discrimination. Some were rather straightforward, others a bit more subtle. Hiring practices that had nothing to do with ability, but everything to do with nationality, were mocked in the following jokes. The situation—a Jew trying to get a job—was so frequent in Jewish humor until the end of the Soviet regime that the jokes consist only of their punch lines:

(6.10) A chief of personnel looks attentively at a Jew in front of him:
"I'm sorry, but your profile doesn't suit us."

(Here the word "profile" has a double meaning—a facial silhouette and the applicant's area of expertise.)

(6.11) A phone call to the Personnel Department:
"My name's Rabinovich. Do you need a specialist like me?"

The hypocritical Soviet hiring system—loudly claiming equality of all nations under Soviet law, while practicing outrageous discrimination—was so widespread that employers assumed it was rather insolent of the Jews to know about it and yet still dare to apply:

(6.12) A Personnel Department head talks to a Jewish engineer:
"We would love to hire a fine specialist like you, but, alas, we need someone with a degree in higher mathematics."
"I majored in mathematics and graduated with honors."
"That's swell! But the job requires also an advanced degree in nuclear physics."
"In fact, I had a double major, in math and physics."
"Wonderful! But, for our Alma-Ata plant, we need someone with these qualifications who at the same time is fluent in the Kazakh language."
"Kazakh is my second language."
"And how long are you going to make fun of me, you kike's mug!"

A number of "personnel department" jokes take place in a circus. The symbolism of the setting underscores the strenuous efforts a Jew had to make to be employed in the Soviet Union. He should have been far superior to any worker anywhere—in circus terms, an acrobat able to perform spectacular stunts:

(6.13) A Jewish performer comes to seek employment in the circus.
"What can you do?" the director asks.
"I can do a triple somersault."
"No big deal. I have artists who can do that."
"Yes, but I'm doing it while sitting on a chair."
"Well, I've seen that done as well."
"But I'm doing a triple somersault while sitting on a chair that rests on a tightrope."
"I'm not much impressed."
"Yes, but I do all these things while playing a violin."
The director says: "OK, you may have a chance here. Show me your act."
The Jew positions a chair on a tightrope, takes a violin in his hands, and makes a triple somersault while playing Paganini's "Scherzo Capriccio."

After the act, he turns to the director, who says: "Well, let me tell you straight, Comrade Rabinovich. You're not Yascha Haifetz."

The message is clear: when it comes to employment, a Jew has to be able to do more than a triple somersault to be on equal terms with the Russians. In another circus joke, the employer is not enigmatic at all about his reason for turning the Jew down:

(6.14) A man comes to the director of the Moscow Circus and puts a little suitcase on his desk. Little mice in black tuxedos run out of it and make a semicircle. They take out their tiny musical instruments from tiny cases and beautifully play Tchaikovsky's "First Violin Concerto."
Director: "Unbelievable! Stupendous!"
"So, can I count on a job offer?"
"No. You can't. Your first violin looks Jewish to me."

It is interesting that, although the nationality of the mice tamer is not mentioned, we sense that he is also Jewish, as his first violin is, so highly inventive is his attempt to get a job. The employer plays a rejection game with the applicant: he pretends that he does not reject him for being Jewish, but only his mouse.

In Art Spiegelman's comic strip "Maus," mice serve as a metaphor for the Jews' precarious existence in Germany as they confront Nazi cats (Bernard Saper 48).[9] In Russian Jewish jokes, the mouse invokes a Russian saying "to behave oneself, be as quiet as a little mouse" (*vesti sebia tikho, kak myshka*). The joke 6.14 indirectly satirizes a notion widespread among Russian Jews at the time—that a Jew could survive in Russia by keeping a low profile, not unlike a mouse careful not to attract a cat's attention.

The following "mouse" joke can be viewed as a mocking cautionary tale aiming at an anti-Semitic stereotype that once in a soft, "cushy" job (in Russian, *teploe mesto*, "a warm place"), Jews tend to sneak in their relatives. Here, this stereotypical assumption is played upon in reverse order: if they follow each other in, maybe they will follow each other out:

(6.15) An officer manager can't get rid of mice, no matter how hard he tries. Finally, he turns to a professional exterminator. The man arrives, opens a briefcase and lets out a small mouse. It disappears into the nearest hole in the wall and soon returns. The exterminator puts it back in his briefcase and leaves.
And—miracle of miracles!—the next day all the mice have disappeared. The manager calls the exterminator, thanks him profusely, and asks:

"By the way, do you happen to have the same kind of little kike?" (For a variant, see Shturman and Tiktin 509.)

If in this joke Jews were treated as pests to be rid of, in the following joke they are also animals, living in the Russian "zoo," to be driven out at the first opportunity:

(6.16) They have a staff reduction in the zoo. They fire the lion Leo (because of his "fifth item"), a parrot (his nose looks like a hook), and a whale: for three days he gave shelter to a Jew named Job who lived there without police registration.

Jokes that addressed various discriminatory practices served a well-defined social function—to solidify the group by pointing out that its members shared a common fate. While evoking the sympathy of members of the Russian out-group toward the plight of Soviet Jews, these jokes expressed the Jewish group's fantasy that they could end their misery by leaving the country in the 1950s and 1960s, long before emigration became a possibility:

(6.17) 1956. Question to Radio Armenia:
"What nationality is the sputnik?"
Answer: "Jewish. Who else could fly away from the Soviet Union with such incredible speed!"

(6.18) 1961. After listening to the news about Gagarin's space flight, Rabinovich shrugs his shoulders:
"To leave the Soviet Union, to fly around the world—and all this only in order to come back? One has to be crazy."

Yet another joke holds that if a Russian Jewish astronaut were sent into space, he would prefer forever remaining in orbit to returning to Soviet territory (Shturman and Tiktin 511).

Searching for Jewish Identity

The jokes of the time performed another important function: they began to shape a sense of new Jewish identity. Indeed, the question that these jokes indirectly posed for the Russian Jewish community was, "what does it take to make one feel Jewish in the Soviet Union?"

In Stalinist and post-Stalinist Russia, most Jews could not openly observe their religion, give their children a Jewish education, or learn about their history and culture. By and large, this has been a nationality that has known neither the languages of its ancestors (Hebrew and Yiddish) nor its history and culture. In most cases, especially true for the younger generation, Soviet Jews have considered Russian their native language and have felt themselves to be part of Russian culture.

Under these circumstances, Soviet Jews have preserved their Jewish identity thanks not to their religion, as has been the case for Jews throughout the world for many centuries of the Diaspora, but primarily to the anti-Semitic tendencies of the host nation, in the forms of spontaneous manifestations within the population and clandestine government regulations. Thus, by exposing the anti-Semitism, the oral humor of the Soviet Jews undoubtedly played a part in their realization that they were not just ordinary Soviet citizens, as they may have wanted to be, but a special group singled out by the Russians to be mistrusted and mistreated in many ways.

Therefore, in the 1950s and 1960s, the years immediately preceding the exodus, Jewish jokes dealing with the "Jewish/non-Jewish" dichotomy were not only an ironic commentary on Soviet-Jewish life but they also reinforced the in-group's cohesiveness by reminding its members of their vulnerability in a hostile environment. No longer a target of direct and open violence, as was the case at the beginning of the century, the Russian Jewish community had lived through the whole period after World War II in an atmosphere of suspicion. Hiding one's Jewish identity became a primary psychological preoccupation. Consider the following item:

(6.19) A telephone is ringing in the communal apartment.
"May I talk to Moishe, please," the voice says.
A neighbor responds: "We don't have anyone like that here."
Another phone call: "May I talk to Misha?"
The neighbor shouts: "Moishe, it's for you." (Shturman and
Tiktin 489)

The joke accurately captures the spirit of the time and succinctly describes the divided world in which Soviet Jewry had been forced to exist. The telephone in the tale is the symbolic outpost between the intimate world in which the Jew can feel relatively secure, being accepted for who he is, and the outside world from which the Jew expects nothing but trouble. Thus, to protect himself from it, he has to hide his Jewish identity.

The joke also conveys the anxiety of the neighbor picking up the receiver. We do not know whether the neighbor is Jewish or not. It really does not matter. In his first reply, he protects not only the Jew but himself as well from the telephone inquirer, for being associated with a Jew in any way was almost as bad as being one.

The postwar period was marked by increased circulation of recycled Jewish Diaspora jokes evolving around the questions: was one Jewish? Did one look Jewish? The recycling of jokes of this kind occurred in direct correspondence to the nature of Jewish humor, with its high degree of historical perspective (cf., Boskin 1987, 61). Through these jokes, the in-group reminded its members that in the Soviet Union it was still much safer to be non-Jewish, as it had been in the Russian empire a century earlier:

(6.20) An opera house. A Jew asks a theatergoer next to him:
"Tell me, please, is Onegin Jewish?"
"No."
After awhile, the Jew fidgets in his seat and asks: "Is Tatyana Jewish?"
"No."
Some time later, the Jew asks:
"What about Lensky? Is he Jewish?"
"Ok, Ok," says the much-annoyed neighbor. "He's Jewish, Jewish, all right. . . ."
"Of course," sighs the Jew. "There was only one Jew in the whole opera, and they killed him. . . ."

With the Israelis' Six-Day War, Russian Jewish humor of the late 1960s attempted to further solidify the in-group by helping to shape the sense of its true identity. The jokes of the period reflect the conflict of interests that Soviet Jews experienced, the perplexed state of mind of a people who found themselves with a double identity: they were officially Soviet citizens, whose loyalty to the state obliged them to express publicly their support for the Arabs in the Arab-Israeli conflict, while all their sympathy belonged to the Jewish state, fighting for its right to exist.

The following jokes, which circulated around the time of the Six-Day War, are not so much funny as indicative of the mood of the time and reflective of the soul-searching of Russian Jews. In these jokes, the double take is deliberate. Considering the well-known fact that the Soviet government had sent rockets and military planes to the Arabs, the jokes play with two meanings of the words "our," "we," and "us," which could interchangeably mean "Soviet" and "Israeli." The source of delight of these little quips is not a witty punch line but the ambiguity itself:

(6.21) "Did you hear?" says one Russian Jew to another, "*Our* radio announced that *our* missiles shot down twenty-five of *our* jets over the Nile."

(6.22) "Abram, have you heard? *We* beat *us!*"

These jokes disparaged the Jewish in-group for the loss of its identity, as if an invisible inquisitor were asking: "Who are you—Jews or obedient and servile Soviet citizens?" The jokes of the period helped to establish the Jewish in-group's demarcation lines by targeting the anti-Semitism of the Russian population and the discrimination practiced by the Soviet government. They were influential in sharpening the existing conflicts between Jewish and non-Jewish groups and they assisted the Jewish in-group in further highlighting and maintaining the boundaries necessary for its survival as an ethnic entity.

In their jokes of the time, Russian Jews expressed not only their despair, their sense that they no longer belonged to the country where they and their fathers and grandfathers were born, but also their wish to go where they hoped their home might be. While the following joke of the 1970s is similar to one in the 1950s (see 6.2), the Jewish protagonist does not simply allude to his plight, but expresses his feelings in a straightforward manner; the punch line became a Jewish proverb of the time:

(6.23) They summoned Rabinovich to KGB headquarters.
"Tell us, Comrade Rabinovich, why did you lie to the Soviet authorities? To the question whether you have any relatives living abroad, in all your papers you answered 'no.' We recently discovered that you have a brother living in Tel Aviv. What do you have to say to that?"
"*He's* living abroad?" Rabinovich cried out. "*I'm* the one who's living abroad!"

"To Leave or Not to Leave"—That Is the Question

With the emigration gate set ajar in the early 1970s, the humor of the Russian Jews took on new social functions. Many of the exodus jokes played an important part in galvanizing the community, in fostering the conflict that the opportunity to emigrate brought about in its wake.

This opportunity was a risky one. An application for emigration was seen by Soviet authorities as a declaration of disloyalty to the regime. Thus, by applying for emigration a Jew had to renounce de facto any possibility of retaining his current status. This usually led to the loss of his job, and significantly impaired his opportunities in the future if he changed his mind and stayed.

Because of the formidable risk that a private decision to emigrate entailed, the conflict within the group evolved around the question of whether the Jews should leave the Soviet Union. The vast majority of Jewish jokes of the time represent the in-group's attempt to solidify itself and shape consensus by ridiculing those who doubted the need to emigrate and by persuading the hesitant ones that there was no other solution to their problems in Russia.

The following samples of jokes from the early 1970s deliver clear messages:
"*There should be no debate about the decision*":

(6.24) Two Russian Jews are standing on a street corner and talking. A third passes by and murmurs out of the corner of his mouth:

"I don't know what you are talking about, comrades, but yes, leaving is a must."[10]

"Only the lunatic stays":

(**6.25**) There are two kinds of Jews—brave and insanely brave. The first kind leaves, the second stays. (Telesin 134)

"Those who stay are stupid":

(**6.26**) Odessa in the year 2000. A conversation in the line for sausage: "Excuse me, madam, my friend and I are arguing. I say you look Jewish, and he says no. Would you tell us please, who's right?" "I am Jewish? I am foolish!" (in Russian: *Ia evreika? Ia idiotka*!)

(**6.27**) There are three kinds of Soviet Jews—those who are leaving, those who want to leave, and those who *think* that they don't want to leave.

"They are not human beings but playthings":

(**6.28**) "What is a Jew of the year 2000?" "A Russian souvenir."[11]

The jokes of the 1970s dealt with every emotional conflict that prevented members of the in-group from making the fateful decision to emigrate. The following jokes addressed the trepidation that many Russian Jews experienced in contemplating a drastic change in their lives—doubts about living in Israel, a virtually unknown country, and their fear of having such human feelings as homesickness:

(**6.29**) A KGB officer summons Rabinovich: "Listen, Citizen Rabinovich, you're annoying us. First, you complained to the UN that you are denied the right to emigrate, and now how do you act? We gave you an exit visa, and first you went to Argentina. Soon you came back and said that you didn't like it there. Then you went to Canada and soon came back again. You didn't like it there either. Last time, you went to Israel, also only to come back. Enough is enough! Here's your final chance: take this globe and point to any country of your choice. You'll go there and that's it! We won't see you anymore." Rabinovich picks up the globe, makes it turn again and again, sighs, puts it back on the officer's desk: "Well, do you have another globe?"

(**6.30**) In Tel Aviv they have opened a new expensive restaurant called "Nostalgia," for Russian Jews. There you have to wait hours to be served. They make you move from one table to another. The

food is horrible. The waiters are rude and insolent. When the bill
arrives, they cheat you. Then they throw you out on the streets
and shout: "Get lost! Go to your Israel, you kike's mug!"

As a way of persuading people to leave for Israel, Jewish joke tellers
evoked fear of persecution. While recycling old in-group jokes told at the
expense of those stereotypical "always scared" shtetl Jews of the turn of the
century, the tellers of jokes like the following now implicitly reminded their
audience that, although Rabinovich might worry excessively, Russia was still
not a safe place for a Jew:

(6.31) Rabinovich's family goes to bed. Rabinovich checks the locks on
the door, turns off all the lights in his apartment, and then goes to
bed himself.
After a short while, he says to his son:
"Niuma, *kindele,* sweet child of mine, I'm not sure I locked the
door. Please turn the lights on, go to the door, and see if
everything is in order."
"Dad, you just did it. I saw it."
"Niuma, my child, please. I can't fall asleep till you do it."
"But, Dad! I'm dead tired. My knees ache. I played soccer all
day long."
"I beg you!"
"Oh, Ok . . . Here I am. Checking the door. It's locked."
"And the big lock?"
"Yes, and the big one."
"And the little one?"
"Yes, and the little one."
"And the chain is also engaged?"
"Yes, it is."
"Oh, thank you, Niumele, thank you."
A few minutes pass in silence. Rabinovich calls to his daughter:
"Firale, *kindele,* I'm not sure I locked the door. Please turn the
lights on, go to the door, and check if everything is in order."
"Daddy, please, Niuma just checked the door. My head is
splitting. I had exams today."
"I beg you!"
"Oh, all right. Here I am. Checking the door. It's locked."
"And the big lock is locked?"
"Yes, the big."
"And the little one?"
"Yes, and the little one."
"And the chain also?"

"Yes."

"Oh, thank you, Firale, thank you."

Again a few minutes pass in silence. Rabinovich turns to his wife:

"Sofochka, my dear . . ."

"No!"

"Please! I beg you!"

"No, no, and one more time no! You've gone crazy with these locks! You locked them. The kids have just checked them twice. Shut up and let me sleep at last!" Silence. Rabinovich produces a huge sigh:

"Ok, as you wish, Sofa. Thanks to you, we're all going to sleep all night long with the doors wide open."

Other jokes made a more direct plea for emigration, claiming that those who thought of staying in Russia were counting in vain on a quiet and peaceful life for themselves: exile and hard labor camps awaited them. The Far East was traditionally associated with exile in Russian consciousness; the following joke invents a slogan hanging on the wall of the Exit Visa Office (*OVIR*):

(6.32) "It's better to have a far relative in the Near East, then a near relative in the Far East."

The implication of imminent doom for Jews on Russian soil is clearly behind the punch line of the following item as well; it may be read as a command addressed to the indecisive:

(6.33) They stop Rabinovich at the customs. He wants to take his parrot along to Israel:

"Our instructions do not allow you to take out living birds. You can take it out of the country only if it's stuffed or a stiff. Not alive!"

"What! What kind of laws do you have in this country! What do you mean, stuffed or a stiff? This is the most intelligent parrot that has ever existed. He speaks twelve languages! He is like a member of my family! How can you be so hard-hearted?"

"Sorry, Citizen Rabinovich, this is the law. If you refuse to obey it, you'll stay here, together with your smart aleck of a parrot. We won't let your birdy out alive."

Stricken with grief, Rabinovich says to the customs officer:

"Is there a room where I can talk to my parrot in private?"

They show him a room. There, he says to his parrot:

"What should we do, my dear! Did you hear what those idiots

said! They let you go only if you're stuffed or a stiff! What
should we do now!"
The parrot thinks for a minute and says:
"Listen, Syoma, stuffed or a stiff, but we have to get the hell out
of this country!"

Since in many jokes a parrot is a stand-in for a Jew (see, for example, 6.16), it is
clear that the bird is brought into this joke for the sole purpose of dramatizing
the choices left to the Jewish community at the time; the joke makes a striking
point: staying in this country is not much different from dying.

As a way of arguing for total emigration, the Jewish in-group created
many jokes addressing their predicament in great detail, exploring every
sore point, everything related to their treatment as second-class citizens.
Many more jokes, similar to 6.9–16, about job discrimination, obstacles in
the way of higher education, ostracism, and harassment began to circulate
among the Russian Jews. For those who questioned the need to emigrate—
arguing that, despite tremendous difficulties, through hard work, persistence,
and ingenuity a number of Jews had managed to find their place in Soviet
society—new jokes appeared appealing to their dignity and sense of fairness.
The jokes addressed the widespread Russian refusal to acknowledge Jews'
achievements, either as individuals or as representatives of their nationality.
Some jokes exposed the tendency of those in power to pretend that there was
no Jewish nationality, thus mocking the party propaganda claims about full
equality in the Soviet Union:

(6.34) A detachment is practicing marksmanship. All Russian soldiers
score rather poorly. Rabinovich is the only one who scores 100
percent. At the end of the day, the lieutenant tells his men:
"You should follow Private Rabinovich. He's a bad soldier, but
he tries. . . ."

(6.35) At the opening of a public concert, the master of ceremonies
announces from the stage:
"The Peoples' Friendship String Quartet is going to perform for
us tonight. Let us welcome Comrade Prokopenko, Ukraine;
Comrade Karapetian, Armenia; Comrade Abdurashidov,
Uzbekistan; and Comrade Rabinovich, Violin."

The jokes, then, were persistent in making the point that all attempts to
escape the Jewish lot on Russian soil had been and would continue to be
futile. The following item is remarkable in its persuasive power. In it, it is a
Russian, not a Jew, who not only acknowledges the sorry plight of Jews in the
USSR, but also sympathizes with them. It is as if the tellers of this joke were

admonishing those who could not acknowledge the reality of their existence in Russia: "You stubborn Jews! Don't you see how humiliating it is to be a Jew in this country! Even some Russians pity you!"

(**6.36**) A new factory manager comes to the engineering department to meet its staff. As they introduce themselves, he goes around the room shaking hands:
"Ivanov."
"Nice to meet you, Comrade Ivanov!"
"Petrov."
"Nice to meet you, Comrade Petrov!"
"Rabinovich."
The manager pats Rabinovich on his shoulder:
"It's OK, it's OK. . . ."

Along the same line of persuasion, the exodus jokes attacked, one by one, alternative solutions to the Jewish problem and insisted on their uselessness. Through humor, the community disparaged those who contemplated escape through such drastic measures as document shifting:

(**6.37**) "I solved my problems once and for all," says one Jew to another. "I've arranged it so the fifth passport item 'nationality' reads 'Russian.' "
"Well, I'm going to disappoint you," says another Jew.
"When they start pogroms, they'll kick you in your face, not in your passport."

At sixteen the children of mixed marriages could apply for a passport, choosing a non-Jewish nationality, but this tactic rarely helped. There were other ways to recognize a Jew, as the following joke suggests:

(**6.38**) A school principal walks into a class and announces: "Finkelshtein, Shapiro, and Ivanov-by-your-mother's-surname should not come to school tomorrow. A delegation from Syria is visiting."

The joke tellers attacked other means that some Jews used to avoid obstacles set up by anti-Semitism—for example, joining the Communist Party, that is, acting in accordance with the American saying, "If you can't fight city hall, join them." The jokes expressed skepticism that Jews would gain anything that way. Despite its proclamation of equality among nationalities, in reality the Communist Party was no less contaminated by anti-Semitism than the state. Sometimes the jokes warned those who contemplated such a move that they were heading for disappointment:

(6.39) They asked a Jew why he didn't want to join the Party. "I'll have duties as a Communist," he answered, "and rights as a Jew."

The setting of the following two jokes is sarcastic; these (and other similar) jokes make a salient point that the party is not a haven for Jews: it won't save any of them from virulent anti-Semitism, even if one is the arch-Communist or the Almighty himself:

(6.40) Paradise. An election campaign for secretary of the local Communist Party is under way. They turn down Karl Marx, who has applied for this post. First, he is of nonproletarian origin. Second, he's Jewish.

(6.41) Paradise. God puts his name on the ballot to run for the post of secretary of the local Communist Party cell.
"Any objections?" the chairman of the election committee asks.
He sees one party member raising his hand:
"I'm against it. The man has a son in Israel."

No less mocking, even merciless, were jokes aimed at those few Jews who contemplated religious conversion:

(6.42) The scene is a public bath.
"Riurik Solomonovich,"[12] says one man to another. "Please do one of two things: either remove the cross from your neck, or put on your trunks."

As a way of convincing the members of the group that they should accept themselves and should not try to change their lot through altering their nature, several turn-of-the-century Jewish jokes began to make new rounds. One such joke reads like a cautionary tale: you cannot count on the possibility of good fortune if you do not remain true to yourself:

(6.43) On his sixtieth birthday Abramovich, a pious man, who observed all the rituals and holidays and led a very modest life of self-discipline and self-denial, decided to give himself some joy, to have a break in his monotonous life. He took out his life savings from a bank and bought himself a new white suit to replace his old black one.
Then he went to a barber and asked him to cut his long beard and to dye his gray hair light blond. He hired a troika and invited the most beautiful young woman to join him on a ride through their town.
Suddenly, as the troika charged through the streets, from around the corner a peasant in a cart crossed their path. Clang,

bang!—and Abramovich was thrown out of the carriage onto the sidewalk, where he hit a tree and died. As soon as he appeared in front of the Almighty, he began to cry out:

"O my Lord! Why such an injustice! All my life I was a pious man. I observed all the holidays and rituals. I saved, I prayed, I tried to please my God as much as a human being can. Only once in my whole life I wanted some happiness, just a little bit of joy. And here I am—dead! How could you, the Justest and the Fairest, allow such a thing to happen?"

The Almighty tore his hair:

"*Oy veis mir,* woe is me, Abramovich! Forgive me! I didn't recognize you!"[13]

Other exodus jokes addressed those in the Jewish community who, instead of trying to change their lot, decided to stall for time, to do nothing, but simply to wait out the bad times in the hope that their lot would improve. The joke tellers attacked this "let's wait it out" tactic with irony and outright mockery:

(6.44) "Will there be the fifth passport item under communism?"
"No. But there will be a sixth: 'Were you a Jew under socialism?'"

As if projecting into the hypothetical utopian future of communism were not enough to underscore the idea that the Jews' existence on Russian soil was doomed, the following joke looks even farther, many millennia ahead, into the imaginary cosmos populated by mutants that only partially resemble humans. Yet even then there is no escape for the Jew, who is still going to be singled out, earmarked as Jewish. The joker implies that while perhaps there is a universal, even cosmic, curse that the Jews are destined to bear, it is only in Russia that they will still be singled out:

(6.45) A group of aliens from the cosmos march through Moscow. One Moscovite asks an alien,
"Tell me, do all of you have six feet?"
"Yes, all."
"And all of you are hymenopterous?"
"Yes, all of us."
"And all with two heads?"
"Yes."
"And with four eyes on each?"
"Yes."
"And all have that little light in the frame above the head?"
"No, only the Jews." (Shturman and Tiktin 511–12)

In this joke, one can spot a self-congratulatory note. The "Jewish" aliens are marked by a light that is located on their foreheads, and light is an archetypal symbol of intelligence. In the intergroup situation, a joke that esteems one of the groups fosters disintegration of the relationship between the groups, broadens the estrangement between them, and keeps the boundaries between them clear (Martineau 122).

The arguments for emigration employed in the exodus jokes that helped to solidify the Jewish community include those concerned with the collective responsibility for the actions of the in-group's members. These jokes stressed the commonality of the Jewish lot. In a situation in which a Jew who applied for emigration would immediately become politically suspect and everybody who was associated with him would also fall from the regime's grace, the jokes reminded the in-group's members of their common bondage: every Jew became accountable for the decisions made by other Jews. A number of the exodus jokes made the point that for those Jews who stayed in the country when the others left, life would no longer be the same. The following joke aims at the double standard of Soviet life in the 1970s, when many people were leaving the country with official permission, yet this fact could not be openly acknowledged:[14]

(6.46) A telephone rings in a communal apartment:
"Can I talk to Comrade Rabinovich?"
"He's not here," a neighbor says.
"Is he at work?"
"No."
"Is he on a business trip?"
"No."
"Is he on vacation?"
"No."
"Did I understand you right?"
"Yes." (Telesin 166)

Although the elliptical quality of this joke is characteristic of many Jewish jokes (Davies 1986, 76), this one is an example of evasion brought to the level of metacommunication. In Victor Raskin's (103) terms, bona fide communication—the straight imparting of information—and non-bona fide communication—joke telling, the text abides by the principles of both types of communication. Taken out of the concrete sociological and psychological situation of the mass emigration of the Jews in the mid-1970s, the joke is hard to understand; indeed, it is hard to see that it is a joke at all. The knowledge of what exactly is unutterable under these specific conditions is what makes the text comprehensible. The very obscurity of the text for the uninitiated makes it comic.[15]

| Reinforcing the Group's Boundaries

While in the intragroup jokes the function of solidifying the in-group is carried out through reinforcement of its image by stressing the unifying aspects of the group's conditions, in the intergroup situation the same function is carried out by aggressive humor aimed at the Russian out-group with the obvious intent to disparage. This kind of humor helped foster the disintegration of the relationship between the Jewish in-group and the Russian out-group.

Unlike anti-Semitic jokes, Jewish jokes featuring the Russians did not so much aim at insult as at making a point in the argument within the Jewish community. They served primarily as demarcation devices that helped to remind the Jewish in-group about its borders, kept is members together, and thus protected its integrity. Although never vicious, Jewish jokes about the Russians have a clear pejorative quality and often resort to crude caricature. The Russian characters act as primitive beings whose world outlook is miserably limited; their sphere of interest is that of mindless consumers of alcohol who often engage in drunken brawls. Consider the following:

(**6.47**) How various people come to a party:
An Englishman comes with a cane in his hand, a Frenchman with a bouquet of flowers, a Russian with a bottle of vodka, and a Jew with a cousin.
How each of them leave the party:
The Englishman leaves with his cane in hand, the Frenchman with the most beautiful woman, the Russian with a beaten-up face, the Jew with a little doggie bag for another cousin, who could not come.

While the joke may be judged as one that disparages the Jews for being overly preoccupied with the well-being of their kin, it is noteworthy that it is only the Russian character whose behavior is uncivilized. The Englishman and Frenchman are introduced in the story, on the one hand, to underscore the Russian's lack of manners, and on the other, to avoid direct comparison between Jewish and Russian characters. Since both the Frenchman and the Englishman are outsiders to Jewish life in Russia, it is clear that the joke was told to emphasize the contrast between a Jew and a Russian.

Consider another item in which reference is made to the typical way the Russians spend their vacations, that is, by going to "rest houses" and sanatoria in which the "patients" typically indulge in drinking and promiscuity:

(**6.48**) "Rabinovich, do you like warm vodka?" a Russian factory manager asks.
"No."
"How about sweaty women?"

"I can't stand them."

"Good. Then you'll be glad to hear that I've scheduled your vacation for January." (Shturman and Tiktin 515–16)

This may be considered just another joke about discrimination. The gentleness of the humor, however, indicates that the teller's true intention is not so much to point out the very fact of discrimination as to attempt to estrange the Russian out-group from the Jewish in-group. The manager asks leading questions, knowing perfectly well that the Jew will say "no" to both. In this way, he manipulates the Jew by making him feel that he is doing him a favor by scheduling his vacation in the cold season. However, the joke is actually on the Russian: "vodka and women" are not really a Jewish pastime. It is if the teller were saying: "Look at the Russians, people we are forced to lived with! Look who has the power over our fate! They not only don't understand us, they also expect us to be their spitting image. What do we have in common with these people after all?"

Attacking the Soviet System

There were, however, two out-groups in the psychological environment of the Soviet Jew —one was (and still is) the Russians as people,[16] and the other was the representatives of the Soviet system as such. In numerous exodus jokes, both out-groups, indifferent to the Jewish fate, fell under attack. The jokes aimed at the Soviet regime and its institutions served two functions—they participated in the process of increasing morale and solidifying the Jewish in-group and helped foster a hostility toward the Soviet system.[17] The exchange of quips aimed at the regime helped to sustain the in-group's cohesiveness and maintain its spiritual health. In these jokes, while disparaging the out-group (the system), humor often tends to esteem the Jewish in-group, thus contributing further to the social distancing between them. Thus, in one joke a Jewish character is assigned by the Party committee to serve as a district propagandist on election day. Because his duty calls for it, the Jew goes from apartment to apartment, inviting people to go to the polls. Forced by the circumstances to represent the regime, and at the same time wanting to dissociate himself from it, he politely knocks on the door and says: "Excuse me, please. They ask me to pass on to you that the Soviet system is the best in the world."

Both out-groups (the Russians as people and the Soviet system) were often attacked simultaneously. The jokes with such a double edge also argued in favor of emigration; they stressed the double misery of Soviet Jewry—as Jews and as Soviet citizens:

(6.49) "Citizen Rabinovich," asked the visa officer, "why do you want to leave our beautiful country, the best in the world?"

"There are two reasons," answered the Jew. "The first reason is that when my neighbor gets drunk, he bangs on the door of my apartment and screams, 'Just wait until we put an end to the Soviet regime; then, we'll take care of all you Jews.' Well, I don't want to wait around until that happens."
"You shouldn't pay attention to such nonsense," said the officer, smiling.
"We all know that the Soviet regime will last forever and ever."
"That's my second reason."[18] (Draitser 1980, 67)

Here representatives of both out-groups are the butt of the joke: the Russian neighbor for his drunken behavior and the officer for his sophomoric enthusiasm about the future of the Soviet regime. At the same time, the joke esteems the Jewish in-group: its representative fools the KGB officer into playing the game of words by his rules.[19]

The following joke makes the same point, that the Soviet system is the main reason for leaving, but it also addresses the uneasiness and trepidation experienced by many Russian Jews about leaving the country in which they had lived for centuries. This uneasiness is expressed by the characteristic Jewish sigh of the female character in the joke's punch line:

(6.50) Abram and Sarah sit in Moscow's Sheremetievo Airport and wait to board their plane for Tel Aviv. They hear a radio announcement:
"Because of the departure for Prague of Comrade Brezhnev and other Politbureau members, the flight to Tel Aviv is postponed for three hours."
In three hours' time, another announcement: "Because of the departure of Prime Minister Kosygin for a visit of friendship to Budapest, the flight to Tel Aviv is postponed for four hours."
Later, again they announce: "Because of the departure of members of the Supreme Soviet for a visit of friendship to Berlin, the flight to Tel Aviv is postponed for five more hours."
"Oy, listen, Abram," Sarah says, "since they've all left, maybe we could stay?"

| Boosting the Group's Morale

While many jokes attacked the weak-willed and laughed at those who wavered, others showed a more tolerant approach. They acknowledged that the choices Jews had to make in leaving the country of their ancestors were hard ones indeed. Jokes of this kind implied that, after all, making hard choices has always been part of Jewish life. To that end, the following joke's setting in prerevolutionary times suggests that the current troubles were not really new. The joke has all the features of a parable, although its moral is rendered with a smile, in the punch line. Its message is a wise one—you can't always count on easy solutions to problems:

(6.51) Two Jews are talking.
"Listen, Haim," says one, "imagine that you are riding in a cart driven by a horse over a huge Russian steppe, and all of a sudden the horse's wooden shaft breaks in half. What would you do?"
"Well," says Haim, "I'd go to the nearest grove, find a small tree, and try to make a new shaft out of it."
"Nonsense!" says his companion. "I told you: you're in a vast steppe. What kind of a grove do you have in a steppe!"
"OK," says Haim, "I'll go to the nearest village and ask a peasant for help."
"What are you talking about! What kind of village? I told you, it's just one endless Russian steppe."
"Well," says Haim, "maybe I should look in my cart for a wooden stick to replace the shaft at least for a time. . . ."
"There's nothing there! Not a thing!"
"OK, OK, I give up. Now tell me. What's the right answer?"
"You know, Haim, the right answer is that it *is* difficult!" (in Russian: *taki trudno!*)

Other Jewish jokes raised the spirit of those who questioned their ability to go through the ordeal of emigration, which usually involved tremendous expenditures in time and energy. Old in-group jokes that portrayed Jews as smart and wise, and able to get themselves out of trouble, began to circulate again. Telling them to each other was a way to provide mutual moral support, as if saying: "Yes, the times are hard on us, but we Jews are not so easy to break, not so prone to despair. We have survived many times in history against great odds, in a hostile environment. We have done it before, we'll do it again." Such jokes imbued the group with optimism based on history:

(6.52) One Jew talks to another:
"Listen, there were the Pharaohs and the Jews. The Pharaohs became extinct, the Jews survived. Then there were the Spanish inquisitors and the Jews. The Inquisitors disappeared and the Jews survived. There were the Nazis and the Jews. The Nazis got busted, the Jews survived. Now there are the Communists and the Jews . . ."
"What are you driving at?"
"Nothing! I just wanted to say that the Jews have managed right up to the final play-offs!"

Telling jokes in which Jews are portrayed as ingenious people who find a way out of any trouble became part of the psychological agenda at the time. Torn between those who, for obvious reasons, feared emigration and those who felt that this unique opportunity, no matter how risky, should not be missed, the group exchanged jokes of the "Jews manage" type. The message of these in-group jokes was one and the same—"we are a nationality of survivors":

(6.53) A nurse warns the obstetrician on duty that one baby is positioned in the wrong way in his mother's womb. "What's the parents' nationality?" the doctor asks. "Jewish." "Don't worry. The baby will find its way out."

(6.54) One day, annoyed with the way people on earth were behaving, God announced that in two weeks he'd let loose another universal deluge. In a short while, he sent an angel to see how people were reacting to the news. Upon his return, the angel reported:
"In the USA, they've begun filing for bankruptcy.
"In England, they play tennis day and night.
"In France, they've begun to make love to each other.
"In the Soviet Union, they've announced a slogan: 'Let's fulfill a Five-Year Plan in two weeks,' and begun a grand drinking party.
"In Israel, Golda Meir has called on her people to learn in two weeks how to live under water."

To build a group's morale, a formal community may organize a lecture about the contributions to humanity of its most distinguished members. The same purpose was served by Jewish in-group jokes that poked fun at its preoccupation with Jewish identity, yet, at the same time expressed pride in belonging to a people of super-achievers. These jokes reaffirmed the group's sense of self-worth:

(6.55) Two passengers on a train are talking about celebrities. A Jew sits nearby and from time to time interjects with a short note about the origin of the celebrity in question.
"Spinoza . . ."
"A Jew."
"Columbus . . ."
"A Spanish Jew."
"Freud . . ."
"An Austrian Jew . . ."
"Bergson . . ."
"A French Jew . . ."
"Chagall . . ."

"A Russian Jew . . ."
"Einstein . . ."
"A German Jew . . ."
"Oh, Jesus Christ and Mother of God!"
"Both Jewish."

Perhaps no other jokes reflected (and helped to sustain) the increased morale of the Jewish in-group as much as the series dealing with the paradoxical situation in which it found itself with the opening of emigration in the early 1970s. One of the most disadvantaged minorities in the USSR throughout most of Soviet history, the Jews suddenly became privileged, due to a special circumstance. Pressured by Western public opinion, the Soviet regime was forced to grant the Jews a virtually exclusive right to emigrate—an exception to its general "sealed border policy."[20] This lucky turn of events for the Jews was accurately captured in the following joke:

(6.56) After Rabinovich applied for emigration, he was called to the party bureau for questioning.
"Comrade Rabinovich, why do you want to leave our beautiful country?"
"I don't want to. But my wife wants to go," said Rabinovich.
"So, let her go, and you stay."
"Yes, but my wife's father also wants to go."
"Let both of them go, and you stay."
"Yes," said Rabinovich, "But my wife's father's sister also wants to go."
"Let all three of them roll the hell out of here, and you stay."
"I wish I could," said Rabinovich with a sigh.
"Why can't you?"
"I am the only Jew in the family."

Thus, Russian Jews were suddenly able to leave the country in which they felt miserable and where they had actually been held hostage to the regime. For those Russians who wanted to take advantage of the situation and also leave the country, there was an off chance of sneaking across the border with the Jewish wave. Russians who had some drops of Jewish blood in their veins and who had hidden this fact now began to seek Jewish status. Relating to the Jews in one way or another became advantageous, and some Russians tried to improve their lot through bogus marriages with Jews (a Russian would marry a Jew only for the purpose of leaving the country legally; once they crossed the borders, they would divorce). Many jokes of the time reflect this unusual situation. For example, in a takeoff on a famous line from the Soviet bestseller *The Twelve Chairs,*[21] "A car is not a luxury but a means of transportation," the following joke arose:

(**6.57**) A Jewish wife is not a luxury, but a means of transportation.

This was also expressed in the form of a Russian *chastushka:*

(**6.58**) Nadoelo mne v Riazani   I am bored with you my darling,
Tantsevat' s toboi kadril'.   Dancing in Riazan'.
Sdelai, milyi, obrezan'e   Let's do a circumcision
I poedem v Izrail';   And off to Israel be gone;[22]

or in a takeoff on a typical question on the Soviet application forms:

(**6.59**) Have you been abroad? If you have been, why did you return?

The virtually exclusive right to choose their country of residence had a tremendously uplifting effect on Russian Jews. As a result, with the emergence of the emigration theme, traditional Jewish humor underwent a complete rebirth. Its typical self-disparaging tendency yielded to self-congratulation; its skepticism gave way to optimism; its self-doubting and sad tone was replaced by feelings of joy. In the jokes of the time, the hidden pride of the underdog whose fortune had suddenly changed for the better can be clearly felt. As if mocking the age-long anti-Semitic stereotype of the "ugly Jew," the Jewish humor of the period shifted to its opposite:

(**6.60**) Question to Radio Armenia:
"Why are Jewish babies born prettier than Russian ones?"
Answer:
"Because they are made for export."

Reaffirming the Group's Identity

The jokes of the period helped Russian Jews to reaffirm their ethnic identity for the first time in recent history. The traditional Jewish jokes that had reflected the preoccupation with seeking ways to avoid irritating the anti-Semites and to better hide their Jewishness were gradually replaced with quite different ones in which one may clearly hear the in-group's call for a complete change of its emotional focus. The jokes helped to solidify the in-group by arguing that if so many attempts at assimilation had failed due to strong Russian anti-Semitism, then now, when the Jews could seek refuge from persecution in Israel, it was time to think of their true national interests.

As we have seen, the early jokes ridiculed the indecisiveness of some of the in-group's members and made it obvious that the time of self-doubt was over. If the Six-Day War of 1967 had produced a split Jewish personality, the jokes of the 1970s and early 1980s strongly argued for the in-group's full identification with Israel.

Furthermore, through the jokes of the time, the in-group insisted on keeping strong emotional ties with the Jewish state even for those Soviet Jews who did not plan to emigrate, who still associated their future with Russia. In one such joke set in the summer of 1982, when Israeli tanks rolled into southern Lebanon, a Jewish student was taking an entry exam in a Soviet college. Despite his excellent knowledge of the subject, the examiner graded him "C," which under the fierce competition meant that he would not be accepted into the college:

(6.61) "Grade according to my knowledge," said the student firmly.
"Otherwise we'll take Beirut." (Shturman and Tiktin 538)

All in all, Israel's military successes gave to Russian Jews an invaluable psychological boost, which the exodus humor clearly reflects. The jokes concerned with the Israeli victories on the battlefields helped to enhance the in-group's morale. These victories were especially celebrated by the Russian Jews, for they were always accused by the anti-Semites of shying away from combat, avoiding military service.

In the post-World War II years, a typical anti-Semitic slur in Russia took the form of a sarcastic question asked of the Jews: "Where were you during the [Great Patriotic] War?" The questioner would immediately provide the equally sarcastic answer: "In Tashkent, I bet."[23] Although the Jewish humorous folklore of the past does, by and large, express Jewish loathing of war, these slurs were insulting and grossly undeserved.[24] As is well documented, many Russian Jews who were able to bear arms fought in the Red Army with astonishing heroism. Many were decorated for their courage on the battlefield, and, percentage-wise, the number of Jewish soldiers and officers with military awards far exceeded many other national minorities living in Soviet territory (see, for example, Shvarts 154–55; Harris 182; Ignatieff 33).

Reversing the Old Stereotype

The unjust treatment of the Jews with respect to their war effort makes only too clear the tremendous relief that they experienced when the news of the astounding Israeli military victories in the Six-Day War reached the Soviet Union. The stereotypical image of the Jew who could not fight was smashed in a matter of a few days. For the first time, being a Jew ceased to mean invariably fearing the enemy and yielding to the aggressor. The very conversion of the fearful Jew into the brave one became the subject of the following joke that could not have existed even a few days before the beginning of the Six-Day War. Considering the awesome reputation of the Cossacks as the most formidable enemies of the Russian Jews—a reputation that goes as far back as the seventeenth century, to the time of Bogdan Khmelnitsky's pogroms, and up to their participation in the infamous pogroms in the beginning of the twentieth—this joke is remarkable:

(6.62) Upon receiving his college diploma, a young Jew was assigned to his first job in one of the little towns (*stanitsas*) on the Don River. His relatives felt quite apprehensive:
"Oy, there are so many Cossacks over there!"
"So what?" answered the Jew. "They have nothing to be afraid of. I won't touch them." (Shturman and Tiktin 511)

It is thanks to Israel's crushing defeat of the Arabs that the Jew in the joke feels strong. With the confidence of the mighty, he can forgive his age-old enemies as long as they are wise enough not to come close to him.

As if unable to savor enough of these feelings of pride that the Israeli victories brought them—establishing for the first time in their history that they were not alone in the world, and that, if worst came to worst, they could count on a Jewish helping hand, not on a benevolent Gentile's—the Russian Jews were especially happy, composing many jokes with the same theme— "The Jews are good fighters":

(6.63) "What is the Six-Day War?"
"It's a week-long festival of Jewish military art held in Arab countries" (Telesin 119).

(6.64) A question to Armenian Radio:
"Do the Jews do battle on Saturdays?"
"We can't say. They started the war on Sunday and finished it by Saturday."

(6.65) Armenian Radio: "How are we going to fight China since we have only 250 million against their billion?"
"We'll fight not by numbers but by skills, the way the Jews fight Arabs."
"But do we have enough Jews?"

(6.66) Once the Communists were fighters, Gypsies were thieves, the Jews were traders.
Now the Communists are the thieves, the Gypsies are the traders, the Jews are the fighters.

(6.67) "How can a Jew become a Communist Party member?"
"On the recommendation of three Arabs."

| Identifying with Israel

In 1982, after Israel's military success in Lebanon, the following joke expressed the Russian Jews' pride in Israeli military skills:

(6.68) The USSR sends new fighter jets to Syria. A Soviet instructor
drills a Syrian pilot:
"This is the takeoff button: you press it, and the plane will
ascend and gain the proper altitude. This is the right turn button.
This one is the left turn button. This button opens fire—of
course, if you have time for that."
"And where is the button for landing?" asks the Syrian.
"You don't need it. The Israelis will take care of that."[25]

General Moshe Dayan quickly became the most popular Israeli. Numerous jokes appeared in which Dayan's standing was compared to that of the most
famed generals in the history of mankind. In one joke, Dayan is considered of
equal standing with Kutuzov, the Russian national hero of the Great Patriotic
War of 1812 against the Napoleonic invasion. The humor in the joke plays with
some similarities between Kutuzov and Dayan—their first names (Mikhail-
Moshe) and the fact that each lacked an eye:

(6.69) Strolling along Moscow streets, two Jews, one local and one
visiting from the West, come up to a statue of a one-eyed general.
"Is this Moshe Dayan's statue?" asks the guest.
"No," answers the host. "It's Moshe Kutuzov's. Dayan's left eye
is missing, and in this statue the general is missing the right one."

The Moscow Jew seems to wish that the statue were dedicated to Dayan:
perhaps he even regards Kutuzov's as Dayan's, with a minor external discrep-
ancy, so great is his pride in having a Jewish military genius. In the Russian
Jewish jokes of the time, Dayan became a legendary figure, larger than life, fit
to enter folklore as a character with power as awesome as that found in scary
fairy tales:

(6.70) Sadat's daughter-in-law is feeding his grandson. The grandson is
not in the mood to eat.
"Eat!" says his mother, but the little one turns his head away.
"Eat!"
Again he refuses.
Sadat comes in, covers one eye with his hand, and demands:
"Well, will you eat now?"
The baby starts eating immediately. (Shturman and Tiktin 535)

The jokes that deal with Israel's military victories, besides enhancing
the in-group's morale, have served another important function. The following
item seems to be just an another Jewish joke about anti-Semitism, but there
is a new overtone in this age-old theme:

(6.71) The judge in the Soviet courts asked a certain Ivanov why he
beat up Comrade Rabinovich.
"Well, it's all too clear," said Ivanov. "I got up in the morning,
and heard over the radio the news: 'Israeli troops counterattack
Arabs.' I ate my breakfast, shaved, and the radio reported:
'Israeli tanks crossed the Sinai Desert.' I rushed to the bus on my
way to work, and from a portable radio I heard 'Israeli infantry
crossed the Nile.' I jumped onto the subway and heard 'Israeli
tanks on the way to Cairo.' I got out of the subway, and as I
turned around the corner—they were already here!"
He pointed at Rabinovich:
"So I made a preventive strike."

It is easy to see that the joke tells not so much about another Jew as a victim
of ethnic hatred as it does of a rather rare admission by an anti-Semite that
the Jews can fight and that they do it well. The joke also promotes the idea of
the in-group's cohesiveness in the face of the anti-Zionist (i.e., anti-Jewish)
propaganda in the country. It seems to be addressed to those Russian Jews
who, in order to survive, attempted to separate themselves from Israel. Such a
course is futile, the joke says: the anti-Semites keep all Jews accountable for
Israel's actions anyway. This sentiment of taking closer to heart all that was
concerned with Israel as a state explains the proliferation of jokes in the late
1960s through the 1970s that deal with the Jewish state in one way or another.
Good-natured humor about Israel and Israelis became increasingly popular
among the Soviet Jews:

(6.72) "Is Israel a small or a big state?"
"Of course, it's big and mighty. Otherwise it would be called
simply Izzi." (Shturman and Tiktin 532)

So great was the Russian Jews' desire to say something good about the
historical motherland that even Israeli jokes poking fun at the lack of manners
among Israelis sometimes acquired a different, upbeat, connotation:[26]

(6.73) An Israeli journalist removed his jacket while sitting at the
Knesset meeting. The speaker of the Knesset asked him who
gave him permission to violate the dress code. The journalist
rose and said:
"The Queen of England, sir."
"What does the Queen have to do with this place?"
"Well," said the journalist. "When I removed my jacket in the
British Parliament, the Queen said to me, 'You'll kindly take off
your jacket at home.'"

In the Soviet Union, this joke was not considered disparaging to the Israelis; on the contrary, it esteemed them. It was perceived as a joke that celebrates Israel as the country in which a Jew is no longer an underdog, but an equal among equals, with whom even the notables of the world are on an even footing.

Thus, Jewish exodus humor assisted the Jewish in-group in controlling the behavior of its members under perilous circumstances, helping them to survive in trying times and in a hostile environment. The jokes pointed out the danger of the biases from the in-group's established behavioral attitudes and standards. They also galvanized conflicts already present in the in-group in order to bring them to the collective consciousness and attempt to resolve them.

Conclusions

Joke telling within a group is a complex activity that resists labeling. The target minority may be rendered with some relation to fact or it may be the product of total invention—for example, Jews in high positions were careful not to hire relatives; jokes of the Soviet period invented their nepotism. A joke may seem to have a clear message for one audience and a different, ambiguous meaning for another. Thus, interpretations may be misleading when ethnic jokes are discussed outside the concrete sociopolitical context of their circulation.

An analysis of the ethnic-joke repertoire in and of itself is instructive about the workings of the folk creative mind. Thus, I have found that a number of jokes in the Russian ethnic repertoire consist of jokes told by a minority and retold within the majority group. Sometimes they are taken almost verbatim, sometimes they are altered by replacing the social-tension scenario of the borrowed item with an ethnic one. Thus, an indigenous minority joke is made to meet the emotional needs of the majority group's tellers.

The majority's pool of ethnic humor may include jokes previously directed at another nationality. For example, some contemporary anti-Ukrainian jokes are made up on the pattern of old Russian anti-Semitic jokes. The majority's repertoire may also include items that "ethnicize" certain generic human foibles. Sometimes, too, old Soviet political jokes are made ethnic by replacing their original target—the Soviet system—with a minority, as is the case with several contemporary Russian jokes about Jews, Ukrainians, and Moldavians. Some Russian ethnic jokes carry a "hidden curse" scenario in which bad things—disease or death—happen to a member of a minority.

My analysis of the repertoire has shown that contemporary Russian ethnic jokes also make use of old stereotypes and create new ones, even if they contradict old ones. This is especially the case with new anti-Jewish jokes in which, contrary to previous folk stereotype, Jews are depicted as incompetent and stupid.

Contemporary Russian ethnic humor, as this study shows, is primarily a result of the gradual stagnation of the Soviet system in the post-Stalinist period and the tension that stagnation created in the mainstream Russian culture. This tension grew over the years of the Soviet regime. On the one hand, the Russians enjoyed the status of a great nation—as a military superpower, a major force during World War II, possessor of nuclear weapons; as a nation that produced world-class literature, theater, music, and ballet; as outstanding in sports and a country of impressive technological accomplishments exemplified in successful space flights. On the other hand, Russia was (and, by and large, still is) a nation with a low and rapidly worsening standard of living. "It is degrading," says the poet Evgeny Evtushenko (13), "that we are still unable to feed ourselves, buying bread, fruit, and vegetables abroad."

Such discrepancies had existed before Brezhnev's time, but the Russians didn't feel singled out for misery when compared with other groups in the Soviet empire; all ethnicities were perceived as sharing a common fate. Popular humor of that time targeted primarily members of the ruling elite, in numerous political jokes.

It was not until the 1960s, when this feeling of common misfortune was violated by the conspicuous consumption of super-achievers among the Georgians (and other ethnic groups) that the Russian folk mind responded to the loss of equilibrium in the "things are tough all over" situation. Jokes about the Georgians expressed not only envy, but a sense of injustice—aimed at their alleged violation of both written law and moral codes of behavior.

The birth of the ethnic stereotype of a Georgian as an uncultured spend-thrift undeservedly enjoying his wealth reflected class stratifications within Soviet society at the time, a process that until then had been, by and large, "ethnic-blind". The appearance of anti-Georgian jokes was the first indication of the rise of the Russians' self-consciousness as a group.[1]

It is noteworthy that the same derision is at the core of current jokes about the so-called New Russians. This ironic nickname is given to the acquisitive, profit-oriented, nascent entrepreneurial class, stereotyped as of little culture and as holding spiritual values in low esteem. The adjective "new" aims to differentiate them from the "old" Russians, as history witnessed them, who, despite dramatic political and social changes, remained true to their perception of themselves as a group—as nonmaterialistic people, much more concerned with cultural and spiritual values than with profit making.

The Soviet system of national wealth distribution, in which the vast major-ity of people were equally poor, corresponded to this self-image. The following joke of the post-Soviet period can be viewed as both self-deprecatory, if seen from the point of view of the materialistic West, and self-congratulatory from the "old" Russians' vantage: they would not bend their beliefs and habits in the face of sweeping political and social changes.

(7.1) "What's business, Russian style?"
"To steal a case of vodka, to sell it off cheap on the streets, and drink up the money." (I. Raskin 85)

It is not by chance, therefore, that it is on Russian soil that the theory of laughter as a way of dealing with shame has gained new currency. Relying on Plato's notion of shame as "fear before expected disgrace," the Russian philosopher Leonid Karassev (63–88) sees laughter as a way of reacting to this fear and covering it up. Although he defines shame as "the tragedy of an individual (87)," it follows that laughter as a defense mechanism may be adopted by a group as well.[2]

My study has suggested that the Russians' need to vent their sense of failure has made them hide their "disgrace" by inventing Chukchi jokes. Appearing at the time of the growth of Russian nationalism, with its claim that the Russians were the most disadvantaged group in the former Soviet Union, Chukchi jokes portray a small and remote minority as intellectually inferior to the Russians. Analysis of a body of these jokes, which have circulated over a period of two decades, has shown that the Chukchis of these jokes are not the real target. Although because of their insignificant number and lack of the the economic power that the Russians have ascribed to Georgians, Ukrainins, and Jews, they hardly fit the concept of an enemy, the Chukchis do fit the psychological construct of "the other" and are "not unlike the self" (Volkan 94). In many respects they are projections.

Used as a vehicle of political satire of the Soviet regime in the 1970s and early 1980s, in the late 1980s and early 1990s they became a metaphor for underdogs, abused and fooled by fate—the Russians themselves. Their presumed dismal living conditions have served to express Russian destitution, and their misery is Russian misery. As a Russian saying of the time goes, "Chukchi is not a nationality; it's a diagnosis." Thus, Chukchi jokes are, in fact, a rather unusual instance of a well-known phenomenon of self-deprecatory folk humor, a veiled form of the Russians' laughter at themselves.

"Fear of disgrace" may account for the appearance of new Russian jokes targeted at Ukrainians as well. Although age-old tension between these groups produced anti-Ukrainian jokes in the past, an explosion of especially fierce items in the late 1980s and early 1990s was caused by the high anxiety evoked by the threat that this economically highly significant group would leave the Soviet Union. Parting with the closely related group was perceived as the loss of the traditional "bread basket," as the Ukrainian Republic was called in the Soviet Union. The pervasive portrayal of Ukrainians as greedy, as insatiable lovers of salt pork (*salo*) in these jokes is most indicative as to this motive.

An attempt to shift feelings of shame to minorities is seen in another genre of folk humor—ethnic nicknames. Although some of them existed earlier, many new ones began to circulate in the last decade because of increased contacts with other ethnic groups, caused by their mass influx into central Russian cities. Many of these nicknames, however, are hardly more than cognitives; they are used to tag a representative of an ethnic group in an offhand manner. A member of a minority group is identified synecdochically, through complexion or a characteristic detail. This could be a feature of a national costume or of a face—the shape of nose, eyes, or the traditional hairstyle, which either characterized a target group in the past, as in the case of the Ukrainians, or is typical for a small ethnic subgroup in the present, as in the case of Hasidic Jews.

Other ethnic nicknames, although purely linguistic in nature (as with a word from an indigenous language as a token identification of a member of a group), when used in the context of Russian, often may carry an offensive connotation—a linguistic phenomenon not unknown in other cultures. Many of these nicknames are used in a strictly pejorative sense.

While ethnic jokes and nicknames are for in-group consumption, they produce a mirror response in the target group. Many minority groups not only use insulting nicknames when referring to the Russians in their midst, but also tell anti-Russian jokes. The phenomenon of "protest humor," as it became known in humor scholarship, is especially developed in the Russian Jewish in-group. Russian Jewish humor, as we have seen, performed the functions of a formal community, replacing many vehicles of self-expression unavailable to the Jews under the regime's clandestine anti-Semitic policies. Jewish in-group jokes helped to increase cohesiveness, provided moral support in dire situations, and sharpened existent conflicts inside the group in order to help resolve them and to help make important decisions concerning its future.

As further evidence that jokes read outside of their cultural and temporal contexts are prone to misinterpretation, my study has shown that the stupidity script, the one most frequently used in Russian ethnic humor, is not a sign of the target group's insignificance for the tellers, as is the case, for instance, with American jokes about Poles, Italians, and Hispanics.[3] Rather the opposite is true. The stupidity script in Russian jokes about the Georgians, Ukrainians, and Jews fulfills the joke tellers' need to lessen feelings of shame in the face of the alleged or seeming economic advantage of these groups over the Russians.[4] All these groups have been featured in idiot jokes because they have been considered undeserving of their well-to-do status in the Russian folk mind. It is assumed that they did not attain their status "through competence in a modern workplace,"[5] but only through their luck in having fertile land (Georgians and Ukrainians) or through economic crimes and scheming (Jews, Georgians, and Armenians).

As is the case with many jokelores of the dominant cultures around the world, the comic device of language distortion serves as another way to put down various out-groups. Due to folk equation of linguistic impairment with mental inferiority, this device may be considered a variant of the stupidity script.[6] Making fun of the ethnic's difficulties with Russian, the language of mainstream culture,[7] most easily accommodates the Russians' need to feel superior toward target ethnic groups.[8]

I have also shown that jokes based on language distortion are especially hostile when a minority group insists on its own, unique, ethnic way of life, on independence from "big brother." By attacking their attachment to their own language, as in jokes about the Ukrainians and Lithuanians, the Russians attack, in fact, their ethnic consciousness, of which language is "a carrier and symbol" (Balzer 10).[9]

Some Russian jokes utilizing the language script imply that all the ethnicities' talk about using their own language is insincere. They just pretend not to understand Russian in order to avoid subordination and insist on using their own language for extortion and other unseemly ends.[10]

Especially versatile and significant is the use of a sexual script in Russian folk humor, both in jokes and *chastushki*. Sexual overindulgence and perversion (from the Russian point of view) are reasons for denouncing the Georgians and Armenians;[11] both are often portrayed as homosexuals or practitioners of pedo- and zoophilia. Totally invented accusations in these folkloric items show the same folk tendency to ascribe negative behavior to "the other," as is the case, for example, in British and American cultures. For instance, what is called a "French kiss" in contemporary British and American cultures was named "Tartar kiss" in medieval Russia (Levin 175). In jokes, the Russians confer crude male chauvinism on the Georgians and love for full-figured women on the Georgians, Ukrainians, and Jews.

The script of a targeted group's asexuality is used in Russian jokes about Jews and Chukchis. Jewish men are usually presented as sexually inadequate and, as a result, their wives as sexually loose (see Dreizin 6). While some *chastushki* are bluntly anti-Semitic (Kozlovsky 136, 189), and a suitor's Jewishness seems a sufficient ground for a girl's rejection (Kozlovsky 194), others portray the Jews as sexually inadequate because they are circumcised, a conclusion that directly derives from the folk belief that the one and only sign of male sexual prowess is the size of his organ.[12] The Chukchis are rendered as sexual losers, mostly because they are perceived as a "conquered" group.

Their inability to keep intact their sexual territory in jokes is consistent with their failure to protect their geographical one.

Yet jokes are highly ambivalent texts. By attacking a target group's intelligence and sexual inadequacy, such jokes, in fact, question a target group's ability to adapt to mainstream modern society and survive as a group. The projected subconscious meaning of these jokes may well be a case of wishful thinking. An implied lack of sexuality essentially means that a target group is incapable of reproducing itself: consequently, its disappearance from Russian soil is only a matter of time. This is consistent, for example, with political pressure exerted upon the Jews after the October Revolution to assimilate with the Russian population. A portrayal of Jewish men in Russian jokes as sexually inadequate and their wives as promiscuous can be viewed as a folk means to achieve the same end.

It is noteworthy that, while there are many jokes in which the Russians portray themselves as drunkards and impotents, in jokes involving foreigners the picture is quite different. It would be hard to find any joke in which a Russian character would admit his inferiority in this matter in relation to another ethnic group.[13]

A degree of animalistic territoriality is frequently reflected in rural *chastushki* that sexually denigrate foreigners and certain ethnic groups, that is, any non-Russian males. It seems that the aim of these *chastushki,* their jocular tone notwithstanding, is to keep away, by means of sexual slander, any intruder on the Russian male's territory. These "nonlocals," in general terms ("*nezdeshnii,*" literally "not one of this locality"), are described as having organs that, by folk belief, are either too small (Kozlovsky 111) or too large, presenting a threat to the health, and even the lives, of the local women (Kozlovsky 113).[14]

In contemporary Russian folklore, as in ancient times, sexual prowess symbolizes fertility, which, in turn, spells the vitality and survivability of a group. Most emblematic in this respect is a Russian *chastushka*-cum-proverb: "We have been fucking and haven't perished; [so, as long as] we keep fucking, we won't perish" (*My ebali—ne propali, i ebem—ne propadem*). That is why, no matter how drunk and undernourished or socially humiliated a Russian character may appear in numerous self-deprecating jokes, he always sexually outperforms any non-Russian contender. Thus, despite the presence of many gloomy jokes (especially those of the post-Soviet period), Russian folk humor reasserts the ultimate optimism of the group.

An analysis of a significant development in the current Russian jokelore shows another sign of hope. As Russian ethnic jokes of the past few decades reveal, although class distinction in the Soviet Union during the Brezhnev period was rather pronounced, ethnic antagonisms followed the current urban American pattern, which runs "not along economic or social lines, but along racial and cultural ones" (Volkan 88).[15] From the late 1950s through the 1980s one could find plenty of jokes about Georgians, Armenians, and Jews flaunting their wealth, but hardly any jokes directed at the Russians' own profiteers in the "shadow" economy and the underground millionaires who flourished in the post-Stalin period. The emerging and widely popular "New Russians" jokelore can be interpreted as a sign of a healthy tendency on the part of the Russian group, of a strengthening of the sense of identity by Russians who have begun to look for culprits within their own group, not outside of it.

As a result, many Russian ethnic jokes have undergone "de-ethnicization," that is, they have appeared in the very same form as before, with one exception: they now ridicule the stupidity, low culture, criminality, and extravagance of a subset of their own group. For instance, exactly the same joke that used to imply that a Georgian or a Jew could buy out all "Mother Russia" (see 2.54) have recently switched the culprit to "a New Russian." (See Eroshkin, et al. 45). Thus, today it is no longer only "the other" who is at fault for the substandard level of living, but also Russians themselves. The joke offered at the end of chapter 2 is worth repeating here:

(7.2) A Georgian boy asks his father:
"Daddy, what nationality am I?"
"You're a Georgian."
"And you?"
"I'm also a Georgian."
"And Mom?"
"She's a Georgian as well."
"So, Uncle Otar's also a Georgian?"
"No. He's a New Russian."

Let us put Russian ethnic humor in a world context. According to Pinderhughes (1982), who studied the group-related paranoid process in thirty-four countries, this process and discrimination seem to be universal.[16] As denigrating ethnic jokes represent "the playful end of the spectrum 'of the ebb and flow of aggression' toward a perceived enemy" (Volkan 100), it is evident that, although Russian ethnic humor also often exhibits xenophobic, racist, or chauvinistic tendencies, overall it is much less spiteful and humiliating than, for example, American ethnic jokelore. In fact, there is hardly a single Russian joke to rival the many American jokes that have been directed at the Irish, Poles, Italians, African Americans, and Puerto Ricans in their utter disdain and contempt for a minority. Furthermore, according to the most comprehensive dictionary of contemporary Russian slang, compiled by Elistratov (1994), Russian derogatory nicknames for even the most hated group (the Jews) are at least 50 percent fewer (around forty words and expressions) than similar slurs in English [Roback 130–32; Spears 143–44, 221 records around seventy items].

One general conclusion may be drawn from this comparison: folk minds work in such a way that if irritation caused by another group can be soothed by words alone, fists are rarely needed. Thus, a plethora of ethnic jokes about a nationality may well prove that the negative feelings about it are fairly manageable and can be discharged in the realm of folk humor.

Contradictions remain, however. Its function as a safety valve notwithstanding, ethnic humor raises the question: is it benign or malicious in its impact? Davies (1990, 9) argues that jokes are "not social thermostats regulating and shaping human behavior, but they are social thermometers that measure, record and indicate what is going on." The situation with ethnic joke telling, however innocent in intention, is much more complicated, however. Humor scholarship is divided on this subject.[17] Although I would agree that nobody tells jokes strictly for the purpose of promoting a negative stereotype, ethnic jokes do have their impact, like any other product of human spirit rendered in artistic forms. After all, entertainment value lies at the core of most works of art and literature, and yet these works have frequently played a great role in shaping many world perspectives, especially those of the young. In this respect, folklore is no less (perhaps even more!) powerful a sphere of human creativity. While all jokes are told primarily for laughter's sake, the pejorative scripts of ethnic jokes are responsible for shaping (often for a lifetime) a negative image of an ethnic group. Ethnic jokes do this whatever their tellers' intentions; their belief in these stereotypes is beside the point.

Asking "to what extent it is permissible to laugh at those who are different from us in some way," Umberto Eco (9) notes that the image of a black man as a crook has disappeared from American films and talk shows and that today nobody dares tell Jewish jokes or to show a typical Italian American, Polish American, or Chinese American in a ridiculous light. Eco believes that

> this is as it should be because jokes of that sort in the end are paving the way for prejudices. . . . Even if there is a difference between comic racism which evokes a smile and fanatical racism which leads to slaughter, quite often they are interconnected; centuries of satirical depiction of Haims and Izzis preceded Hitler's anti-Semitism. Therefore refraining from mockery of other nationalities becomes a necessity, a demand of civilization.

Russia is hardly an exceptional example of the worldwide tendency to develop prejudices and preconceived notions based on folklore, but it offers a striking example of the pervasiveness of folklore's influence. I have found no evidence that Russian scholarship recognizes negative attitudes sustained by the jokelore. It is the Russian folk who understand the Chukchi jokes as "diagnosis" of their own problems. Russian scholars, however, lest they exacerbate ethnic tensions, tend to deny their presence in current ethnic jokes (see, for example, Shmeleva and Shmelev 1996).

Analysis may ill comport with laughter, usually associated with spontaneity and release, but an examination of the elements—both positive and negative—involved in ethnic humor develops new perspectives—the underlying motive of this study.

Notes

Chapter 1: The Repertory of Contemporary Russian Ethnic Jokelore

1. The Gypsies are featured, rather prominently, in humorous rural *chastushki*. Their treatment varies. In some, they appear in a traditional image of fatal lovers. In others, they are rendered as cheats and thieves (e.g., in Starshinov 2:158–61).
2. Dr. Leonid Karassev of the Russian State Humanist University told me the following:

   A Koriak is waiting for his flight to board at the Moscow Airport. He walks up to an automatic fortune teller that promises to tell the nationality, age, and flight number of anyone who deposits a coin. His fortune reads: "A male Koriak, age 25, flight 101 to Chita."
   Amazed at the machine's ability, he goes to the men's room and disguises himself as a woman. He deposits another coin, and the machine shows again: "A male Koriak, age 25, flight 101 to Chita."
   The Koriak again enters the men's room and disguises himself as a very old man. He looks in the mirror and believes it's impossible to recognize himself. Again he drops in a coin. The machine shows:
   "A male Koriak, age 25, would have already departed on flight 101 to Chita if he hadn't made a fool of himself."

   There is also a variant of this joke involving a Georgian (Ivanova 1996, 109).
3. For world distribution of similar ethnic scripts, see Davies 1990, 11–12, 42, 52, 103.
4. There are some cases, however, when the opposite is true—that is, the lower class laughs at the attempts to assimilate made by the upper crust of the group—the rich—as happened, for example, among nineteenth-century German Jews (see Ziv 51).

5. As Oring (134) notes, the charge of Jewish self-hatred is erroneous, for it is made by someone outside of the group who sees Jews as a whole, that is, on an ethnic, not a social, basis. Therefore, an outsider's perception of an ethnicity as self-hating if it tells jokes seemingly about itself shows a racist (or at best uninformed) and stereotypical attitude toward that group.

6. The American comedian Jackie Mason provides a psychological insight into the reason for such behavior:

> Jews are professional victims who practically beg their persecutors to keep persecuting them, 'cause Jews feel so guilty for their own existence that they're ready to accept the blame for anything. [Jewish leaders] do this out of their own sick fears, their own persecution complexes, their Jewish paranoia that if you raise your voice, you're gonna somehow cause trouble and lose the fight. (Quoted in Kasindorf 42)

7. In 1911, in Kiev, the anti-Semitic Black Hundred group accused Mendel Beilis, a laborer, of murdering a Christian boy for ritual purposes. In 1913, at the trial, which brought worldwide protest, Beilis was fully acquitted of the charges (Harris 162–64).

8. For an in-depth treatment of the notion of self-effacing humor, see Oring 122–34.

9. Quoted in Ehidelman 194.

10. See Draitser 1994, 171–72.

11. For a variant joke about a *melamed* (teacher) of Chelm and Rothschild, see Spalding 120.

12. A similar story about Herschel Ostropolier can be found in Spalding 45–46.

13. In the following item, ethnic identification is more subtle for a nonnative speaker:

> "Semyon, how are you doing? What's new?"
> Semyon says sadly: "My wife's cheating on me."
> "You did not understand me, Syoma, I asked what's new?"

> Although there are many Russians named Semyon, in contemporary Russian jokelore Russians are traditionally featured as Ivan, Vasia, Kolya, or Vladimir (as in the series of sexual jokes about the little Vovochka). The name Semyon in jokes is Jewish, reflecting the fact that many Russian Jews give their children, instead of a preferred name such as Samuel (Samuil in Russian transliteration), the closest sounding Russian name.

14. The following account by the poet Igor Guberman, who served a prison term for writing his satirical anti-Soviet verses, shows that "clannishness" of Jews is such a strong part of the Russian stereotype that neither facts nor logic deter the accusers. Prisoners in Stalin's work camps, where sentences were served for both political and criminal offenses, learned that there were more Jews in the Gulag than there were members of any other minority in proportion to their total populations. One criminal remarked disapprovingly: "Look what an awful people! Not only do they crawl in everywhere. They also squeeze in their own kind" (cited in Lvovich 20).

15. For a similar observation about the appearance of "feeble-minded Jews" in contemporary Russian jokelore, see Grafov 16.

16. See, for example, in Russian proverbs collected by Dal: "A German is an adroit fellow; he can shit in a bottle" (*Nemets khiter—v butylku nasret;* Carey 76).

Chapter 2: "I Didn't Buy My Driver's License: My Brother Gave It to Me for my Birthday": Russian Jokes about Georgians and Other Southerners

1. Bay leaves were another popular item sold by the Georgians, which prompted the Russians to nickname them "laurel businessmen" (Elistratov 223).
2. In addition to its regular meaning, the Russian word for "faces" (*litsa*) in Soviet bureaucratese also means "persons."
3. Quoted in Ehidelman 193–94.
4. On the inclination of a majority group to project its own unwanted traits on an alien group, see Davies 1982, 386.
5. In true-to-life descriptions of some Russians, even minor characters have been portrayed as outstandingly stingy. Thus, in a famous story by Gorky (54), "The Twenty Six and One," a bakery owner covers with tin the windows of the damp cellar where his workers toil from early morning until ten at night so that they "couldn't give any bread to beggars and to their unemployed comrades, who were starving." The bakery owner calls his workers "crooks," and gives them rotten innards for dinner instead of meat.

    In time, Russian jokelore of the 1990s will admit the existence of this vice in the majority group. Numerous jokes about the Russian *nuoveaux riches,* the so-called "New Russians," attack their stinginess, lack of compassion, and avarice:

    A New Russian's wife asks her husband:
    "They came to ask for donations for a high school swimming pool. How much should I give them?"
    "Give them two . . . no, three—buckets of water." (Eroshkin et al 37)

    A homeless man stumbles upon a luxurious villa in Barvikha [a Moscow expensive suburb], sees the mistress of the house on the threshold, and says:
    "Dear lady, help me! I haven't seen meat for two weeks!"
    "What a misfortunate man!" says the mistress and shouts to her maid:
    "Niura, bring over a meat rissole, show it to him."(Erokaev 92)

6. On the "second economy" in the former Soviet Union and its impact on the nation's morale, see Grossman 172–97, Wiles 198–213.
7. See also Venclova 322–23.
8. Citing several published sources, Shlapentokh (213) states that a widely developed system of bribe taking existed throughout the former Soviet Union.
9. The spelling of the first name in this joke (and in many others where this name is used to identify a Georgian) proves that its teller is a Russian. He transfers the ending of some of Georgian surnames—*iia,* as in Beriia—to the first name, which in Georgian is invariably Gogi. Astafiev falls into the same trap in his infamous sketch "Catching Gudgeons in Georgia," as Ehidelman (194) points out.
10. There is a variant of this joke involving a Chukchi.
11. In the original, the Caucasian is nicknamed *abrek* (archaic, probably, from the Ocetian word *abreg,* "daredevil"), once used by northern Caucasian peoples to

denote an exile chased out by his own clan and who usually turned into a drifter or robber (Prohkorov 1: 7). For other nicknames of the Georgians, see chapter 5.

12. Such a script is also used in the United States in jokes about blacks and Hispanics (V. Raskin 194; Boskin 1979, 31).
13. There is also a synonym for this neologism with a man of another Southern nationality as the target—"to behave like an Armenian" (*priarmianivat'sia;* Elistratov 363). Armenians are also often portrayed in Russian jokes as pedophiles:

> A court hearing in Erevan on the rape of a boy. The Armenian judge asked the defendant:
> "Tell us, how did this unfortunate accident occur?"
> "It was a bright, sunny day," the defendant began with delight in his voice.
> "The ray of sun played on the boy's sweet little behind . . ."
> The judge interrupts the defendant: "Do not arouse me!"

14. For example, as described in Saltykov-Shchedrin's work (Draitser 1994, 75–77).
15. There is also a variant of 2.45 (see I. Raskin 314) in which, instead of the female singer, a male Italian singer is featured as the object of the Georgians' desire.
16. This proverb is a modified version of an old one in which, instead of a Georgian, an Armenian was named as the superior wheeler-dealer.
17. Cf. a popular rhyme, a sample of Russian Jewish "protest" humor: "If there is no water in the faucet, it means the kikes drank it all" (*"Esli v krane net vody—znachit, vypili zhidy"*).

Chapter 3: Salt Pork in Chocolate: Russian Jokes about the Ukrainians

1. For an American variant of essentially the same joke, but involving an Irishman, a Pole, and an Italian, see Davies 1990, 63.
2. As often happens in folk mythology, stereotyping overrules facts. In the Soviet period, this clannishness was, by and large, uncharacteristic of the Jews. On the contrary, the opposite was often the case. Because of meager employment opportunities due to secret government regulations and everyday anti-Semitism, as a rule the Jews in hiring positions did not dare to employ other Jews for fear of being accused of this very trait—clannishness.

   Shturman and Tiktin's (412) dating of the joke—from the 1950s—is rather doubtful. Strong anti-Ukrainian feelings were not a part of the Russian folk worldview at the time, and the Jewish emigration to which the joke alludes was a much later development. I would place the item in the late 1970s, or even later.
3. A version of 3.3 suggesting the Ukrainians' treacherous nature:

> In a Ukrainian school:
> "Who will do any work for half a liter of vodka?"
> "The Russkies (*Moskali*)!"
> "Who loves money, the way you children love bananas?"
> "Kikes!"
> "And who will sell their own mother and father for a ruble?"
> "But we sing very beautifully!" (I. Raskin 428)

4. The Ukrainian proverbs listed in Roback's (216–18) dictionary of international slurs depict the Russians as sly, foul-mouthed, treacherous, and "worse than the devil himself."

5. According to Armstrong (28), such a "title" belongs to a large ethnic group "low in social mobilization, yet close to the dominant ethnic group in major cultural aspects. . . . In terms of social mobilization, the younger brothers are rural, low in education and access to skilled occupations and mass media, and low in geographical mobility except when transplanted by the dominant nationality."

6. See also an interview with a literary critic of the nationalistic right, Vadim Kozhinov (160–70), in which he speaks of Russians, Ukrainians, and Byelorussians as "three branches of one and the same people," and claims that "these three branches should be on one tree." M. Nazarov (30–44) also offers a concept of "Slavic brotherhood" possible in a "post-totalitarian future."

7. Tolpygo (150–51) gives a rather crude, but overall truthful, metaphor of the Russians' attitude toward Ukraine: "In respect to Ukraine, the Russians have developed the syndrome of the abandoned wife who runs to a party committee: 'My husband has left me, he is a bastard and a pervert—get him back for me!' "

8. Compare with Russian jokes where the butt is clearly a Russian:

"Comrade conductor, wake me up before the Ivanovka station ."
"Are you getting out there?"
"No, but I want to see my neighbor oversleep his station." (Genis 2:62)

God grants one wish each to an Italian, an Englishman, a Frenchman, and a Russian. The Italian says: "I want Italians to be the world's finest singers." The Englishman says: "I want Englishmen to be the world's finest horse-men."
The Frenchman says: "I want French women to be the world's most beauti-ful."
The Russian says, "I want my neighbor Ivan's mare to drop dead." (Will 70)

9. Compare with the following Russian item:

A man is riding in a streetcar and repeats: "Damn, motherfucker!"
"What happened?" his neighbor asks.
The man explains to him quietly. His neighbor hears him out and says:
"Damn, motherfucker!"
People begin to get angry: two men are swearing in a streetcar. They call a militiaman. He listens to the men and explains:
"Citizens, his wife gave birth to twins and both babies are—little black ones!"
The whole streetcar:
"Damn, motherfucker!" (Genis 2:214)

10. Compare with the following Russian joke:

An American tells a Russian: "I have three cars. I use one of them when driving to work. Another one is for visiting friends. And I take my third one when I vacation in Europe."

The Russian: "Well, I go to work by streetcar, and when I visit my friends, I use our subway."
"And what about Europe?"
"When it comes to Europe, I go there by a tank."

11. It is easy to compare this item with many Russian anti-Semitic jokes. By the same token, although some anti-Semitic acts have taken place on Ukrainian, as well as on Russian soil, in the post-*glasnost* period, contrary to predictions expressed in this joke, the Ukrainian push for autonomy has not increased the frequency of such acts. Such overtly anti-Semitic societies as *Pamiat* and *Edinstvo* took root on Russian, not Ukrainian soil. Tolpygo (152) states that "Ukrainian anti-Semitism today is not local but imported [from Russia]." He also finds Ukrainian anti-Semitism "far less acute than in Russia," and calls Russia's anti-Semitism "an ugly (and frightening) caricature of Ukrainian anti-Semitism" (150).

12. An example of the opposite—a Ukrainian who finds regular Russian names strange and funny:

In a Ukrainian hospital, a doctor is reading a patients' file. He shows it to a colleague, laughing:
"Look, Chernozhopenko [Black-ass-enko], what a funny name—Zaitsev [an ordinary Russian name]!

13. In fact, as early as 1959, according to Soviet census data, 52.5 percent of the Ukrainian population was engaged in nonagricultural work (Rockett 128).

14. In the post-WWII period, a couple of Ukrainian stand-up comedians, Timoshenko and Berezin (who used their stage nicknames—Tarapunka and Shtepsel), as well as Ukrainian humorist Ostap Vishnia and others, enjoyed all-Union fame and popularity.

15. One of my consultants, a Russian with a college degree in history from Moscow State University, insists that there is no such thing as a Ukrainian language; at most it is a rural Russian dialect. This opinion is rather widespread and characteristic of an overall condescending attitude toward the Ukrainians on the part of many Russians. A similar script of disparagement of a nationality insistent on its own identity is seen in a joke about Lithuanians circulated among the Russians during the late 1980s, when Lithuania was beginning its drive for secession from the Soviet Union. As the onomastic rules of Lithuanian allow the addition of the *s,* as in *-as, -ius,* or *-is,* to otherwise Russian-sounding names, the linguistic device employed in the following joke is adding the ending *-as* to a typical Russian dog's name and *-s* to the sound of its barking. (As Professor Jules Levin of the University of California, Riverside, observes, the Lithuanians often give the most popular Russian dog name, "Sharik," to their dogs):

In a Lithuanian village a woman calls her dog:
"Sharik! Sharik!"
Not a sound from the doghouse.
"Sharik! Sharik!"
Stubborn silence.

"SharikAS!" shouts the woman.
The dog jumps out of its house:
"GavS! GavS!" [BowS-wowS].

The joke is also a disparaging and condescending commentary on the Lithuanian insistence on independence as a petty matter, "a dog's barking." By implication, the joke tells Lithuanians that they should "know their place."

16. A reference to the flag colors of the short-lived Ukrainian state under the Rada during the civil war years.

17. Rockett (115) cites a scholarly estimate showing that while about 40,000 households in Uzbekistan were "dekulakized," in the Ukraine this number was at least five times greater. According to Robert Conquest (306), the subsequent "purely man-made famine" of 1932–33 was also aimed primarily at the Ukrainians, claiming five million of its victims in the Ukraine out of the total seven million Soviets who perished during this disaster.

18. Rockett (88) cites the following reasons why the Ukrainians were considered politically suspect by the Kremlin: "The strong peasant traditions and lack of an industrial proletariat among Ukrainians are regarded as major factors that steered them away from the Bolshevik political ideology."

19. *Salo* as a derogatory connotation of the Ukrainians has been used not only in the realm of private joke telling, but in the mass media as well. Thus, on July 24, 1995, in the course of the KVN program (abbreviation of "*Klub veselykh i nakhodchivykh*" [The Club of the Jolly and Witty]) aired by the major Moscow Ostankino Television Studio, the following joke was told:

"Would [the president of Ukraine] Kravchuk kiss the Wailing Wall during his visit to Israel?"
"Yes, if it was smeared with *salo*."

20. Other Russian ethnic slurs regarding food are related to Tartars, who are assumed to be connoisseurs of horse meat, to Koreans as dog eaters, to Jews as chicken eaters (Dreizin 3), and to Moldavians as lovers of *mamalyga,* a porridge made out of corn flour. The shapelessness of this dish apparently gives the connotation of flaccidity and spinelessness in slurs in which a person called "mamalyga" is assumed to be lazy and weak-willed.

21. There was even a Russian joke of that time that made this point:

A mother brought her skinny son to a doctor to see what was wrong with him. The doctor examined the boy and said:
"There's nothing wrong with him. He just needs more vitamin C [pronounced in Russian as "tse"]. You should give him *sal'TSE, masliTSE.* [a little salt pork, a little butter].

22. It would be interesting to compare this image with the image of the Russians as primarily eaters of cabbage (a low-calorie food), drawn by an Italian, Aldo Buzzi (34), at the turn of the century:

For Russians, cabbage is the principal food. It is served at almost every meal, as a first course, second course, vegetable, salad, perhaps dessert:

cabbage soup (*shchi*), borscht, cabbage-filled rolls (*pirozhki*), cabbage pie à la Muscovite (*pirog*), red cabbage, sauerkraut tart, etc. The smell of cabbage soup impregnates public offices. Cabbage in Russia is eternal. The muzhik says, "The worm eats the cabbage and dies before the cabbage."

In a few words Chekhov sketches the portrait of a Russian eater: "On his beard he had little pieces of cabbage, and he gave off the odor of vodka." "What I desire," said Pushkin, "is quiet and a pot of cabbagesoup, the biggest possible."

Borscht, on the other hand, is the cabbage soup of Little Russia (Ukraine), capital Kiev, a country of heavy eaters, where a chicken is considered a simple appetizer, where the best sausages are made, and where the proverb "The best bird is the sausage" was born.

Chapter 4: Taking Penguins to the Movies: Russian Jokes about the Chukchis

1. This joke needs some explanation for those readers who have not been exposed to the barrage of Soviet propaganda. In many Soviet texts, the names of Marx and Engels were most often treated together and pronounced in speeches in one breath. Lenin's real name, Ulyanov, has also often appeared in print together with his pseudonym. "*Slava KPSS*" [Glory to the Communist Party of the Soviet Union] was one of the most ubiquitous Soviet slogans; the Chukchi confuses "Slava" with the Russian diminutive for Vsevolod, Viacheslav, or Mstislav—Rostropovich's name.

2. Some features of Chernenko's appearance made such a joking suggestion plausible: his small stature, dark hair, and high cheekbones were characteristic of the Asian physical type.

3. Cf., for example, Rubina's (82) article in which she states that all [Soviet] Uzbek literature was created by a few literary "work horses." According to her, a Russian poet whom she identifies only as "Iliusha N." was responsible for the entire Uzbek poetic output. For his labor, he was allowed "once in ten years to publish a slim collection of his own talented verses." One of my consultants, a Russian Jewish journalist and writer, wrote novels for a semiliterate Georgian and published them in Moscow as a translation from the Georgian. Then these books were translated into Georgian and published in Tbilisi as original prose. Honoraria for both publications would be split by both parties. Such a practice was rather widespread in the Soviet period.

4. A variant of this joke was widespread in Eastern Europe, referring to encounters with illiterate Russian scientists.

5. On Russian perception of the notion of "Soviet" as Russian, see a quote from Abram Terz (Andrei Sinyavsky) in chapter 5, p. 102.

6. According to Clem (26), Daniel Bell "singled out the Soviet Union as a country in which ideology has become largely a rhetorical exercise. At this writing [1988], the Bolshevik revolution is some seventy years in the past, and one suspects that the ideological fervor characteristic of the early decades of the Communist regime is difficult for today's average Soviet citizen to understand at best."

7. A similar German Jewish joke was told at the time of Hitler's ascendance to power (see Lipman 166–67). Another joke of the period of stagnation also expresses an important feature of the time—the weakening of the regime's will to persecute the dissatisfied:

> Rabinovich walks around the town, looking into shop windows: "Oh! Out of meat! Out of coffee also! Out of milk!"
> A plainclothes KGB man comes up to him:
> "Shut up! We shot people like you in 1937!"
> "Understood, understood. Everything's understood."
> Rabinovich returns home and says to his wife:
> "You know, Sarah, I understood it all. They're out of bullets as well."

8. Clem (26): "Other attempts to divert attention away from socioeconomic reality, such as the massive campaign to perpetuate the memory of the Great Patriotic War (1941–1945), are probably not much more effective than are appeals to revolutionary zeal."
9. See chapter 2, pp. 37–38.
10. "From an adaptive outlook, the sharing of ethnicity within a group necessarily has a healing effect because it provides emotional borders that protect the individual's self and the group's self from injury. This border helps to create the concept of enemy even when there is no clearly defined enemy, which in turn shores up the group's (and the individual's) sense of self. Shared ethnicity provides the individual and the group with support and a perceived means of psychic survival." (Volkan 93)
11. For example, see chapter 5 (p. 115) on Russian proverbs about Tartars and reference to their traditionally low social status in Russia in Zholkovsky (18). Also see Astafiev's racist characterization of Mongols as having "slant-eyed mugs" (*raskosye mordy*) in his sketch "Fishing for Gudgeons in Georgia" (cited in Ehidelman 195). There is enough folkloric evidence that the Chukchi is a collective image of an Asian man. Thus, in a contemporary Russian hippie joke, Tsoi, a Russian pop singer of Korean origin, is mocked as a dumb Chukchi (Lurie 1989, 148, 151).
12. In fact, some early versions of Chukchi jokes were jokes involving the Eskimos (e.g., see V. Raskin 200).
13. On use of this comic device in satirical literature, see Draitser 1994, 148.
14. More distant is the sound association of the initial morpheme of the word (*chu*) with several words with negative connotations, such as *chudnoi* ("strange, eccentric"), *chuzhoi* ("a stranger"), and *chumazyi* ("a dirty one").
15. The name of a Chuckhi's home is *iaranga;* calling it *chum,* using a rather generic name for a tent of skins in Siberia and far northeastern parts of Russia, is another proof of the joke tellers' unfamiliarity with the real life of the Chukchis.
16. The joke is backdated, that is, of a later origin; at the time of the experiment in space involving two dogs, there were no Chukchi jokes in Russian jokelore. It is noteworthy that a similar Russian joke exists that involves another Asian man who is also nameless—a Vietnamese (see Shturman and Tiktin 362).
17. The folktale type # 1699, according to Aarne's (484) classification.

18. In this joke, the implication is, of course, that the Georgian also wound up on a dirty road because of his lack of knowledge of the Russian language. For a similar joke, involving a Moldavian instead of a Chukchi, see Ivanova 1996, 113–14.

19. Cf., a contemporary proverb in Kozlovsky (233): "One who has not fucked a Buriat woman hasn't been to Siberia" (*Kto buriatku ne ebal, tot v Sibiri ne byval*). That is, one should not believe that he had really visited the region if he hadn't "tasted the local delicacies." Analyzing Lermontov's *A Hero of Our Time*, Barbara Heldt (29) talks about Pechorin's "squarely Russian imagination that sees [. . .] conquest of women as a corollary of the Russian imperialistic conquest and 'civilizing' of the people of the Caucasus."

20. There is an American version of this joke involving a garbageman who finds a penguin in a city dump, puts a baseball cap on him, and takes him to a baseball game.

21. I came across only two jokes suggesting that the Chukchis were unclean (see I. Raskin 456; Ivanova 1994, 210).

22. In the following joke, however, the Russian characters are able to endure the discomfort because they are adequately supplied with alcohol:

> The Japanese invented a freezer that could bring the temperature to -1,000 degrees Celsius [approx. -1,770 Farenheit]. They announced a prize: whoever remained in the freezer the longest would be given the island of Hokkaido.
>
> A Frenchman tried first and asked that he be given a woman and a case of wine. But he didn't last more than a minute when the temperature dropped below -200 degrees.
>
> Then an Englishman tried. He sat with a woman and a case of whisky until the temperature read -300 degrees.
>
> The only other contender was Ivan, very drunk. He said to the Japanese: "Give me a milk-can of moonshine and bring in my buddy."
>
> They gave him what he asked for. They closed both men in the freezer and watched the thermometer; the temperature dropped below the limit in an hour. One little Japanese [in Russian: *iapioshka*—both derogatory and condescending] said to another:
>
> "Well, let's take these 'icicles' out. They're probablyalready dead."
>
> The other little Japanese opened the freezer and saw the two friends sitting opposite one other, drinking moonshine.
>
> Suddenly, Ivan banged the Japanese over his head and asked his buddy: "Did I do the right thing?"
>
> "Of course, you did the right thing. It's cold in here, and he goes and opens the door." (Genis 1:207–8).

23. The artistic device of Russian folk humor—to treat another ethnicity as Russians whose labors have changed their facial features and their complexions—can be seen in Russian jokes about other groups, most often blacks and Chinese. Usually differences in the appearance of a nationality are interpreted as deformations or disfigurements of the normal [read: Russian] image as a result of suffering or

deprivation. Thus, there is a contemporary Russian saying: "work as hard as a Negro" (*vkalyvat', kak negr*). Although generally the Chinese in Russian jokes are treated with animosity, stemming from tensions between the nations that began shortly after Stalin's death, with Mao-Tze Tung vying for world leadership of the Communist movement, in the following item artistic considerations overrule the political; the Chinese are seen as fellow suffering brothers who have endured the same political system:

"Who are the Chinese?"
"They are Russians who became cross-eyed and jaundiced from an excess of Marxism." (Dubovsky 345)

24. A variant collected by Shturman and Tiktin (312):

Two Chukchis are sitting in their hut.
"You know that Chernenko's a blockhead, after all."
"Not so loud. Otherwise, they might deport us . . ."

It may well be that the series was born from a single joke told in 1967 during a recess at the Union of Soviet Writers meeting convened to condemn Solzhenitsyn (recorded by Shturman and Tiktin 366). A Chukchi writer, Yury Rytkhehu, was one of the few who attempted to defend Solzhenitsyn against the attacks of the vast majority of proregime writers denouncing him as a slanderer—a campaign initiated and inspired by the KGB and the party:

Yury Rytkhehu is not afraid to defend Solzhenitsyn. The farther they exile him, the closer he'll be to his native land. But if we defend him?

25. Quoted in Boston 92.
26. On Shtirlits joke series, see Belousov 104–17.
27. It does not come as a surprise that, parallel to the recent jokelore about the "New Russians," in which Russian social upstarts sport stylish crimson jackets and drive the latest model of Mercedes, the "New Chukchi" jokes have also appeared, in which crimson is the color of the Chukchi's skies and, instead of the 600 series of Mercedes, he possesses the 600th deer (Erokaev 110).

Chapter 5: On "Chuchmeks," "Egg Yolks," and Other Strangers: Contemporary Russian Ethnic Nicknames, Proverbs, and Sayings

1. In their study of post-Soviet threat perception as it is expressed in Russian public opinion, Sayrs and Lindsay (247) conclude that "the immediate threat from within the [former Soviet] Union is greater than perceived external threats."
2. In part, such a huge disparity may be explained by the absence of Russian written sources for such comparisons. This was caused by the ban in the USSR on the collection and publication of such politically sensitive material, since antagonism among various peoples of the Soviet Union contradicted the official proclamation of "invincible friendship" among all of them.
3. There are a few exceptions, however. Thus, the name of a venereal disease still carries the euphemistic name "French (or Parisian) head cold." Another epithet,

"a frogman" (*liagushatnik*), a reference to the presence of frogs in French cuisine, has reappeared recently.

4. In contemporary Russian slang, there is a cognitive nickname for a German, "hans" (*gans*). Also, the expression "on German terms" (*na nemetskii schet)* is used when a Russian proposes dinner in a restaurant on condition that the others pay for their own meals. (Cf. "go Dutch" or "Dutch treat" in British and American culture). The implication of the German name for the arrangement is that a true (read: generous) Russian would pay the entire bill.

5. As for the objects of xenophobic feelings, contemporary Russian school-age children's folklore (Lurie 1992, 26–27), however, follows an outdated adult pattern. Most frequently, it expresses nineteenth-century Russian sensibilities—that is, animosity toward Poles and Germans.

6. Roback (315) perceptively finds it influenced by the phonetic resemblance of the Russian words to the Japanese names. There are several comic routines for Russian schoolchildren that parody the Japanese language (among others); most such parodies are scatological. For instance: *khochu-pisi, khochu-kaki* ("I want to piss, I want to shit").

7. The material for this chapter is drawn primarily from Elistratov's dictionary and two other publications: Shlyakhov and Adler 1995; Yuganov and Yuganova,1994, as well as from my thirty years of observations in Russia and several field trips made since 1990.

8. The title of the dictionary is an obvious misnomer. Webster's (1981, 60) defines argot as a "more or less secret vocabulary and idiom peculiar to a particular group." However, in this volume many entries not only circulate both inside and outside the capital, but also are understood and used by many people, not necessarily members of a specific group. In fact, the dictionary presents a rather mixed bag. Besides words that belong to argot per se (in the form of the so-called thieves' language [*blatnaia fenia*] as well as the talk of prostitutes, drug pushers, and drug users), it also has a number of entries that, while initially coming from colloquial Russian, had already entered the literary norm either a long time ago (e.g., "refusenik" [*otkaznik*], "a person who refuses to return from a trip abroad" [*nevozvrashchenets*]; or, rather recently, "lawlessness" [*bespredel*], "an informal gathering" [*tusovka*], "a quarrel" [*razborka*], etc.). While some entries belong to the professional jargons of various groups, the bulk of the vocabulary consists of words that best qualify as slang and that are used by a wider audience: students, blue-collar workers, Bohemian artists, and businessmen whom the compiler lists among his informants.

Most ethnic-related entries in the volume fall under this last category. According to *Webster's New Dictionary of Synonyms* (239), slang "implies comparatively recent invention, the appeal of the words or phrases to popular fancy because of their aptness, picturesqueness, grotesqueness, or humorousness, and usually an ephemeral character."

Many of these words are not literal denominators. They are emotionally colored, have attitudinal character, and present facetious figures of speech, which makes them part of the realm of popular humor.

9. In the past, Presnia was a working-class neighborhood on the outskirts of Moscow. Shlyakhov and Adler (56) also include a derogatory female name, Dun'ka. Two other newly coined nicknames of certain types of Russians in Elistratov's (248) dictionary are diminutives of Dmitry. One of these nicknames, *Mitek,* denotes a member of a St. Petersburg artist group who works in a pseudo-Russian style and leads a peculiarly stylized Bohemian life; the nickname is a diminutive form of the first name of the group's leader, Dmitri Shagin. The other is "Mit'ka," a nickname of a street policeman (in thieves' argot).

10. In Russian, the word *enoty* is made up to fit both meanings, that of Japanese money and the animals, for intentional humorous characterization (a hint at the relatively short Japanese, a device not exceptional in the realm of popular humor).

11. For a similar technique used in America, see Allen 29–34.

12. The first is patterned on a Russian name, Georgii; the second on the pattern of Georgian last names, as, for example, Guliia or Beriia.

13. Elistratov (24) mistakenly translates *"ara"* as "listen," probably because the two words are often coupled in Georgian conversation: "No, listen . . ." Shlyakhov and Adler (4) also wrongly interpret it as "a pal" in Georgian.

14. The last nickname also sounds like a food item, a date, in Russian.

15. The second meaning of the word is "a peach." The word is sometimes mockingly pronounced with a typical Caucasian nonpalatalized accent—*pehrsik.*

16. In the train conductors' jargon, "to sell a Chinese female" (*tolknut' kitaiku;* Elistratov 196), has nothing to do with prostitution, but means the collection of a fee for linens already used by sleeping-car passengers. The word *kitaika* suggests the yellow of the soiled linen.

17. Contributed by Ruth Mathewson.

18. This slur also has a belittling suffix, *-enok,* denoting cubs, as in *kotenok,* "a kitten," or *porosenok,* "a piglet."

19. On the semiotic significance of the Georgians' caps, see chapter 2, p. 38.

20. On nicknames of various nationalities in the United States dealing with unusual food from an outsider's vantage, see Allen (47–56).

21. Another term used is *banderlogi,* "disorderly monkeys," after the characters of Kipling's *The Jungle Book.*

22. "All the markets are bought up by the khazars" (*"Vse bazary kupili khazary"*; Elistratov 516).

23. Another term is "the Comanches" (*komanchi*).

24. One of these expressions, a saying used when addressing a person with whom one does not want to talk: "Get lost like a kike in Dachau" (*"Svoboden kak zhid v Dakhau"*; Elistratov 423), is especially insensitive toward the ethnic group's collective pain.

25. On sound associations of this name, see chapter 4, p. 82.

26. It is clear from the context that the word "Soviet" is used in terms of "Russian." The etymology of such folk perception of the word "Soviet" as "one of ours" (*svoi*) is discussed by Abram Tertz (Andrei Sinyavsky) (see p. 102). Derogatory meaning of *chuchmek* is also seen in the context of Brodsky's (32) play *The Marbles.*

27. The proverb refers to the Jewish stereotype that Dreizin (6) calls "The Clever One,"

that is, the vision of a Jew as "a cold, solitary, reserved, secretive and rational creature. . . . The typical [Russian] attitude to 'The Clever One is hatred.'"

28. "Russians think they're better than us. That's the root of the [inter-ethnic tension] problem," says [Tartar nationalist leader Marat A.] Milyukov. "Even an alcoholic Russian—a bum and a scoundrel—is convinced he is higher on the human scale than a Tartar." [Quoted in Williams A6]

29. There is also the expression: "sly as one hundred (or two hundred) Chinese."

Chapter 6: "He's Abroad? I'm the One Who's Abroad": Contemporary Jokes Told by Russian Jews

1. See, for example, Ziv 49.

2. In general, Russian political jokes of the time showed a strong tendency to borrow from Jewish folklore. Starting in this period, there was a gradually increasing process of "judafication" of Russian political jokelore. In regard to borrowing from Jewish humorous folklore in political joke telling, see Benton 42.

3. Another Jewish joke underscores the fact that anti-Semitism is so deep-seated in the Russian soul that everything irritating or even just unpleasant is associated with a Jew: "An anti-Semite walks into cold water: 'Brr, damned kikes!'" (See also V. Raskin 236–37.)

4. See Louis Rapoport's book, *Stalin's War Against the Jews;* cited in Friedberg 21.

5. Cf., a German Jewish joke about the prediction that Hitler would die on a Jewish holiday; that is, any day he dies is going to be a Jewish holiday.

6. It became a practice of the generation of Russian Jews who had their Jewish names in their passports to cover up their Jewishness by referring to each other in public by made-up Russian names. For example, my late mother, Soybel Volfovna, whenever she needed to address my father on the street, would call him not by his real name, Abram, but by the closest-sounding Russian name, "Arkadii." Correspondingly, she would introduce herself to strangers with the Russian equivalent of her name, "Sof'ia Vladimirovna."

7. One story in evidence of the Russian tendency to find a Jew in anyone with a foreign-sounding last name:

[A famous actress of the Malyi Theater,] Vera Pashennaia, didn't like an actor named Kenigson. Once she said angrily, "They've taken on Jews in the Malyi Theater. When that kind of thing has ever happened before!" Kenigson flared up and said: "Vera Nikolaevna, I'm a Swede." Pashennaia returned in her deep voice: "Swede, Swede, lousy Swede." (In the original: *shved parkhatyi,* on the pattern of a widespread anti-Semitic slur: *zhid parkhatyi,* "lousy kike"). (Lvovich 20)

On a personal note: my friend Eugene Genrikhsen, an ethnic Russian who carried the Norwegian surname of his step-grandfather, was often harassed by our schoolmates, who perceived him as Jewish just because his last name sounded foreign to a Russian ear. Cf., a Russian Jewish one-liner: "Don't beat me, don't beat me. 'Grandmaster' [in Russian *Grossmeister*] is my title in chess, not my surname."

8. Some other jokes of the same nature:

> An entrance exam in a Soviet institution of higher learning.
> Questions to a Russian student:
> "When was the Great October revolution?"
> "In 1917"
> "And when did the Great Patriotic war end?"
> "In 1945."
> "Correct. You got an A."
> Questions to a Jewish student:
> "When was the Great October revolution?"
> "In 1917"
> "And when did the Great Patriotic war end?"
> "In 1945."
> "And how many Soviet people perished?"
> "Twenty million."
> "Name them all."

> "What's a miraculous miracle?" (*chudo-iudo*)
> [a play on the words *iudo* and *Yid* in Russian]
> "It's a Jewish kid accepted this year by Moscow State University."

If a Jewish student finally succeeded in entering an institution of higher learning, he would be subject to discrimination after graduation. All students were then assigned to work for three years in a place of the government's choosing; Jewish students would be given the worst assignments—that is, in areas farthest from the European center of the country. This practice is venomously attacked in the following joke:

> As they finished college, three honor students, two Russian and one Jewish, are given work assignments. One Russian student gets a job in Moscow, the other in Leningrad. As for the Jewish student, he is sent to the remote northern provincial town of Archangelsk, hundreds of miles from Leningrad. At a graduation party all three honor students are asked to say a few words. Both Russian students toast the Communist Party for the care and consideration they were given while attending the college. The Jewish student also raises a glass and says:
> "I am also grateful to the Communist Party. And my special thanks go to the czarist government for selling Alaska to America."

9. On the image of a Jew as a mouse in Kafka, see Saper 48.
10. A variant of this joke mockingly refers to the Soviet ideological cliché:

> "What is proletarian internationalism?"
> "I don't know what proletarian internationalism is, but leaving is a must."

11. A joke with a similar theme puns on the "Jewish" name of the famous ship, the *Aurora Cruiser* (in Russian, *kreiser "Avrora"*), which signaled the beginning of

the October Revolution: " By the year 1990, the only Jew left in Leningrad will be *Aurora Cruiser.*"

12. To a Russian ear, this is an obviously unnatural cluster of an unmistakably Russian first name and an explicitly Jewish patronymic.

13. Cf., a variant of this classical Jewish joke in Saper 51.

14. An exception to the rule were the newspaper articles that usually smeared the names of those who left the country.

15. Essentially the same joke in Shturman and Tiktin's (503) collection is dated 1952 (but there it implies that Rabinovich is absent because he is imprisoned, a theme characteristic of jokes of the late 1940s and early 1950s, when government-inspired hunts for embezzlers and swindlers of state property were taking place. If the criminal was Jewish, his identity would be emphasized and invariably publicized. Thus, if we compare these two virtually identical jokes, the timeframe alone provides a different reading of the same punch line. It is noteworthy that in both jokes the Jew has no place in Soviet society; he is isolated either internally or externally.

16. The "Russians" in these Jewish jokes denote not only ethnic Russians but other non-Jewish nationalities in the Soviet Union, such as Ukrainians, Belorussians, and Lithuanians, that show a general lack of sensitivity toward the Jews, ranging from badly concealed hostility to open anti-Semitism.

17. As in the cases discussed in Martineau (119).

18. The punch line of this joke is characteristically "Jewish." Often in Jewish humor, the Jewish protagonist does not attack his target head-on, but achieves the same goal through sly verbal maneuvering. As if fearful of being accused of criticizing the powerful, he usually avoids actually uttering the incriminating words themselves. This circumlocution permits the Jewish protagonist to wear an innocent mask.

19. Jokes attacking the regime's attempts in the early 1970s to curtail emigration by imposing obstacles of all kinds, including the demand for high payment for having obtained a Soviet diploma or refusing exit visas on the grounds of possession of unspecified state secrets, served the same end—boosting the Jews' morale:

> The agricultural instructor from the regional party committee addresses the collective farmers. He speaks about how profitable it is to breed chickens. From each chicken one could have so many rubles in annual income.
> He is interrupted by a collective farmer:
> "How much does a Jew with an education pay for the right to leave the country?"
> "Four and a half thousand rubles," replies the instructor. "But let us not get distracted."
> Then the instructor talks about sheep breeding and how profitable it is.
> He is again interrupted:
> "And how much does a Jewish engineer pay if he wants to leave?"
> "Around eight thousand . . . But to continue, comrades."
> And he talks about cattle breeding. From each head of cattle one can get so much in annual income.
> "And what if a Jew has a Ph.D.?"

"Twelve thousand."

"Well, maybe then it's more profitable to breed Jews?" (Telesin 133).

In this joke, while the in-group is given a high value (almost literally—the message is "the Jews are worth big money"), the Soviet system as the out-group is depicted as inept and incapable of solving its problems. The farmers in the joke do not take the government's instructor seriously; they have no faith in the system whatsoever. We are left with the feeling that they know only too well that nothing good will come of the instructor's advice anyway.

20. Armenians and Germans were two other minorities who had the right to apply for emigration, according to a special Soviet decree. Officially this policy was worded as "the right to emigrate granted to nationalities, the majority of which live in the capitalist countries."

21. The novel by Ilf and Petrov, first published in the late 1920s, became immensely popular; selected lines entered Soviet urban folklore.

22. This *chastushka* was translated from the Russian with the assistance of Joseph Brodsky.

23. An anti-Semitic joke circulating currently in Russia refers to this episode, of which Tashkent became emblematic. The joke plays with the double meaning of the expression "hot spots" as both "a place of high tension" and that of "hot climate"; "a warm place" is interpreted in direct and figurative meanings, that is, as "a much sought after place of comfort." The Jew is stereotyped as one who abhors combat and hard physical work and "always finds a warm place for himself":

A Jew talks to himself in distress:
"During the whole Great Patriotic War [1941–1945], I was in the hottest spots—once in Tashkent, another in Ashkhabad [another Central Asian city]. I returned from there and thought of living quietly, to work for a while—but no such luck! All the warm places were taken by the Russians: in the boiler rooms and near the open-hearth furnaces. . . ." (Ivanova 1994, 365)

24. While referring to real events, the anti-Semites deliberately misinterpreted them. Indeed, during the first months of Hitler's invasion of the USSR, Tashkent and other cities of Soviet Central Asia and the Urals were chosen for resettlement of the civilian population, some of whom were Jewish, evacuated from the European part of the country to rescue it from the rapidly advancing German troops. For Russian anti-Semites, however, Tashkent connoted Jewish cowardice, although it was obvious that the Jewish population in particular was at most risk if captured by the Germans. Such Nazi atrocities as the mass murder in Babi Yar and the killings of the Jews in Kaunas, Minsk, Odessa, and other cities with considerable Jewish populations were the best proof of the impending danger.

25. According to Shturman and Tiktin (484), the Russian Jews' response to Israeli victories as apocalyptic reflected Israeli and foreign news reports. This only partly explains the phenomenon, however. The scholars have overlooked the simple fact that we are dealing with folklore, in which, by its very nature, myths are essential; in them, there is always good versus bad, smart against foolish, weak against strong.

26. This phenomenon of different readings of the same joke is not infrequent; it depends on the speaker's and hearer's set of preconceived notions about the characters in a story and the implied psychological and sociological climate of the milieu in which the joke circulates.

Conclusions

1. "Sharing of primary sentiments [among which there is the need to have an enemy] is universal and developmental and may be strengthened by stress and humiliation. Group members may turn to shared targets not only to patch up a disturbed sense of self, but also to establish grounds on which to reunite for mutual support and strength." (Volkan 90)
2. I would argue that Karassev is not quite right in characterizing shame as a sudden reaction; it could also be a result of a gradual realization of a disgraceful situation.
3. Only a few jokes about the Chukchi can be compared with American jokes in this respect (see chapter 4).
4. Clem (14) concludes:

> From the middle to the end of the 1970s . . . Jones and Grupp found that the rate of improvement in minority educational attainment and access to white-collar jobs slowed markedly, and minority higher education enrollment rates actually dropped, due to a decline in the growth of the Soviet economy and the inability of the system to provide space in schools and universities for the burgeoning minority population. Thus, the most recent data indicates that, despite the tendency toward socioeconomic equalization, important differences remain between the relatively privileged Russians and achiever groups on the one hand and most minority ethnic groups on the other.

5. For a list of other "undeserving groups" around the world, see Davies 1990, 103.
6. Practically all Russian ethnic jokes employ the universal comic script of language distortion. However, this script rarely appears alone. It does occur in those cases when a specific mispronunciation of Russian words serves as a means of national identification and functions as the sole ground of an ethnic character treatment, as in Jewish jokes about a Jew who, after pronouncing a word in what is considered a typically Jewish way, is denied employment (cited in chapter 5, p. 102). The comic effect of language distortion is also the sole source of entertainment in stories involving Georgian, Japanese, or Chinese characters (e.g., a joke about a Japanese tourist riding in a Moscow taxi).
7. "Soviet scholars generally agree that fluency in the Russian language enhances the non-Russians' chances for social mobility. This is, of course, related to the fact that most higher education in the USSR is conducted in the Russian language. Thus, in terms of ethnic stratification, Russians have an advantage over non-Russians by having acquired the official language of the Soviet Union early in life" (Rockett 138).
8. Pipes (464) notes that "only 3 percent of Russians speak a second (Soviet) language, which . . . is the lowest percentage of any ethnic group in the USSR to do so,

whereas among the minorities the percentage of Russian-speakers is typically 15–30 percent, and often exceeds 50 percent."

9. It would be wrong, however, to fully equate language and consciousness. Thus, an educated member of an ethnicity in Russian territory, even if he is most nationalistically inclined, may stress the importance of knowing Russian, one of the world languages, if for no other reason than that often information is available in the state language only. As Owen Lattimore (quoted in McCagg 261) points out:

> The Russians don't need to forbid the use of any minority language nor do the Chinese, because it works the other way—if you want a better career in the Soviet Union you learn Russian, same thing in China. This is something that applies to any small nation. . . . You may work for the survival of the Breton or the Welsh languages, but Lloyd George went on to a brilliant career because of his eloquence in English.

10. Two examples:

> A master-sergeant conducting a morning inspection sees that a Chukchi is wearing dirty boots.
> "Chukchi! I give you one minute to clean your boots."
> "Mine don't understand you."
> "I assign you an additional tour of duty."
> "Mine don't understand you."
> "I assign you two additional tours of duty."
> "Mine don't understand you."
> "Three additional tours of duty."
> "You have no right to do that." (Ivanova 1994, 210)

> A Ukrainian arrives in Georgia in his car. A Georgian traffic cop stops him and begins to harangue him:
> "You violated the rules. Here's a piece of paper. Write explanations in the Georgian language."
> The Ukrainian insists that he hasn't violated any rules, and that he can't write in Georgian. The cop keeps demanding:
> "I don't care, write your explanations in Georgian."
> The Ukrainian thinks and thinks, then wraps a ten-thousand-ruble bill in a piece of paper and gives it to the Georgian.
> The Georgian unwraps it and says:
> "Hey, you said you don't know any Georgian, and you've already written half of your explanations." (Ivanova 1996, 111)

11. On sexual overindulgence as a satirical device in literature, see Draitser 1994, 74–78, 182.

12. I have found no proof in Russian folklore of Dr. Stern's (240) observation that Russians portray stereotypical Jews as "tireless sexual performers." Usually both jokes and folk rhymes play down the sexuality of the Jews, and there is more than one reason for this.

    First, because according to Russian popular physiognomy (see chapter 2,

p. 49), a man's nose is telling as to the size of his male organ, and, stereotypically, the Jews are portrayed as rather long-nosed, the unconscious penis envy may well be the source of scornful remarks about the Jews as lovers.

Furthermore, there is not only a psychological but also a social reason behind presenting the Jews as sexually inadequate, both in jokes and in *chastushki*. Some Russians stereotype the Jews as formidable sexual competitors, thanks to a belief that Jewish husbands are better breadwinners (Gray 56). Some Russian mothers encourage courtship of their daughters by Jewish young men for want of a better lot than their own. According to a stereotype, a Jewish husband, unlike a Russian one, would not indulge in alcoholism and wife beating.

The Russian awareness of the Jews as a potential threat to their sexual territory is seen in the following jokes:

An old Jew is sitting on a beach with his young grandson.
"Listen, Moishe. Do you like that blonde in the red bathing suit?"
"I like her, Grandpa."
"And that brunette with a puffy little tushi?"
"I like her," says the grandson shyly.
"And that redhead with her high bust?"
"Yes, grandpa . . ."
"Then remember, Moishe, in order to have them, you have to study hard."
(Soloviev 2:28)

In a train, a young man and a girl strike up a conversation. The young man asks, "What kind of people do you like most of all?"
"Well, maybe, the American Indians because they are strong and brave and the Jews because they can adjust to any living conditions."
"Then let me introduce myself: Chingachgook Aron Moiseevich." (Soloviev 2:42)

Perhaps this explains the existence of some *chastushki* evidently intended for those Russian girls for whom a suitor's Jewishness is not by itself a deterrent to courtship. For instance, to discourage sexual contacts with the Jews, one *chastushka* (Kozlovsky 197) suggests that they suffer from gonorrhea.

13. Should a Russian cross the national border or confront a stranger, miraculously his masculinity becomes not only strong, but legendary, something out of a fairy tale:

One Russian decides to escape to Alaska and become a citizen of that state.
"You see," they tell him, "to become a citizen of Alaska, you should fulfill three conditions: eat a pot of raw fish, give a handshake to a female polar bear, and spend a night with an Eskimo woman."
The Russian agrees and leaves. In a while he appears again:
"I ate the pot of raw fish, I spent a night with the female polar bear, but where is that Eskimo woman whose hand I have to shake?"

(There is an American version of this joke featuring a Texan who wants to become a citizen of Alaska).

A Russian reporter asks a visiting French woman about her impressions of Russia. She says:
"Well, I wish the Russian men were more virile."
"Oh, yeah?" says the Russian. "I'll be back in a few minutes."
Soon he comes back with a bottle of vodka, a large box of condoms, and a pack of cotton.
"Well," says the French woman. "Vodka and condoms I understand. But why do you need cotton?"
"The cotton is not for me, it's for you—to stick into your nostrils so that you won't be bothered by the smell of burning rubber." (See also V. Raskin 202–3.)

14. In one *chastushka* (Kozlovsky 114) girls are warned against "malicious," sexually "overendowed" Kyrgyzs. It is noteworthy that no such concern about females is expressed when, in other *chastushki,* it is a Russian man who is a proud possessor of a formidable, often superhuman, sexual organ.

    Some *chastushki* express nationalistic sexual tendencies quite overtly. In one of them (Kozlovsky 46), it is said with pride that a woman did not "put out" either for a German, or for a Jew, but saved her "narrow" (that is, in male folk view sexually most desirable) vagina for one of her own, for a Russian man. In another (Kozlovsky 57), Chuvashians get settled in a Russian woman's vagina, and the *chastushka* calls for guarding the place and deporting the intruders.

15. Of course, displacement of discontent onto minorities is found in many cultures. For example, in the second part of the nineteenth century, since to express their resentment against the Russian conquerers was unsafe, the Georgians turned it against the Jews who began to settle in Georgian towns after the abolition of serfdom. This period accounts for the largest number of "blood slanders" not only in comparison with those in the rest of the Russian empire, but with those of the whole world. These "blood slanders" resulted in pogroms, the most notorious of which was the one in Kutaisi (Svetlova 7).

16. Cited in Volkan 88.

17. For a discussion of positive and negative aspects of ethnic joke telling, see Schutz 165, Boskin and Dorinson 81, Dundes 116, LaFave and Mannell 116–17, Whitfield 196, and Nilsen 219.

Bibliography

Aarne, Antti. *The Types of the Folktale: A Classification and Bibliography.* English ed. Translated by Stith Thompson. Helsinki: Suomalainen Tiedeakatemia Academia Scientiarum, 1961.

Allen, Irving Lewis. *Unkind Words: Ethnic Labeling from Redskin to WASP.* New York: Bergin & Garvey, 1990.

Anekdoty (Jokes). Moscow: Ehkspress-Kniga "Oniks," 1994.

Apte, Mahadev L. *Humor and Laughter: An Anthropological Approach.* Ithaca: Cornell University Press, 1985.

Armstrong, John A. "The Ethnic Scene in the Soviet Union: The View of the Dictatorship." *Journal of Soviet Nationalities* 1, no. 1 (1990): 14–65.

———. "The Soviet Ethnic Scene: A Quarter Century Later." *Journal of Soviet Nationalities* 1, no. 1 (1990): 66–75.

Bakhtin, Mikhail. *Tvorchestvo Fransua Rable i narodnaia kultura srednevekov'ia i renessansa* (Works of Francois Rabelais and the popular culture of the Middle Ages and the Renaissance). Orange, Conn.: Antiquary, 1986.

Balzer, Marjorie Mandelstam. "Nationalism in the Soviet Union: One Anthropological View." *Journal of Soviet Nationalities* 1, no. 3 (fall 1990): 4–22.

Barron, M. L. "A Content Analysis of Intergroup Jokes." *American Sociological Review* 15 (1950): 88–94.

Barsky, L. A. *Ehto prosto smeshno ili zerkalo krivogo korolevstva/Anekdoty: analiz, sintez i klassifikatsiia* (That's just funny, or the mirror of the crooked kingdom/ Jokes: an analysis, synthesis, and classification). Moscow: Kh.G.S., 1994.

Belianin, V. P., and I. A. Butenko. *Antologiia chernogo iumora* (Anthology of dark humor). Moscow: PAIMC, 1996.

Belousov, A. F. "Mnimyi Shtirlits" (Imaginary Shtirlits). In *Uchebnyi material po teorii literatury. Zhanry slovesnogo texta: Anekdot* (Study material on theory of literature. The genres of a word text: An Anecdote) edited by A. F. Belousov, 104–17. Tallinn: Tallinn Pedagogical Institute, 1989.

Benton, Gregor. "The Origins of the Political Jokes." In *Humour in Society: Resistance and Control,* edited by Chris Powell and George E. C. Paton, 33–55. New York: St. Martin's Press, 1988.

Borev, Yury. *Staliniada* (Staliniad). Moscow: Sovetskii pisatel', 1990.

———. *Fariseia* (Pharisee). Moscow: Konets veka, 1992.

———. *Istoria gosudarstva sovetskogo v predaniiakh i anekdotakh* (History of the Soviet state in anecdotes and jokes). Moscow: RIPOL, 1995.

Boskin, Joseph. *Humor and Social Change in Twentieth-Century America.* Boston: Trustees of the Public Library of the City of Boston, 1979.

———. "Beyond Kvetching and Jiving: The Thrust of Jewish and Black Folk Humor." In *The Jewish Wry,* edited by Sarah Blacher Cohen, 53–79. Detroit: Wayne State University Press, 1987.

Boskin, Joseph, and Joseph Dorinson. "Ethnic Humor: Subversion and Survival." *American Quarterly* 37, no. 1 (1985): 81–97.

Boston, Richard. *An Anatomy of Laughter.* London: Collins, 1974.

Brodsky, Joseph. *Mramor* (The marbles). Ann Arbor: Ardis, 1984.

Buzzi, Aldo. "Chekhov in Sondrio." *New Yorker,* September 14, 1992, 34–43.

Carey, Claude. *Les proverbes erotiques russes.* The Hague: Mouton, 1972.

Chapman, A. J., J. R. Smith, and H. C. Foot. "Language, Humour and Intergroup Relations." In *Language, Ethnicity and Intergroup Relations,* edited by H. Giles, 137–69. London: Academic Press, 1977.

Clem, Ralph S. "The Ethnic Factor in Contemporary Soviet Society." In *Understanding Soviet Society,* edited by Michael Paul Sacks and Jerry G. Pankhurst, 3–30. Boston: Unwin Hyman, 1988.

Conquest, Robert. *The Harvest of Sorrow: Soviet Collectivization and Terror-Famine.* New York and Oxford: Oxford University Press, 1986.

Davies, Christie. "Ethnic Jokes, Moral Values and Social Boundaries." *British Journal of Sociology* 33, no. 3 (September 1982): 383–403.

———. "Jewish Jokes, Anti-Semitic Jokes and Hebredonian Jokes." In *Jewish Humor,* edited by Avner Ziv, 75–98. Tel Aviv: Papyrus, 1986.

———. *Ethnic Humor around the World.* Bloomington: Indiana University Press, 1990.

Dezhnov, Iu. B., ed. *Anekdoty . . . Anekdoty? Anekdoty!* (Jokes . . . Jokes? Jokes!). 4 vols. Moscow: DataStrom, 1993.

Dmitriev, A. V. *Sotsiologiia iumora* (Sociology of humor). Moscow: Rossiiskaia akademiia nauk, 1996.

Dolgopolova, Zhanna, ed. *Russia Dies Laughing: Jokes from Soviet Russia.* London: Andre Deutsch, 1982.

Dovlatov, Sergey. "Belym po chernomu" (White over black). *Novoe Russkoe Slovo,* October 27, 1989, 4.

Draitser, Emil, ed. & comp. *Forbidden Laughter: Soviet Underground Jokes.* Bilingual ed. Translated by Jon Pariser. Los Angeles: Almanac, 1980.

———. *Techniques of Satire: The Case of Saltykov-Shchedrin.* Berlin and New York: Mouton de Gruyter, 1994.

Dreizin, Felix. *The Russian Soul and the Jew.* Lanham, Maryland: University Press of America, 1990.

Dubovsky, Mark, ed. *Istoriia SSSR v anekdotakh (1917–1992)* (History of the USSR in jokes (1917–1992). Smolensk: Smiadyn', 1991.

Dundes, Alan. *Cracking Jokes: Studies of Sick Humor Cycles and Stereotypes.* Berkeley: Ten Speed, 1987.

Eco, Umberto. "Umet' smeiat'sia nad soboi" (To be able to laugh at oneself). *Novoe Russkoe Slovo,* September 8, 1989, 9.

Ehidelman, Natan. "Perepiska iz dvukh sovetskikh uglov" (Correspondence from two Soviet corners). *Time and We* 93 (1986): 192–97, 199–200.

Eisiminger, Sterling. "Ethnic and National Stereotypes and Slurs." *American Humor: Interdisciplinary Newsletter* 7 (fall 1990): 9–13.

Elistratov, V. S. *Slovar' Moskovskogo argo* (Dictionary of Moscow argot). Moscow: Russkie slovari, 1994.

Erokaev, S., ed. *Zhizn' udalas'* (Life's a success) St. Petersburg: "DiK," 1997.

Eroshkin, S., A. Slastenov, Ia. Rozybakiev, and V. Berdnikov, comps. *Malinovye parusa: Anekdoty pro novykh russkikh* (The crimson sails: Jokes about the New Russians). St. Petersburg: "DiK," 1997.

Evtushenko, E. "Priterpelost' " (The habit to bear it) *Literaturnaia gazeta* 19 (May 11, 1988): 13.

Flegon, A. *Za predelami russkikh slovarei* (Beyond the Russian dictionary). Troitsk, Moscow Region: Rike, 1993.

Freud, Sigmund. *Jokes and Their Relation to the Unconscious.* New York: Norton, 1963. Originally published as *Der Witz und Zeine Beziehung zum Unbewussten.* Leipzig and Vienna: Deuticke, 1905.

Friedberg, Maurice. "The Price of an Obsession." *New Leader* February 11–25, 1991, 20–21.

Genis, M. V., ed. *Zabavnye anekdoty* (Entertaining jokes). 3 vols. St. Petersburg: Dilia, 1994.

Goldstein, Jeffrey H., and Paul E. MaGhee, eds. *Psychology of Humor.* New York and London: Academic Press, 1972.

Gorky, Maxim. "Dvadtsat' shest' i odna" (Twenty six and one). In *Tsaritsa potseluev* (The tsarina of kisses), edited by N. Popov, 54–63. Moscow: TOO Vneshsigma, 1993.

Grafov, Eduard. "To, chto pozvoleno byku . . ." (What is allowed to a bull . . .). *Literaturnaia gazeta,* 35 (August 26, 1992): 16.

Gray, Francine du Plessix. *Soviet Women: Walking the Tightrope.* New York: Doubleday, 1990.

Grossman, Gregory. "Inflationary, Political, and Social Implications of the Current Economic Slowdown." In *Economy and Politics in the USSR: Problems of Interdependence,* edited by Hans-Hermann Höhmann, Alec Nove, and Henrich Vogel, 172–97. Boulder and London: Westview, 1986.

Harris, David A. *The Jewish World.* New York: Liberty, 1989.

Harris, David, and Israel Rabinovich, eds. *The Jokes of Oppression: Humor of Soviet Jews.* Northvale, N.J.: Jason Aronson, 1988.

Heldt, Barbara. *Terrible Perfection: Women and Russian Literature.* Bloomington and Indianapolis: Indiana University Press, 1987.

Hertzler, Joyce O. *Laughter: A Socio-Scientific Analysis.* New York: Exposition, 1970.

Ignatieff, Michael. "In the Center of the Earthquake." *New York Review of Books,* June 12, 1997, 31–33.

Iudin, Iu. I. "Narodnyi anekdot, smezhnye folklornye zhanry, literatura" (A popular joke, adjacent folkloric genres, literature). In *Uchebnyi material po teorii litera-tury. Zhanry slovesnogo texta: Anekdot* (Study material on theory of literature. The genres of a word text: An Anecdote), edited by A. F. Belousov, 77–86. Tallinn: Tallinn Pedagogical Institute, 1989.

Ivanova, O. Iu, ed. *Anekdoty i tosty* (Jokes and toasts). Moscow: Aurika, 1994.

———. *Anekdoty i tosty* (Jokes and toasts). Smolensk: Rusich, 1996.

Kalbouss, George. "On 'Armenian Riddles' and Their Offspring 'Radio Erevan.' " *Slavic and East European Journal* 21, no. 3 (1977): 447–49.

Karassev, L. V. *Filosofiia smekha* (Philosophy of laughter). Moscow: Rossiiskii gosu-darstvennyi gumanitarnyi universitet, 1996.

Kasindorf, Jeanie. "Jackie Mason Tries to Talk Himself Out of Trouble," *New York Magazine* 22, no. 41: 40–43.

Kharkover, V. I., ed. *Anekdoty* [Jokes]. 3 vols. Moscow: Vikhr', 1993.

Klier, John D. "*Zhid:* Biography of a Russian Epithet." *Slavonic and East European Review* 60, no. 1 (January 1982): 1–15.

Kozhinov, Vadim. "Ia zaviduiu Izrailiu" (I envy Israel). *22* 68 (1989): 160–70.

Kozlovsky, Vladimir, ed. *Novaia nepodtsenzurnaia chastushka* (The new uncensored chastushka). New York: Russica, 1982.

LaFave, Lawrence, and Roger Mannell. "Does Ethnic Humor Serve Prejudice?" *Journal of Communication* 26 (summer 1976): 116–23.

Legman, G. *Rationale of the Dirty Joke: An Analysis of Sexual Humor,* series I. New York: Castle Books, 1968.

Levin, Eve. *Sex and Society in the World of the Orthodox Slavs, 900–1700.* Ithaca: Cornell University Press, 1989.

Lipman, Steve. *Laughter in Hell: The Use of Humor during the Holocaust.* Northvale, N.J.: Jason Aronson, 1991.

Loginov, K. K. "Materialy po seksual'nomu povedeniiu russkikh Zaonezh'ia" (Mate-rials on sexual behavior of the Russians of Zaonezhie). In *Seks i ehrotika v russkoi traditsionnoi kul'ture* (Sex and eroticism in traditional Russian culture), edited by Toporkov, A., 444–53. Moscow: Ladomir, 1996.

Lurie, V. F. "Materialy po sovremennomu leningradskomu fol'kloru" (Materials on contemporary Leningrad folklore). In *Uchebnyi material po teorii literatury. Zhanry slovesnogo texta: Anekdot* (Study material on theory of literature. The genres of a word text: An Anecdote), edited by A. F. Belousov, 118–51. Tallinn: Tallinn Pedagogical Institute, 1989.

———. "Kratkaia antologiia fol'klora mladshikh podrostkov" (A short anthology of the folklore of young adolescents). In *Shkol'nyi byt i fol'klor: Uchebnyi material po russkomu fol'kloru* (Everyday school life and folklore), part 1, edited by A. F. Belousov, 5–44. Tallinn: Tallinn Pedagogical Institute, 1992.

Lvovich, Boris. "Akterskaia kurilka" (The actor's smoking room). *Novoe Russkoe Slovo,* June 20, 1996, 20.

Martineau, William. "A Model of Social Functions of Humor." In *Psychology of Humor,* edited by Jeffrey H. Goldstein and Paul E. McGhee, 101–25. New York and London: Academic Press, 1972.

McCagg, William O. Jr. "A Conversation with Owen Lattimore." In *Soviet Asian Ethnic Frontiers,* edited by William O. McCagg Jr. and Brian D. Silver, 246–65. New York: Pergamon, 1979.

Middleton, R., and J. Moland. "Humor in Negro and White Subcultures: A Study of Jokes among University Students." *American Sociological Review,* 24 (1959): 61–69.

Nazarov, M. "Vselenskie korni i prizvanie slavianskoi kulturu" (The universal roots and the calling of Slavic culture). *Posev* 7 (1989): 30–44.

Nilsen, Don. *Humor Scholarship: A Research Bibliography.* Westport, Conn.: Greenwood Press, 1993.

Oring, Elliot. *Jokes and Their Relations.* Lexington, Ky.: University of Kentucky Press, 1992.

Petrosian, Evgeny. *Evgenii Petrosian v strane anekdotov* (Eugene Petrosian in the country of jokes). Moscow: Tsentr ehstradnoi iumoristiki, 1994.

Pinderhughes, C. A. "Paried Differential Bonding in Biological, Psychological, and Social Systems." *American Journal of Psychiatry* 25:5–14.

Pinkus, Benjamin. *The Jews of the Soviet Union: The History of a Nationality.* Cambridge and New York: Cambridge University Press, 1988.

Pipes, Richard A. "Reflections on the Nationality Problem in the Soviet Union." In *Ethnicity: Theory and Experience,* edited by Nathan Glazer and Daniel R. Moynihan, 453–65. Cambridge, Mass.: Harvard University Press, 1975.

Prokhorov, A. M., ed. *Bol'shoi Ehtsiklopedicheskii slovar' v dvukh tomakh* (Great encyclopedic dictionary in two volumes). 2 vols. Moscow: Sovetskaia ehntsiklopediia, 1991.

Rabinovich, E. G. "Ob odnom iz predpolozhitel'nykh istochnikov 'chukotskoi serii' " (About one of the hypothetical sources of the "Chukotka Series"). In *Uchebnyi material po teorii literatury. Zhanry slovesnogo teksta: Anekdot* (Study material on theory of literature. The genres of a word text: An Anecdote), edited by A. F. Belousov, 100–103. Tallinn: Tallinn Pedagogical Institute, 1989.

Raskin, Iosif. *Ehntsiklopediia khuliganstvuiushchego ortodoksa* (Encyclopedia of a rowdy orthodox man). St. Petersburg: Ehkho; Haifa: L.Y.S., 1995.

Raskin, Victor. *Semantic Mechanisms of Humor.* Dordrecht: Reidel, 1985.

Reik, Theodor. *Jewish Wit.* New York: Gamut, 1962.

Repina, Irina, and Yury Rostovtsev, eds. *Anekdoty nashikh chitatelei* (Jokes of our readers). Vol. 15. Moscow: TOO "Anons," 1995.

Riordan, Jim, and Sue Bridger, eds. *Dear Comrade Editor: Readers' Letters to the Soviet Press under Perestroika.* Bloomington and Indianapolis: Indiana University Press, 1992.

Roback, A. A. *A Dictionary of International Slurs* (Ethnophaulisms). Cambridge: Sci-Art, 1944.

Rockett, Rocky L. *Ethnic Nationalities in the Soviet Union: Sociological Perspectives on a Historical Problem.* New York: Praeger, 1981.

Rubina, Dina. "Na paneli: Zametki 'literaturnogo metra' " (On the streets: Notes of a "literary maestro"). *Marina* (April–May 1995): 82–84.

Saper, Bernard. "A Cognitive Behavioral Formulation of the Relation between the Jewish Joke and Anti-Semitism." *Humor: International Journal of Humor Research* 4, no. 1 (1991): 41–60.

Sayrs, Lois W., and James M. Lindsay. "Threat Perceptions." In *Public Opinion and Regime Change: The New Politics of Post-Soviet Societies,* edited by Arthur H. Miller, William M. Reisinger, and Vicki L. Hesl, 241–58. Boulder: Westview, 1993.

Schroeder, Gertrude. "Soviet Living Standards in Comparative Perspective." In *Quality of Life in the Soviet Union,* edited by Horst Herlemann, 13–30. Boulder: Westview Press, 1987.

Schutz, Charles E. "The Sociability of Ethnic Jokes." *Humor: International Journal of Humor Research* 2, no. 2 (1989): 165–78.

Shafarevich, Igor. "Rusofobia" (Russophobia). In *Nash sovremennik* 6 (1989): 167–92; 11 (1988): 162–72.

Shlapentokh, Vladimir. *Public and Private Life of the Soviet People: Changing Values in Post-Stalin Russia.* New York: Oxford University Press, 1989.

Shlyakhov, Vladimir, and Eve Adler. *Dictionary of Russian Slang and Colloqual Expressions.* New York: Barron's, 1995.

Shmeleva, Elena, and Aleksei Shmelev. " 'Inorodtsy' v russkikh anekdotakh" (Minorities in Russian jokes). *Moskovskie novosti* 11 (March 17–24, 1996): 40.

Shturman, Dora, and Sergey Tiktin, eds. *Sovetskii Soiuz v zerkale politicheskogo ankdota* (The Soviet Union in the mirror of a political joke). Jerusalem: Express, 1987.

Shvarts, S. *Evrei v Sovetskom Soiuze s nachala vtoroi mirovoi voiny (1939–1965)* (The Jews in the Soviet Union from the beginning of World War II). New York: American Jewish Labor Committee, 1966.

Simmons, Donald C. "Protest Humor: Folkloristic Reaction to Prejudice." *American Journal of Psychiatry* 120 (1963): 567–70.

Simons, G. L. *Sex and Superstition.* New York: Barnes & Noble, 1973.

Sinyavsky, Andrei (Abram Tertz). "Anekdot v anekdote" (A joke inside of a joke). In *Odna ili dve russkie literatury?* (One or two Russian literatures?), edited by George Niva, 167–79. Lausanne: L'Age D'Homme, 1981.

———. "The Literary Process in Russia." In *Kontinent,* 77–118. Garden City, N.Y.: Anchor and Doubleday, 1976.

Slezkine, Yuri. *Arctic Mirrors: Russia and the Small Peoples of the North.* Ithaca and London: Cornell University Press, 1994.

Smetanin, V., and Donskaia, K. eds. *Anekdoty o narodnykh geroiakh: Chapaev, Shtirlits, chuckha* (Jokes about popular heroes: Chapaev, Shtirlits, the Chuckhi). Moscow: DataStrom, 1994.

Soloviev, D., ed. *Izbrannye anekdoty* (Selected jokes). 2 vols. Moscow: Reklama, 1992.

Solzhenitsyn. Alexander. *Kak nam obustroit' Rossiiu* (How we should manage Russia). Moscow: Patriot, 1991.

Spalding, Henry D. *Encyclopedia of Jewish Humor: From Biblical Times to the Modern Age.* New York: Jonathan David, 1969.

Spears, Richard A. *Slang and Euphemism; A Dictionary of Oaths, Curses, Insults, Sexual Slang and Metaphor, Racial Slurs, Drug Talk, Homosexual Lingo, and Related Matters.* New York: New American Library, 1982.

Starshinov, Nikolai, ed. *Razreshite vas poteshit'* (Let us entertain you). 2 vols. Moscow: Stolitsa, 1992.

Stern, Mikhail, with August Stern. *Sex in the USSR.* New York: Times Books, 1980.

Svetlova, Svetlana. "Gruzinskie evrei" (Georgian Jews). *Forwaerts* (Russian edition), 31, no. 135 (June 8–12, 1997): 7.

Telesin, Yulius, ed. *Tysiacha odin izbrannyi sovetskii politicheskii anekdot* (One thousand and one selected Soviet political jokes). Tenafly, N.J.: Hermitage, 1986.

Tolpygo, Aleksei. "Oskolki i nasledniki. Ukraino-rossiiskie otnosheniia: konflikt sverkhzadach" (Fragments and heirs. Ukrainian-Russian relations: A conflict of super-agendas). *Druzhba narodov* no. 2 (1995): 148–52.

Vasmer, Max. *Russisches Etymologisches Worterbuch.* Heidelberg, 1950–58. Russian translation: *Ehtimologicheskii slovar' russkogo iazyka v 4-kh tomakh)* (Etimological dictionary of Russian language in 4 vols.). 4 vols. Moscow: Progress, 1986.

Venclova, Tomas. "Ethnic Identity and the Nationality Issue in Contemporary Soviet Literature." *Studies in Comparative Commusinsm* 21, no. 3/4 (autumn/winter 1988): 319–30.

Volkan, Vamik D. *The Need to Have Enemies and Allies: From Clinical Practice to International Relationship.* Northvale, N.J. and London: Jason Aronson, 1994.

Webster's New Collegiate Dictionary. Springfield, Mass.: Merriam, 1981.

Webster's New Dictionary of Synonyms. Springfield, Mass.: Merriam, 1982.

Whitfield, Stephen J. "Political Humor." In *Humor in America: A Research Guide to Genres and Topics,* edited by Lawrence Mintz, 195–211. Westport, Conn.: Greenwood, 1988.

Wiles, Peter. "Political and Moral Aspects of the Two Economies." In Economy and Politics in the USSR: Problems of *Interdependence,* edited by Hans-Hermann Höhmann, Alec Nove, and Henrich Vogel, 198–213. Boulder and London: Westview, 1986.

Will, George F. "Gorbachev and the '1946 Rules.' " *Newsweek,* September 25, 1989, 70.

Williams, Carol J. "The Ethnic Patchwork is Fraying." *Los Angeles Times,* August 21, 1995, A1, A6.

Wilson, Christopher P. *Jokes: Form, Content, Use and Function.* London: Academic Press, 1979.

Yuganov, I., and F. Yuganova. *Russkii zhargon 60–90x godov* (The Russian jargon of 1960s–1990s). Moscow: Pomovskii i partnery, 1994.

Zhabotinsky, Vladimir (Zeev). *Izbrannoe* (Selected works). Jerusalem: Biblioteka Alia, 1978.

Zhelvis, V. I. "Invektiva: opyt tematicheskoi i funktsional'noi klassifikatsii" (The invective: An attempt at thematical and functional classification). In *Ehthnicheskie normy povedeniia* (Ethnic norms of behavior), edited by A. K. Baiburin, 296–321. Leningrad: Nauka, 1985.

Zholkovsky, Alexander. "Seks v ramkakh" (Sex in frames). *Novoe literaturnoe obozrenie* 6 (1993–94): 15–24.

Ziv, Avner. "Psycho-Social Aspects of Jewish Humor in Israel and in the Diaspora." In *Jewish Humor,* edited by Avner Ziv, 47–71. Tel Aviv: Papyrus, 1986.

Subject and Names Index

Anti-Semitic humor. *See* Nationalities Index: Jews; Russian jokes about, in *chastushki*

Anti-Semitism, 101–2, 123–29, 168n. 11, 179n. 24, 183n. 15

Astafiev, Victor, 37–38, 43, 80, 107, 171n. 11

Beilis, Mendel, 164n. 7

Belov, Vasily, 80

Brezhnev, Leonid, 79

Brodsky, Joseph, 109, 179n. 22

Bulgakov, Mikhail, 106

Chapaev, Vasily, 98, 126

Chastushki, 114, 158, 183n. 14; on Chuvashians, 183n. 14; on Germans, 183n. 14; on Gypsies, 163n. 1; on Jews, 157, 181n. 12, 183n. 14

Chekhov, Anton, 169n. 22

Chernenko, Konstantin, 77, 170n. 2, 173n. 24

Chuk and Gek (Gaidar), 82

Comic scripts in jokes about various groups
linguistic, 157, 180n. 6; Chukchis, 85–86, 181n. 10; Georgians, 35, 48–49, 86, 181n. 10; Jews, 102; Lithuanians, 168n. 15; Ukrainians, 64, 67–68, 168n. 12

low culture: Chukchis, 90–91; Georgians, 46–47, 51–52; Ukrainians, 66–67

sexual, 157–58; Armenians, 157, 166n. 13; Chukchis, 86–87, 157; Georgians, 49–54, 157; Jews, 33, 158, 164n. 13, 181n. 12; Russians, 182n. 13

stupidity, 156–57; Chukchis, 84, 88–90; Georgians, 28, 45–46, 48, 156, 163n. 2; Jews, 32; Ukrainians, 57, 65–66

Dead Souls (Gogol), 38

Dovlatov, Sergey, 81

Eco, Umberto, 160

Engels, Friedrich, 76

Envy and ethnic jokes, 45, 73, 80, 154

Ethnic jokelore, repertory of. *See* Repertory of ethnic jokelore

Evenings on a Farm near Dikanka (Gogol), 69

Evtushenko, Evgeny, 154

Folk laughter (general), 120

Food jokes about: Koreans, 72; Ukrainians, 71–73, 169n. 19

Food nicknames for and slurs of: Asians in general, 110–11; Caucasians or Transcaucasians, 110; Central Asians, 110; Jews, 169n. 20; Koreans, 169n. 20; Moldavians, 169n. 20; Tartars, 169n. 20;

"Second economy," 38

Sexual comic script. *See* Comic scripts

Shafarevich, Igor, 80

Sinyavsky, Andrey, 94, 98, 101

Slurs: 101, 103, 105, 112. *See also* Idioms;
Nicknames; Food nicknames and slurs
collective denigration, 114; ethnic
invectives, 111–14; newly coined:
cognitive, 106–11; obsolete, 103–4;
"reverse," 113; Russian: idiomatic, 115–16
of various groups: Americans, 111; any
Asians, 82–83, 108; Blacks, 108–9;
Chechens, 108; Chinese, 116; Evenks
(Tungus), 113; French, 103, 173n.
3; Georgians, 113; Georgians of
Russians, 119; Germans, 103–4,
119; Gypsies, 113; Japanese, 104;
Jews, 112–13, 159, 176n. 7; Jews of
Russians, 119; Koreans, 113; Kyrgyzs,
106; Moldavians, 111; Nanai, 113;
Poles, 104; on provincial Russians,
105, 175n. 9; Tartars, 157; Turks,
114; Udmurts, 113; Ukrainians, 58;

Ukrainians of Russians, 105, 119;
Westerners in general, 108, 111

Sociolinguistics, slurs as, 112

Solzhenitsyn, Alexander, 61, 173n. 24

Sound symbolism, 82, 113, 171n. 14

Stalin, Joseph, 35–36, 46, 69, 124

Stereotypes, 20, 75; of various groups:
Armenians, 166n. 13; Asians, 81;
Chukchis, 76, 84, 88, 94, 105; Chinese,
105; Georgians, 35, 37–39, 45, 47–48,
54, 57, 80, 87, 154; Germans, 33;
Gypsies, 163n. 1; Japanese, 104; Jews,
24, 32, 57, 80, 84, 88, 105, 175n. 27,
181n. 12; Turkomen, 81; Ukrainian, 69,
73, 80, 87; Uzbeks, 81

Stupidity comic script. *See* Comic strips

Taras Bulba (Gogol), 110

Twelve Charis, The (Ilf and Petrov), 146

Xenophobia, 19

Zhabotinsky, Vladimir, 23

Zoschenko, Mikhail, 66

Nationalities Index

African Americans, 102. *See also* Blacks

Americans: their humor compared to Russian humor, 70, 87, 90–91, 108, 156, 159–60, 172n. 20, 182n. 13; nicknames for and slurs of, 106–7, 111

Armenians: in idioms, 115, 166n. 13, 16; their riddles, 21; in Russian jokes, 157, 166n. 13; slurs of, 106–7, 109; stereotype of, 166n. 13

Asians: nicknames for and slurs of, 82–83, 107–11, 114; stereotype of, 81

Asians, Central (Kyrgyzs, Tadzhiks, Turkomen, Uzbeks): in idioms, 175n. 22; nicknames for and slurs of, 106, 109–11, 175n. 21, 23. *See also* Asians

Azeris, 102

Blacks, 102; humor compared to Russian-Jewish humor, 120; in idioms, 172n. 23; in jokes, 58, 109; as scapegoats, 81; slurs of, 108–9, 171n. 11

Buriats, in idioms, 172n. 19. *See also* Asians

Caucasians. *See* Transcaucasians

Chechens, slurs of, 108

Chinese: in idioms, 116, 175n. 16, 176n. 29; in jokes, 60–61, 92, 116, 172n. 23; nicknames for and slurs of, 110, 116; stereotype of, 105. *See also* Asians

Chukchis: and anti-Soviet jokes, 76–78, 96–98, 173n. 24; as benign ethnic men in jokes, 87–94; and economy, 79–80; as "ethnicized" jokes, 28; jokes about them, 75–100; with linguistic script, 85–86, 181n. 10; living conditions of, 75; with low culture script, 90–91; nicknames for and slurs of, 83; origins of, 75–76; and other nationalities, 83–84, 86–87, 92; reasons for targeting, 79–86; recycled as jokes about Ukrainians, 27; as Russian proxies, 77, 94–100, 173n. 27; with sexual script, 86–87, 157; stereotype of, 76, 84, 88, 94, 105; with stupidity script, 84, 88–90

Chuvashians: in *chastuhski*, 183n. 14. *See also* Asians

Englishmen: in jokes, 172n. 22

Eskimos, 82: in jokes, 171n. 12, 182n. 13; Russian nickname for, 109. *See also* Asians

Estonians, 18

Europeans (general): nicknames for them by Kazakhs, 110

Evenks, slurs of, 113. *See also* Asians

Finns, nicknames for and slurs of, 107

BOOKS IN THE HUMOR IN LIFE AND LETTERS SERIES